I Want a Love I Can Feel

BY DR. JOYCE CRIDER-ANDERSON

DORRANCE PUBLISHING CO
EST. 1920
PITTSBURGH, PENNSYLVANIA 15238

The contents of this work, including, but not limited to, the accuracy of events, people, and places depicted; opinions expressed; permission to use previously published materials included; and any advice given or actions advocated are solely the responsibility of the author, who assumes all liability for said work and indemnifies the publisher against any claims stemming from publication of the work.

All Rights Reserved
Copyright © 2021 by Dr. Joyce Crider- Anderson

No part of this book may be reproduced or transmitted, downloaded, distributed, reverse engineered, or stored in or introduced into any information storage and retrieval system, in any form or by any means, including photocopying and recording, whether electronic or mechanical, now known or hereinafter invented without permission in writing from the publisher.

Dorrance Publishing Co
585 Alpha Drive
Pittsburgh, PA 15238
Visit our website at *www.dorrancebookstore.com*

ISBN: 978-1-6495-7129-8
eISBN: 978-1-6495-7639-2

Introduction

In my role as a Nurse Practitioner, I spend a lot of time talking to patients. What I have come to verify that we are told in research is that many health problems are associated with or triggered by our thoughts and feelings. What I have come to realize is the missing component in many lives is love. You hear it expressed in such words as "There is no love here, I am not wanted, nobody cares about me." You hear it expressed in songs – "Everybody needs somebody (to love), Open the door to your heart (and let love come running in), I wanna be your everything, Make me yours."

Because we are created in the image of God, if God is love, if His nature and character are love, then we must have the ability to reflect that nature in our character as well. In Mark 12:30, 31, God gives us two commands that summarize His moral law, "And thou shalt love the Lord thy God with all thy soul and with all thy mind, and with all they strength: this is the first commandment. And the second is like; namely this: thou shalt love they neighbor as thyself." Implied in the second command is the third command to "love thyself" with the strong implication that if I am to love you, I must know how to love myself. The evaluation tool that Jesus uses to evaluate our discipleship is love. John 13:35, "By this shall all men know that you are my disciples, if ye have love one to another."

The covenant that God makes with the fallen, sinful human race is restated in Hebrews 8:10. "For this is the covenant that I will make with the house of Israel after those days, saith the Lord; I will put my laws into their mind, and write them in their hearts, and I will be to them a God, and they shall be to me a people." Character, we are told in the writings of Ellen White, a well-known author, is made of thoughts (mind) and feelings (heart). She further states that the only thing we will take from this world into heaven is our character.

"God" is love. 1 John 4:16 His nature is love. His law, a transcript of His character, reflects His love for His created universe. Everything in God's created universe is governed by law. For this book, we will define law as a principle that has universal applications that does not change. Every law has specific intended outcomes and violation or breaking of the law also results in specific outcomes.

In this book, we will look at the characteristics presented in God's word that stem from the definitive concept that "God" is love. 1 John 4:16 The Bible is a descriptive of the patterns of interaction of God with created beings that throughout its pages identifies characteristics and action principles that give us a picture of love. When we see God's interactions with creation, we see the characteristics and principles of love because love is His nature. His "law" is love and the elements of His law are the guiding principles for those created in His image to know, give, and receive love.

There is a lot of confusion surrounding the word LOVE. What is love? How do I know when I love someone? How do I know when someone loves me? What does love look like? This book attempts to help explore a deeper understanding that supports either answers to/or further inquiry into those questions. We will look at three underlying principles describing love:

1. Love always desires the best interest of the loved
2. Love moves the loved from A to B, B being a better place for the loved than A
3. The lover gives something of value to himself that benefits the loved

We will look at four inter-related components of love

1. Mental – knowing the loved, thoughts of the loved
    a. I will put my law in your mind
2. Feelings – many feelings associated with love
    a. I will write my law on your heart

3. Spiritual - Laws of love – right thoughts, right feelings, right behaviors
4. Physical component of love –used to help mediate the inter-related components- manifested usually in presence, time, and touch

Because the great void in many lives seems to be dealing with the "feelings" component of love, we will spend a lot of time looking at feelings. A very beloved friend told me that "feelings in many situations serve as a judgment spark (based on personal knowledge). which ignites or extinguishes the motivation to engage." Ellen White, noted author, supports this statement in her writings when she says that feelings are the basis for choosing actions. Jesus wept when Lazarus died. The angels in heaven were so sad when they were told that Jesus was to die to implement the plan of salvation, they stopped singing songs of praise. God got angry when His people, the Israelites, were mistreating the poor. God, Jesus, the angels – have feelings and those feelings led to some very specific, identifiable behaviors. We are created in His image, so it is only natural that humans also have feelings. Just as in God, Jesus, and the angels, those feelings lead to some very specific, identifiable behaviors, so do ours.

Reading the Bible with the thought in mind that "God is love" presents a unique opportunity to have a paradigm shift from thinking of Biblical commands as a list of do's and don'ts that one engages in to go to heaven or keep from going to hell. The thinking pattern shifts to viewing Gods commands as the mechanisms by which the Source of Love (God the Father) and Love (Jesus) demonstrate how to love God, self, and others as God has commanded.

With these thoughts as an introduction, the prayer objective of this book is that when the reader has finished reading it, he/she is further empowered to

- Know and Love God as supreme
- Know and Love our neighbor as I
- Know and Love myself
- Know and obey the law of love especially as it relates to the heart (feelings)
- Know and experience the deep role that music plays in feeling and expressing love

Contents

Introduction . . . . *iii*
Chapter 1 What is Love? *1*
Chapter 2 What's in it for Me? *63*
Chapter 3 I just want to feel good! *115*
Chapter 4 Love God Supreme? What is that all about? *169*
Chapter 5 I Love Myself so that I Know How to Love You . . *219*
Chapter 6 I Love you as I Love Myself *271*
Chapter 7 Sex and Love *281*
Chapter 8 Music and the Expression of Love *301*
Chapter 9 Where do I go from here? *305*

Tributes:

Special recognition is deserved by several loved ones who helped inspire the writing of this book: My husband, Vincent, who has demonstrated key love characteristics identified in 1 Corinthians 13– chief of which is patience. My daughters, Maija and Joylin, who have consistently modeled aspects of what God's love looks like. My son Ronald, who has played a key role in helping me recognize the "feeling" aspect of love. Matthew Calhoun, my third grandson, whose questions require deep soul searching answers. Malik Calhoun, the eldest grandson, whose statements trigger reminders of questions still unanswered from my own youth. Malcolm Calhoun, the middle grandson, whose deep ideological values and statements at such a young age makes one aware of what youth today are struggling with. Devon Anderson-Neal, my first grandchild, a registered nurse, and a contributing author of this book, whose kind and gentle way of presenting herself models caring and compassion not often seen in one so young. Many unnamed friends whose patterns of interactions with superiors, peers, subordinates, co-workers, spouses, children, and families have been a lifelong source of inspiration of what unconditional love looks like in practice.

Contributing authors:

Devon Anderson-Neal is a registered nurse living in Hawaii. She shares thoughts about love from the perspective of a young single female whose profession is known for caring and from experiences learned from an early in life walk with God.

Dennis Love is an African-American male that shares from life experiences as a husband and former Probation Officer and what he has learned about love simply by living life and living up to his last name, Love.

David Anderson is an African-American dentist that shares thoughts about love from years of experience in his occupation, his years as a husband and father, his Christ-walk experience, and from his work and research in bioethics.

Salih Crider is an African-American male computer technologist who shares his experiences and collateral torments from the perspectives of a single male that walks and talks with God.

Danielle Parham is a married nurse practitioner and mother of two that shares her perspectives of love from her professional experiences, her experiences in marriage and motherhood, and her walk with God.

Author - Joyce Anderson is a married nurse practitioner/nurse educator that shares her perspectives from her personal walk with God, her experiences in marriage and love, experiences as a mother, and as a nurse practitioner/educator.

How to read the book

The book is written to carry its reader on a walk with love. It is written primarily in the first person, so that the reader can hopefully relay the experiences to him/herself so that love becomes a reality for the individual and is not viewed as something that happens to someone else. It is suggested that the reader claim this bible promise before reading each section, so that the Holy Spirit will help understand love and how it applies in the reader's life. "If ye then, being evil, know how to give good gifts unto your children: how much more shall your heavenly Father give the Holy Spirit to them that ask him" (Luke 11:13)?

Music has been shown through research to have a tremendous impact on human behavior. Classical music is known to increase the number and depth of brain waves that support the growth of intelligence. Music is used in therapy to help with emotional growth and needs. Recognizing the importance of music's impact on humans in so many ways, this book will recommend a song(s) that the reader can hear by searching youtube.com. The suggested song(s) will hopefully help the reader understand how we express our heart (feelings) in music that we listen to. The topic discussed will be the theme in the song suggested for that reading. Either a religious or secular song(s) may be suggested. The secular songs are intended to help us understand the spiritual concept of " loving others as myself" relationship, feelings, and communication concerns that are similar to the same components in a loving relationship with God, feelings that Jesus wants developed in us, so that when we interact with others, it is truly from the heart. The youtube.com suggestion will be listed at the end of each reading in the following manner:

YT: "GOD IS" BY JAMES CLEVELAND

The book is intended to generate deep thoughts, questions, feelings, and very specific prayers and conversations with God specifically about the subject area/bible verse in each reading related to knowing and loving God, self, and others with practical applications. It is intended to be read daily as part of a devotional exercise in developing growing positive, saving relationships with God, self, and others. A suggested pattern is read one page each day in the evening before going to bed using the following methods:

- Begin with prayer – praising God, thanking Him for all that He has done in your life specifically on that day.
    - Claim the promise of Luke 11:13 so that the Holy Spirit is guiding your thoughts/feelings
    - Ask Him for specific knowledge pertaining to your own state of love with Him, yourself, and others to be gained in the reading
    - Pray very specifically by name for those that you are engaged in loving –spouse, family, church members – anyone that the Holy Spirit brings to your mind

- Read one topic and complete the assignment at the end of the page.
    - Start with the bible verse. Talk to God about the verse. Ask Him to help you see His promises/privileges in the verse and ask for His power – His Spirit in you- that will enable you to carry out

the responsibilities/commands/laws associated with the verse
- Example: John 17:3 "And this is life eternal, that they might know thee, the only true God, and Jesus Christ, whom thou hast sent.
  - Promise/privilege – have eternal life
  - Command/law/responsibility – Know the only true God and Jesus Christ who He sent
- Then read the writing to gain specific knowledge related to
  - What love looks like and your own strengths, weaknesses in those areas.

- What did God help you get out of the reading? Write in the space provided in the book. For growth and the best outcomes, please be very specific in your communication with God. Talk to Him knowing that He is present with you and as you would talk to a friend or to your father. He is both.
  - Love looks like_____

  - My strength in this area_____

  - My weakness in this area_____

  - My prayer: (example) Dear God, You have promised ***that I can have eternal life***. You have told me that it is in my best interest to ***know You, the only true God, and Jesus whom You sent***. *I want to live eternally in Your presence. Please empower me through Your Spirit to know You. Please change my weakness in this area into a strength. Please continue to show me how and empower me to love You, love (whoever God inspires you to pray for eg. my husband), and love myself as You have commanded.*

    - In the underlined portion write God's promise(***eternal life*** in the example above) that He has made in the verse that you read and your responsibility (***know God and Jesus who He sent*** in the example above) that goes with that promise.

Spirit-led self evaluation In 2 Corinthians 13:5 God gives the love command "Examine yourselves…prove your own selves. Know ye not your own selves, how that Jesus Christ is in you…?" Promise: **_Know that Jesus is in you_**. Responsibility – **_examine yourself, know yourself, whether you be in the faith_**. Knowledge of where we are in our relationship with God, self, and others is a crucial first step in growing in love. Ask God to help you know what your strengths and weaknesses in a given area are. Then pray for growth in those areas, more strength in the strong areas, and changes from weakness to strength in the weak areas. Prayer is crucial to having the Holy Spirit lead and guide in this important matter. Simply pray, "Lord, you have told me that I can know myself and know that You are in me. You have told me to examine and know myself. I need Your help, so that I know where I am and where I need to go. Please honor Your promise to help me.

♥

Chapter 1
What is Love?

"Love is eternal. Love is all encompassing. Love is a blessing. Love is a curse. Love is pain. Love is joy. Love is forgiveness. Love is letting go. Love is holding on. Love is unconditional. Love is never being alone. Love will make you do wrong. Love is the opposite of hate. Love is blind. Love hurts. Love is worth fighting for. Love is everlasting. Love is bigger than one's self. Love is faith. Love is about others. Love is God.

Love is something that we truly don't understand at times. We take love for granted. We can be terrible at expressing love. We have a tendency to confuse love for things that can be very superficial. Love can fit just as nicely in a small box we keep hidden to ourselves or screamed from the rooftops for the world to hear, and its impact can be equally potent in both situations. Love is a multiplier of everything that we ever experienced or ever wanted to experience; our joys and pains, our wins and our losses, our hopes and our fears. It is great when love comes out right. When the outcome is less than favorable, well, we blame everything and everyone in sight."

- Salih Crider, The Human Experience of Love

God is Love
1 John 4:8 "...God is love."

His nature is love and His law, a reflection of His character, is the law of love.

"Is" – a state of being verb – past, present, future. God's love for me has always been, is continuously, and will be forever. His love has nothing to do with me deserving it, earning it, or being worthy of it. God loves me! He intends for me to love Him, love "me," and love others like I love myself. I cannot earn His love. There is nothing I can do to show that I deserve it or I am worthy of it. There is nothing that I can do that will make Him stop loving me. He loves me because that is just who He is!

Love existed in the beginning. Because of love, all things were made. Love creates. Love is the light of all mankind. Love shines in the darkness. The power of love is in the word.

The three commands that He gives in His word can be summarized as: Love God, love your neighbor as you love yourself. He shows me in His word what this love looks like and what He looks at in me to evaluate whether I am demonstrating whether I love Him, myself, and others. Know that when God tells us to do something, inherent in the command, is the power to carry it out.

Because of my sinful nature, God knows that I cannot love Him, myself, or others on my own. Thus it is "Christ in me, the hope of glory" that loves through me.

As we go through this book, we will focus on three principles of God's love that are seen in reading the Bible, His words of love given to me:

1. The Lover wants only what is best for the loved.
2. Love moves the loved from point A to point B, point B being a better place for the loved than point A.
3. The lover has something of value that he/she gives that benefits the loved.

Love looks like _____

My strength in this area _____

My weakness in this area _____

Dear God, You have promised_____

You have told me that it is in my best interest to_____

I praise Your name for helping me to_____

YT: "God is" James Cleveland
YT "Don't look back" Temptations
YT "I want to know what love is" Foreigner

HIS LOVE SEEKS WHAT IS BEST FOR ME.

Romans 8:28 "And we know that all things work together for good to them that love God, to them who are called according to his purpose."

Love wants only the best for the loved in all things. Love wants me to "prosper and be in good health." (3John 1:2) All things - not just one or two or even a few - work together for my good.

This means that for all the dimensions of man –physical, spiritual, emotional, mental, social – God wants only the best. In all of these areas, all things work together for the good that God intends for me to have. He wants me to prosper and grow in all of these areas. He wants me to be in good physical health, good emotional health. He wants me to have the best social relationships. And He wants me to grow spiritually and mentally.

Inherent in each command that God gives me is the promise of His power to carry it out. When He tells me that all things will work together for good – when He tells me that He wants me to prosper and be in good health, He is at the same time telling me that He will empower me to be sure that what He has commanded can happen if I cooperate with Him to get it done. When He tells me to love Him, myself, and others – He has promised to empower me to do just that.

For physical, spiritual, emotional, mental, and social health, instructions in God's word show me how to cooperate with Him for my best outcomes. A few examples of cooperating with God to achieve my best good include the following. I eat right and get enough sleep to have good physical health. I control my anger when someone mistreats me. I am happy when things are going well. I study my math and feel really proud when I get a good grade. I hug my friend and feel warm all over from the hug.

Love looks like _____

My strength in this area _____

My weakness in this area _____

Dear God, You have promised_____

You have told me that it is in my best interest to_____

I praise Your name for helping me to_____

YT "Victory in Jesus" Yolanda Adams
YT: " You're the best thing that ever happened to me."
Gladys Knight and the Pips

His love moves me from where I am to a better place.

1 John 3:14 "We know that we have passed from death unto life because we love the brethren…"

Love moves me from death to life. Love always moves me to a better place.

Most people prefer life to death. God's promise to me is to move me from death to life. 1 John 5:13 reassures me to "believe on the name of the Son of God, that ye may KNOW that ye have eternal life." I **_know_** I have eternal life because I believe on His name – not because of my goodness but because of His goodness. Not because I am worthy but because His righteousness makes me worthy.

In all that God seeks to do in my life, He always moves me to a better place in life than I was in before. I smoked cigarettes. He gave me the victory over smoking cigarettes. My physical health is in a better place. I was overweight and taking heart medicine because my blood pressure was too high. I lost weight, now my blood pressure is in the normal range. I do not need to take blood pressure medicines now. I am in a better place. I was lonely and depressed. He sent a friend to cheer me up. I am in a better place in my eternal life journey.

He reassures me again in Romans 8:28 that "all things work together" for my good because I love Him and I am called according to His purpose.

God wants to always move me to a better place. I can cooperate with God in that movement by asking Him where am I now? Where do You want to move me to? Am I loving myself physically by exercising for better health? Am I showing that I love myself spiritually by being "one" with my spouse? Am I loving others and myself emotionally by following the instructions for emotional health in Ephesians 4:32 "Be ye kind one to another, tenderhearted, forgiving one another, even as God for Christ's sake hath forgiven you?"

Love looks like _____

My strength in this area _____

My weakness in this area _____

Dear God, You have promised _____

You have told me that it is in my best interest to_____

I praise Your name for helping me to_____

YT "You make me feel brand new" **Stylistics**
YT "Make me over" **Wintley Phipps**

HIS LOVE GAVE ME SOMETHING HE VALUED TO BENEFIT ME.
John 3:16 "For God so loved the world that He gave His ONLY begotten Son, that whosoever believeth in Him, should not perish but have everlasting life."

True love gives something that the lover has that is valued by the lover that he/she gives to the loved one that will benefit the loved one. God gave His ONLY Son, so that I would not perish, but I, by believing in His Son, can live forever.

What was God feeling when He made that decision? What was Jesus feeling when He agreed to die for me? Jesus, when He was in the Garden of Gethsemane the night before He was crucified, was feeling it! He did NOT want to get on that cross and die for me! He was an emotional wreck! His sympathetic nervous system was in overload evidenced by the sweating of "great drops of blood" as He was praying. He got up to check with His "friends," and they were asleep. God sent an angel just to strengthen and encourage Him.

So He kept praying, even more earnestly, and He said to His Father "Father, if Thou be willing, remove this cup from me." I think what He meant was I don't want to die! I don't want to do this, Father, help me! But then because He looked forward and saw me, hopeless, sinful, and with no options but death that would forever separate me from Him, loving me so much, even more than He loved Himself, He said to His Father, "Nevertheless not my will, but Thine be done."

I have wondered how God "felt" as He watched the men that His Son had created put those nails in Jesus' hands. Watched as those men that He was giving His Son's life for, push that sword into His side, spit in His face. Humiliated Him by putting a crown of thorns on His head and taking off His clothes in public. The Father watched and did nothing. The angels watched and did nothing.

And Jesus, knowing that He could tell the angels to stop it, knowing that He did not have to die, just prayed, "Father forgive them! They don't know what they are doing." What love! For me!

Love looks like _____

My strength in this area _____

My weakness in this area _____

Dear God, You have promised _____

You have told me that it is in my best interest to _____

I praise Your name for helping me to _____

YT "Alabaster Box" CeCe Winans
YT "He could have called ten thousand angels" Ncandweni

HIS PUTS HIS LOVE, REFLECTED IN HIS LAW, IN MY THOUGHTS AND FEELINGS.

Hebrews 8:10 "…I will put my laws into their mind, and write them in their hearts; and I will be to them a God, and they shall be to me a people."

Love shares with me the expectations desired of me- thoughts, feelings, and behaviors.

Mind (thoughts) and heart (feelings) make up character. Character is the only thing that I will take from this life to heaven. God puts His law in my thoughts and writes them in my feelings so that I can develop a character like His. When God breathed His breath into man, man became a living soul. Man was created in His image, before sin, with a perfect character based on the law of God's love, the only standard of moral perfection that God has given. Every law that God has given is permanent and everlasting. God, in moving me to a better place, from death to life, is working with me to develop that character that I will take to heaven and continue to grow throughout eternity.

Jesus said just before His death in John 17:4, "I have glorified thee on the earth: I have finished the work which thou gavest me to do" and in John 15:10 "…I have kept my Father's commandments, and abide in His love." The summary of His law in Luke 10:27 is "Love the Lord they God with all thine heart…all thy soul…with all thy strength and thy neighbor as thyself."

Character development occurs over my lifetime. I am constantly learning to love God, love myself, and love others in fulfillment of His law. Because in His love, knowing what is best for my best outcomes, He has commanded me to do this, He empowers me through His indwelling Spirit to make it possible. By His power only, I can love Him. I can love others. I can love myself. I have no excuse. That is the essence of the development of my character – my thoughts and my feelings, the only thing I can take from this earth to heaven. God uses my behaviors displaying my character to evaluate whether I love as He has so instructed me.

Love looks like _____

My strength in this area _____

My weakness in this area _____

Dear God, You have promised _____

You have told me that it is in my best interest to_____

I praise Your name for helping me to_____

YT "Stand" by Donnie McClurkin
"Drinking from my saucer" Jabez

TO KNOW HIM, IS TO LOVE HIM. HE WANTS ME TO KNOW HIM. John 17:3 "And this is life eternal, that they might know thee the only true God, and Jesus Christ, whom He has sent."

Love knows the loved. Presence. Being. Time. All are important in getting to know someone. Knowing someone requires that the person must be willing to reveal himself and I must have the capability of knowing them. God provides both for me.

I must know Him, so that I can have the eternal life He has promised me. Knowledge can be "book" learning or by experiment. I can read in my science book that orange juice is found to be an acid by putting it on pH paper and the color changes to red. That is book knowledge. When I put the orange juice on the PH paper and see the color of the paper change to red, I have experimental knowledge of how to know it is an acid. God wants me to have experimental knowledge of Him.

God has told me that He will put His love in my mind and write it on my heart. He reveals Himself to me in His word, in nature, through interactions with others, through His interactions with me. He wants me to feel His presence, to joy in His goodness, to feel pleasure even when I hear His name.

He provides the opportunity for me to take a good look at Him – inside and out. He tells me in Hebrews 4:16 to "come boldly to the throne of grace." In Romans 12:2, He tells me to be transformed "by the renewing of your mind that you may PROVE what is that good and acceptable and perfect will of God." In Malachi 3: 10 "…prove Me now herewith…" Part of my getting to know Him is to come to Him, to test Him and allow Him to prove to me that what He says is true. Wow! I cannot imagine trusting my own ability to do something that I would say to somebody – I will prove it to you. Yet this is a method He has given me, so that I may know Him experimentally.

Carla Thomas sings in a song, "Look at his eyes, how they hypnotize. He's got everything a girl could want. Man, oh, man – what a prize…he's all the joy I could find in a boy." Although God in His love, in this world of sin, sometimes allows me to have these experiences with man, how often do I find myself looking to find in man, what ultimately I know I will find in God?

Love looks like _____

My strength in this area _____

My weakness in this area _____

Dear God, You have promised_____

You have told me that it is in my best interest to_____

I praise Your name for helping me to_____

YT "Just one look" Doris Troy
YT "So you would know" Brooklyn Tabernacle Choir
YT "Since I met you baby" Ivory Joe Hunter

HE WANTS TO BE WITH ME.
Matthew 1:23 "…they shall call His name Emmanuel… God with us."

Love wants to be with the loved. "Be" another state of being word. Be with me – continuously, round the clock, every moment, every hour, ever day – forever. Presence. God, the Creator of the Universe. Lord of lords. King of kings. Wants to be with "me." Wow! Wonderful and scary at the same time. Why would He want to be with me? I am nothing. I am nobody. I have nothing. I know nothing. Why would He waste His time with me?

God was with Daniel in the lion's den. He was with the Hebrew boys in the fiery furnace. He wrestled all night with Jacob. He came down every evening to "be" with Adam and Eve in the Garden of Eden. He walked by Moses to allow him to see Him and proclaimed to him who He was. He sent an angel from His presence to tell Mary that she, an unmarried teenager, was going to have a baby and to reassure her that even though she could be stoned to death because of it, that God was with her. They were all nothings. Nobodies. Had nothing. Knew nothing. Just like me.

Jesus lived on this earth for thirty-three years – Presence. With men and women, just like me. He cried with Mary and Martha when Lazarus died. He had dinner at Simon's house. He let Mary, a prostitute, touch Him. She washed His feet with her tears and dried them with her hair. He let the woman with an issue of flowing blood for twelve years touch Him and be healed. His heart was broken when he saw the widow weeping for her dead child and he brought the child back to life and gave him back to his mother.

Be with me. Presence, time, knowing me. Allowing me to get to know Him. Thinking about me. Psalms 139:16, "How precious are thy thoughts unto me, O God! How great the sum of them!" This is what His love looks like. He tells me "I will NEVER leave you, nor forsake you. Hebrews 13:5. My mother, my father, my husband - may leave me."

"Just to be with you, thrills me through and through. You can break my heart and I'll be a fool for you – forever," Marvin Gaye says in his song.

A friend once said to me, "I didn't leave my marriage, my marriage left me." I may break Jesus' heart by leaving Him. Jesus will not be my fool, but even when I break His heart, He will never leave me, nor forsake me. He just waits for me to come back.

Love looks like _____

My strength in this area _____

My weakness in this area _____

Dear God, You have promised _____

You have told me that it is in my best interest to _____

I praise Your name for helping me to _____

YT "The Love of God" Wintley Phipps
YT "Forever" Marvin Gaye

HE WANTS ME TO BE WHERE HE IS.

John 14:3 "And if I go and prepare a place for you, I will come again, and receive you unto myself; that where I am, there ye may be also."

Love makes and keeps promises. Love wants me to be where he is. The Lover does not lie, He can be trusted. The Lover accepts me into His personal space. The Lover goes away for a while, yet doesn't leave me, and reassures me that He will come back. The Lover wants me to be in His personal space. Jesus is the Lover here. His desire for me is so strong that He told me I am going to make a place for you in My personal space. Then He told me, I am going to come back and get you to make sure that you are where I am.

His personal space, his physical space. His emotional space. His social space. His intellectual space. He wants to be sure I have a nice, safe place to be with Him, so He is going to make sure I have a place to live. He wants me to share happy and joyous times with Him. He wants me to socialize with His other friends, family, and His other created beings and have some good times. He wants to exchange deep thoughts about everything with me. I cannot wait for that part! I have so many questions to ask Him. He wants me to start here and now but keep it going forever when He comes back to get me.

Where can I be with Him in His personal and social space now? He told me in Matthew 18:20 "...where two are three are gathered in My name, there I am in the midst of them." Where is His emotional space now? Romans 12:15 tells me to join Him in rejoicing with those that rejoice and weeping with those that weep. He invites me, as did David in Psalm 3:4, to cry to him when I am sad, lonely, or scared. In His intellectual space, He has given me His written word. He has given me nature. He has given me you –to have those deep discussions about Him. He often, not always, answers my "why" questions.

Love looks like _____

My strength in this area _____

My weakness in this area _____

Dear God, You have promised _____

You have told me that it is in my best interest to_____

I praise Your name for helping me to_____

YT "He's coming back again" New Jersey Mass Choir
YT "Cry to me" Solomon Burke

He wants me to be "one" with Him and with each other. John 17:21 "That they all may be one; as thou, Father, art in me, and I in thee, that they also may be one in us; ... **23** I in them, and thou in me, that they may be made perfect in one; and that the world may know that thou... hast loved them as thou hast loved me."

Love desires "oneness" with the loved. Unity. That I can be one with Him. He in me – so that I can be made perfect in oneness. He in others, so that we can be "one." Sort of like a family I guess.

A triangle has three different sides, but it is one triangle. Jesus and I are one. He, God, in the form of the Holy Spirit dwells within me to accomplish this. Galatians 2:20 "...I live; yet not I, but Christ liveth in me..."

Have you ever noticed how married couples that have been together a long time start to look and act alike? A lot of their "oneness" is mediated physiologically through the exchange of genetic material, DNA, during the act of sexual intercourse. When He is in me and I am "one" with Him, I act like Him. I talk like Him. I do the kind of things He does. I even look like Him. 1 John 3:2 "Beloved, now are we the sons of God, and it doth not yet appear what we shall be, but we know that when He shall appear, we shall be like Him; for we shall see Him as He is."

The Lover wants me to have that same "oneness" with others that love Him that He has with me. The same Holy Spirit is in all that love Him and the expected "oneness" can be achieved when I cooperate with Him to make it happen. If He has told me to do it, remember He always tells me to do what is in my best interest. At the same time, His indwelling within me provides the power to carry out the command. You hear the same desire for "oneness" expressed in the saying, "Why can't we all just get along?"

Love looks like _____

My strength in this area _____

My weakness in this area _____

Dear God, You have promised _____

You have told me that it is in my best interest to_____

I praise Your name for helping me to_____

YT "Make us one" Philip Bailey
YT "Endless love" Lionel Ritchie, Diana Ross

HE WANTS TO CHANGE MY CHARACTER SO I CAN BE A BETTER PERSON, SO THAT I CAN BE LIKE HIM WHEN HE RETURNS TO GET ME. Romans 12: 1, 2 "I beseech you therefore brethren, by the mercies of God, that ye present your bodies, a living sacrifice, holy, acceptable unto God, which is your reasonable service. And be not conformed to this world: but be ye transformed by the renewing of your mind, that ye may prove what is that good, and acceptable, and perfect will of God."

Love asks me to sacrifice – my body – physical, spiritual, emotional, and social. Love asks that I not give in to what the "world" thinks, but what He thinks. Love does not want me to do or think like the "world" thinks but have my thoughts changed by Him. Knowing that love ALWAYS seeks what is in my best interest, that is a pretty reasonable request. He is saying to me the "world" doesn't love you, I do. Don't let the "world" pull you away from me. You know that I love you. I died for you – is the "world" willing to do that for you? I gave up my glory in heaven for you. Is there anyone else that you know that is going to give up "everything" for you? I know you better than anybody else in the world. Let me have control of your thoughts, and when you do that, you can know for sure what is my acceptable and perfect will. What I want from you. What is best for you. Let me put my laws into your mind, so that your thoughts will work to produce your best outcomes. I really do love you, more than you can ever really know or understand.

1 John 3:2 "...but we know that, when he shall appear, we shall be like him; for we shall see him as he is. Be like Him. Submissive. Respectful. Performed the duties of a son, brother, friend, citizen. Spent quiet time with those who understood what He was about. Acted independently as needed. Used the scriptures only as His rule of law. When He saw that the requirements of God and requirements of society were in collision, He chose to follow the requirements of His Father. Focused on His mission. Loved His brothers, even though they misunderstood Him. Treated them with unfailing kindness, even though they had different values. Sacrificed Himself for the good of others. All of these are aspects of Jesus' character that I have read about and that He wants me to have in my own character. I want to be like Him. Please change me to be like You.

Love looks like _____

My strength in this area _____

My weakness in this area _____

Dear God, You have promised _____

You have told me that it is in my best interest to _____

I praise Your name for helping me to _____

YT "I surrender" Brooklyn Tabernacle Choir
YT "A change is going to come" Sam Cook
YT "Order my steps in Your word" GMWA Women

HE WANTS ME TO KEEP HIS WORDS IN MY HEART.
John 14:23 "…If a man love me, he will keep my words and my Father will love him, and we will come unto him, and make our abode with him."

Love wants me to keep His words in my thoughts and in my feelings. Keep. Hold on to. Retain. Possess. Remember. Understand. Honor.

Words are powerful. Power is the ability to do something, to influence behavior or outcomes, the force to move something. Proverbs 18:21 "Death and life are in the power of the tongue…" John 6:63 "It is the spirit that quickeneth (give life)… The words that I speak unto you, they are spirit and they are life." Love gives me words that give life. Remember He has told me that He wants me to pass from death to life. He arranges to do that by giving me His word. He wants me to hold on to His word in my thoughts and in my mind, so that I will have life.

Psalm 119:105, "Thy word is a lamp unto my feet, and a light unto my path."

With that life comes His Father's love. With that loves comes their presence, abiding with me – staying with me – in MY personal space. My physical space. My emotional space. My social space. My intellectual space. Some of His words that come to mind that I have kept in my heart - I love you. I want you. I want to hear your voice. I think of you a lot. Don't forget me. I want to be with you. I want you to be where I am. Powerful words. That motivate me. Words that encourage and strengthen me. Words that tell me to keep going. Words that give light for me to stay focused on my path.

When I keep His words in my heart, He will make His abode with me! He will live with me! Lord of lords. King of kings abiding with me! Forever! Love's words are always powerful to move me to a better place. From death to life.

Love looks like _____

My strength in this area _____

My weakness in this area _____

Dear God, You have promised _____

You have told me that it is in my best interest to_____

I praise Your name for helping me to_____

YT "Speak" Myron Butler & Levi
YT "Keep my words" Numinous
YT "I wanna be where you are" Jackson 5

HE WANTS ME TO BELIEVE IN HIM.

Hebrews 11:6 "But without faith it is impossible to please him: for he that cometh to God must believe that He is and that he is a rewarder of them that diligently seek Him."

Love wants me to believe in the Lover. I must believe that He "is," even though I can't see Him. I must believe that He rewards me when I diligently seek Him.

Hebrews 11:1, "Now faith is the substance of things hoped for, the evidence of things not seen." I can't see the air that I breathe. The substance that proves that the air exists is my life. Two minutes without oxygen, and I am unresponsive. Six minutes without it and I am physically declared dead.

I believe that He exists because of the faith that He himself gives me to believe in Him. One night there was a really bad rainstorm where we live in the country. My granddaughter asked to bring the horse into the garage to get him out of the storm. My quick response was God will take care of your horse in the storm just like He takes care of the other animals. She decided to help God out, and at nine-years-old, she slipped out of the house during the night and slept on a blanket on the ground by her horse.

The evidence of His existence, the hope that He provides me to prove His existence – I woke up this morning. I have food. When I am hurting, He feels my pain. When I need a friend, He sends me one. When I have pain, He has provided internal pain medicine, endorphins, to take care of it. When I have a cut, He provides the healing processes through the inflammatory process to heal it. When I need wisdom to make a decision, I ask Him and He tells what is in my best interest to do but leaves the choice to me. When I spend hard work and time searching for Him, He rewards that by helping me to find Him – in His word- in my relationship with my husband – in my relationship with you. I know this because He told me – John 17:23 –" Thou in me and I in them." He is in all those that believe in Him and diligently search for Him. Thank you, friend, for allowing Jesus to be in you, so that when I am looking for Him and I come to you, I see Him in you and you become evidence of His existence.

Love looks like _____

My strength in this area _____

My weakness in this area _____

Dear God, You have promised _____

You have told me that it is in my best interest to _____

I praise Your name for helping me to _____

YT "I believe for every drop of rain that fails" MS Thatcher
YT " I believe in you and me" Whitney Houston

HE WANTS ME TO TELL HIM THAT I LOVE HIM.
Psalm 18: 1 "I love you, Lord, my strength." Love wants to hear me say, "I love you." Talk to me, my love. I love to hear your praises. I long to hold you in my arms at night. Words are so powerful. They effect change and accomplish things in my life that I want accomplished. The Lover wants to hear me say, "I love you" – such powerful words when they are true. Then He is ok with me telling Him why. My strength – You empower me to do the things You want me to do. He wants me to talk to Him – in the morning, in the noontime, at night. He wants to hold me close in His arms when I talk to Him. He wants me to feel comfortable when I talk to Him. He wants me to feel safe when I talk to Him. He wants me to know I am accepted into His space. When I am telling Him why I love Him, He knows that it is also reinforcing how He feels about me to me, so that my love for Him will continue to grow. He wants me to talk to Him in private. Matthew 6:6, "…when thou prayest, enter into thy closet, and when thou has shut thy door, pray to thy Father which is in secret… "

I love You, Lord. When I look at You up on that cross. When I see you sitting on Your throne that You have gifted to me as Your heir. When I see and hear You in Your High Priest garments in the Most Holy place, holding up Your nail pierced hands, pleading, "My blood, My blood," for me. It brings tears to my eyes. I feel so happy and safe when I am with You. I think about You all the time. What rationale reason would I have for not loving someone who loves me like You do? You know everything about me – when I sit down, when I rise up – even the number of hairs on my head. You are with me every moment. You think about me with good thoughts. You have never said an unkind word to me. You have never mistreated or disrespected me. You have never lied to me. You will love me forever! You sacrificed Your own feelings and needs to make sure I could spend eternity with You. You accept me in to Your personal space. You desire me to be in Your presence. You told me You are going to come back and get me, so I can be where You are forever.

"Talk to me, I love the things you say. Tell me you love me so. Hold me close. Can't you see, darling, I love you so," Little Willie John.

Love looks like _____

My strength in this area _____

My weakness in this area _____

Dear God, You have promised_____

You have told me that it is in my best interest to_____

I praise Your name for helping me to_____

YT "Talk to me" Little Willie John
YT "Talk to me-Love Jesus" Sunflower girl
YT "I love the Lord, He heard my cry" Whitney Houston

HE WANTS ME TO TRUST HIS JUDGMENT MORE THAN I TRUST MY OWN.

John 16:8, "And when He is come, He will reprove the world of sin, and of righteousness, and of judgment."

Love wants me to trust His judgments and decisions. Is this good or bad? Is this right or wrong? Judgment calls are different than decisions. Judgments are based on law. Decisions are based on critical analysis of a given situation based on intended outcomes or goals. God is the only one capable of making judgment calls. It makes sense that the One that gave the law knows best how to interpret it. He gives me the power of choice to make decisions based on the thoughts and feelings He has put in my mind and written on my heart. God, who knows the end from the beginning and knows everything there is to know about me, is also best at advising me on the decisions that I must make.

God wants me to make decisions that are in my best interest and in the best interest of those He has given me to love like myself. He provides the standard for making those decisions in His laws of love. He will also make the judgment call as to whether I have met that standard. My judgment and decision making are very faulty. He wants me to trust His judgment better than I trust my own. He wants me to ask Him before making decisions. Feelings are the signal that motivate me to engage or not engage in making a decision, but it is not wise to make the final decision based on feelings alone. That is why God wants me to trust His judgment better than my own.

Trust, a necessary part of love, does not come all at once. It comes from experiencing the best outcomes based on the advice given to make decisions. Honesty is a key ingredient needed for trust. Time, talking to Jesus regularly, testing and proving Him as He has told me to do, being in His presence, "knowing" Him. He has never lied to me. I see consistently that He does exactly as He has said He would do. My outcomes based on following what He has told me to do have been far better than they would have been had I followed my own feelings. There is no reason not to trust His judgment more than I trust my own.

Love looks like _____

My strength in this area _____

My weakness in this area _____

Dear God, You have promised _____

You have told me that it is in my best interest to _____

I praise Your name for helping me to _____

YT "I TRUST IN GOD" CLARA WARD
YT "YOU MUST BELIEVE ME" IMPRESSIONS

He wants me to choose and submit to Him.

Joshua 24:15, "And if it seem evil unto you to serve the Lord, choose you this day whom ye will serve…but as for me and my house, we will serve the Lord."

James 4:7, "Submit yourselves therefore to God. Resist the devil and he will flee from you.

Love gives me the option to receive love or not receive love. Love does not force itself on me. Choice is one thing that God gives me that He refuses to control. He writes His law on my heart, but He says I must choose to obey it. He shows me what He can do for me. He tells me how much He loves me. He takes care of me every day. He provides for my needs. He gives me the opportunity to know Him. He shows me the outcomes that will happen if I choose someone or something over Him.

Deuteronomy 30:19, "…I have set before you life and death, blessing and cursing; therefore choose life, that both thou and thy seed may live." Life or death. Blessing or cursing. My choice. But He does not force me to choose life. He leaves that up to me. He wants me to understand that my choices do not impact just me; my choices affect my "seed" – my children, and those others that I love. Choices have outcomes. My choice for best outcomes demonstrates that I love God, myself, and others.

Submission is an informed response to love. God wants me to submit to Him. He knows that it is in my best interest to do so. He knows that my best outcomes come when I submit to His judgment, His leadership, His laws that He puts in my thoughts and writes on my feelings. His love. He loves me so much and desires that I choose and submit to Him, but He will not force me. He makes Himself available, but He leaves the choosing and submission in my heart and in my hands.

Love looks like _____

My strength in this area _____

My weakness in this area _____

Dear God, You have promised _____

You have told me that it is in my best interest to _____

I praise Your name for helping me to_____

YT "I choose You again" Wintley Phipps
YT "Make me yours" Bettye Swan

I am His child.

1 John 3:1-2, "Behold what manner of love the Father hath bestowed upon us, that we should be called the sons of God... Beloved, now are we the sons of God...but we know when He shall appear, we shall be like Him...

Love recognizes my position, status in the relationship. Now! I am His son. Male or female. When he appears, I will be like Him. Where did I get THAT DNA? Adam's DNA is still in me. I still look and act like him. But God, who loves me, said that I am His son and I will be like Him. Colossians 1:27, "...Christ in you, the hope of glory." Love privilege – be His son. Love response/responsibility – be like Him when He appears.

Christ in me, the Holy Spirit in me, empowers me to "be" like Him. Growth is often imperceptible and occurs over time. An apple is an apple at each stage of its development, but it continues to grow to maturity over time. Christ in me – His thoughts. His feelings - lead to His behaviors. I will grow to be like Him so that when He appears, I will "be" like Him. Because of God's love, His grace – giving me what I don't deserve – salvation and His mercy – not giving me what I do deserve, death, I am His child.

Galatians 4:7 "...if a son, then an heir of God through Christ." Revelation 1:6 " And hath made us kings and priests unto God and his Father... Because I am His son now, I am an heir to His throne, a king, a priest. Now. Male or female. Me – an heir to His throne. Me – a king. Me –a priest. Christ in me, the hope of glory!

What love! He allows me to be His son. His heir. A king. A priest. Undeserving, nobody, nothing, me. A song I learned as a child has the refrain, "Be like Jesus, this my song. In the home and in the throng; Be like Jesus, all day long! I would be like Jesus." I will be like Him when He appears because I am His child.

Love looks like _____

My strength in this area _____

My weakness in this area _____

Dear God, You have promised _____

You have told me that it is in my best interest to _____

I praise Your name for helping me to_____

YT "Lord lift us up" Bebe and Cece Winans
YT "I am His child" Hillside's interpretation

HE KNOWS WHAT I NEED BUT HE NEEDS ME TO KNOW THAT I NEED IT.

Matthew 6:8, "…for your Father knoweth what things ye have need of before ye ask Him. **Phillipians 4:19,** "But my God shall supply all your need according to His riches in glory by Christ Jesus."

Matthew 7:7, "Ask, and it shall be given you; seek, and ye shall find, knock, and it shall be opened."

Love helps me to know my needs. Love knows and takes care of my needs. Maslow, a renowned psychologist, describes five levels of human needs in a hierarchy moving from the basic physiological needs (air, water, food, sleep, etc.) to the highest need of self-actualization (to be all that I can be). His list includes the need to be safe, the need to be loved and belong, the need to be esteemed and recognized. All of these needs fit within what God wants for me and how He himself has made me. His love tells me that He has the ability to and will take care of all these needs.

His love always seeks what is best for me. He knows that I need oxygen. He created the water cycle to have a continuous available supply to meet the sixty percent of water that makes up my body, so that it can function. He knows that I want to be happy and feel good about myself. He knows that I need to feel whole, complete. He sends His angels to watch over me to keep me safe and fight battles for me. He knows that I need love. He recognizes that I need to be recognized and acknowledged, so He told me that I am His Son, an heir to His throne, a priest in His kingdom. He wants me to be the best that I can be, so He places His Spirit in me so I can cooperate with Him to be like Him.

He knows everything I need to live, to survive. I think I know lots of times, but the truth is I really do not know, and I certainly do not know how to meet those needs most of the time. That's why He tells me to ask Him. It reinforces for me when I ask Him, that His judgment is better than mine. It reinforces that He has everything I need. He tells me in His word how to live to have my best outcomes while living in this world of sin. He leaves the choice up to me whether I will listen and obey Him - whether I will ask, seek, knock. He honors His promise to give, let me find, and open. Many times I have not because I ask not or I ask with the wrong motive, so I don't get what I ask for.

James 4:2-3, "…ye have not because ye ask not. Ye ask and receive not, because you ask amiss; that ye may consume it upon your lusts."

Love looks like _____

My strength in this area _____

My weakness in this area _____

Dear God, You have promised _____

You have told me that it is in my best interest to _____

I praise Your name for helping me to _____

YT "Oh, it is Jesus" Andre Crouch
YT "Lady Soul" Temptations

HE WANTS ME TO SHARE THE GOOD THINGS HE HAS GIVEN ME WITH OTHERS.

Matthew 10:8, "Heal the sick, cleanse the leper, raise the dead, cast out devils: freely ye have received, freely give."

Psalm 23:5, "…thou anointest my head with oil; my cup runneth over.

Love gives. A lover has something he values that he gives to the loved that benefits the loved.

I cannot pour from an empty cup. God makes sure that my cup is full even to the point of excess that it runs over. Shall I just let the excess run over, or shall I put it to the good use God says is in my best interest and in the best interest of those that I love like I love myself? The cycles that we see in so many areas of nature help me to understand how giving works. In the water cycle, the rain falls to the earth where it fills the ocean. The temperature causes the rain to evaporate into the sky. When the clouds are full to overflowing, it rains and the water comes back to the earth again.

Giving benefits the lover as well as the loved. If I am constantly pouring from my cup, God is constantly refilling it. If I don't pour from my cup, what it is inside will rot after a while. If I drink it all myself and deplete the supply, where will the needed continuous supply come from? I hear the problem of depletion and misuse of supply that does not recycle appropriately in the environment in the term "climate change." The same thing happens in my love life. Luke 6:38, "Give, and it shall be given unto you; good measure, pressed down, and shaken together, and running over, shall men give into your bosom. For with the same measure that ye mete withal it shall be measured to you again." Love knows that it is in my best interest to give. If my hand remains closed to keep whatever God has placed in it, how can I expect Him to keep giving to a hand that is closed? The same happens with love – when I give it, I will get it back. It is in my best interest to give love back to God and give love to others.

Love looks like _____

My strength in this area _____

My weakness in this area _____

Dear God, You have promised_____

You have told me that it is in my best interest to_____

I praise Your name for helping me to_____

YT "I GIVE MYSELF AWAY" SUNBEAMS CHOIR
YT "EVERYBODY NEEDS SOMEBODY TO LOVE" SOLOMON BURKE

HE WANTS TO OCCUPY MY PERSONAL SPACE.
Revelation 3:20, "Behold I stand at the door and knock: if any man hear my voice, and open the door, I will come in to him, and will sup with him, and he with me."

Love occupies my personal space. The Lover will enter my personal space when I open the door to my thoughts and feelings and let Him in. He knocks and calls out my name to get my attention. He stands at the door of my heart, waiting for me to say yes. When I open the door, He comes in. We have dinner together with my three children. What a conversation we have at that meal! He tells me all about Himself – what He likes, what He did when He was a little boy, what His family is like, what it was like living in Nazareth, about the time His mother took Him to Jerusalem and He was left behind at the temple by Himself. Why He got angry in the temple and what it felt like to turn over those tables. He tells me how different and special that I am. How unique I am. He tells me what He is doing in the Most Holy place. He talks about the twenty-four elders that came forth from their graves and are in heaven with Him now. He helps me understand what I need to do to get along with my boss. Then He holds me in His arms and tells me how much He loves me, how much He enjoys His time with me. He said just what I needed to hear.

Now, He says, it's my turn. We go in the bedroom and I tell Him I am having trouble sleeping because I am worried about my child on drugs. I take Him in the kitchen and show Him how low on food I am with three mouths to feed. I tell Him thank you for helping me find a good paying job. Then I start crying because I just don't know how to handle my husband's affair– should I get a divorce? Should I stay? He listens quietly. He reassures me that He will never leave me, that He will do everything He can to support me. He reminds me of my options and tells me to consider what my long term outcomes are intended to be. He asks me questions to make me consider the consequences of the choices and decisions that I must make. Then He leaves the choice up to me. We quietly lay down to sleep with Him holding me in His arms. What an evening!

Love looks like _____

My strength in this area _____

My weakness in this area _____

Dear God, You have promised_____

You have told me that it is in my best interest to_____

I praise Your name for helping me to_____

YT "The Potter's House" Tramaine Hawkins
YT "Open the door to your heart" Darrel Banks

HIS HEART IS BROKEN IF I DECIDE TO LEAVE HIM.
Matthew 23:37, "O Jerusalem, Jerusalem, thou that killest the prophets, and stonest them which are sent unto thee, how often would I have gathered thy children together, even as a hen gathereth her chickens under her wings, and ye would not."
Luke 19:41, "And when He was come near He beheld the city, and wept over it."
Ephesians 3:17-19, "That Christ may dwell in your hearts by faith…rooted and grounded in love…to know the love of Christ which passeth knowledge…"

Love wants me to stay with Him forever. We both will miss the warmth, the tenderness, the trust, the good feelings that we shared when we were together. I am moving from life to death if I leave Him.

Once He comes into my space, He doesn't leave. It's His dwelling place now. We work together to make sure everything is kept clean and that we are available to each other at all times. He does everything He can to make sure I don't leave Him or put Him out. Once I leave, it is not easy to come back. My pride gets in the way. I get caught up in a lot of other "stuff." Lot's wife turned around to look at what she was leaving behind and turned into a pillar of salt. Judas left and ended up hanging himself.

Babies at the very least fail to grow if they are not physically touched. If they do not experience touch at all, they can die. Two key hormones are released during touching, as well as during sexual intercourse. Oxytocin, a hormone needed by the new mother to bond with her newborn baby, increases bonding and trust. It does the same for married couples. Endorphins, released when I am touched, do a lot of things in the body, but they are responsible for two very important functions. They are the body's " feel good" hormones. Endorphins also support the immune function to decrease disease. When I fail to have these hormones released, I can get physically ill and can fail to grow in trust in my relationships.

Like a hen gathers her chickens. That's the comparison that He makes for what He does with those that He loves and those that love Him. The warmth going from the mother hen to the chickens is nothing compared to the warmth that He wants to give to me. The safety and shelter of her wings over her chicks, He wants to make sure I have. The good feelings the chicks feel when they are so close to the mother hen is what He wants me to feel when I am close to Him. I will stay because I need to and like to be touched.

Love looks like _____

My strength in this area _____

My weakness in this area _____

Dear God, You have promised_____

You have told me that it is in my best interest to _____

I praise Your name for helping me to _____

YT "Stay" Maurice Williams
YT "I cried a tear because of you" Lavern Baker

He asks about my goals and answers my questions.
John 1: 38-39, "Then Jesus turned, and saw them following, and saith unto them, 'What seek ye?' They said unto him, Rabbi…where dwellest thou? He saith unto them, 'Come and see.' They came and saw where he dwelt, and abode with him that day…"

Love asks me questions about what I want. Love answers my questions. Love increases my desire to follow Him and be where love is. Love recognizes that I am following and engages me in conversation.

"What seek ye?" What are your goals? What do you want? "Where do you live?" I am not going to tell you, I am going to show you. "Come and see." Come on in. This is where I live. Can I get you anything to eat or drink? Make yourself at home. Mi casa es su casa – my house is your house.

I wonder what the rest of that day was like for the two disciples. Did they share their other goals with Jesus? Did He ask them more questions? What was His response to what they wanted to personally accomplish? Did they help Him clean His house? Did they help Him fix dinner? Did He share His hurts and pains with them? Did He talk about His brothers? Did they share their fears? Did they talk to Him about sex? Did they talk about how to fix things around the house- carpenter things? Did they talk about the sheep in the field? Did they crack jokes? What were their takeaways from that day spent with Jesus? How did it change their lives? Did they leave saying we've got to do this again soon?

Have I shared my goals, my wants, my needs with Jesus? Do I ask Him "why" questions? How questions? What next questions? Have I followed Him to His house? What did I do when I got there? Was I comfortable in His presence? Did I help Him fix dinner? Did I crack jokes with Him? What were my takeaways when I left? When will I go back again?

Love looks like _____

My strength in this area _____

My weakness in this area _____

Dear God, You have promised _____

You have told me that it is in my best interest to _____

I praise Your name for helping me to_____

**YT "Come and go with me to my Father's house."
Hawkins Singers
YT "Welcome home baby" Shirelles**

He wants me to be confident, courageous, and carry out the dreams He has placed in my heart.
Matthew 19:26, "But Jesus beheld them, and said unto them, With men this is impossible: but with God all things are possible." **Deuteronomy 31:6,** "Be strong and of a good courage, fear not, nor be afraid of them: for the Lord thy God, he it is that doth go with thee; he will not fail thee, nor forsake thee."

Love gives me confidence, courage, and helps me live my dreams.

Joseph had a dream that one day his brothers would bow down to him. Genesis 37:8-10. It came true in Genesis 43:26 "…and bowed themselves to him to the earth." Nebuchadnezzar had a dream of an image. Daniel helped him to understand that his kingdom, Babylon, represented the head on that image and that Babylon would become a ruling nation in the world. History bears out that the dream came true. Jesus had a goal in His mind when He extended grace. Titus 2:11, "For the grace of God that bringeth salvation hath appeared to all men." Salvation is possible through Jesus' life, death, and resurrection.

Shall I live my life like Ahab, afraid of Jezebel and what she might say or do? Shall I run like Elijah because someone threatens to kill me? Shall I be bought with money like Judas whose goal was to have money? Shall I be like Lot's wife always looking to the past and wishing things were the way they used to be?

Joel 2:28, "…I will pour out my spirit…and your sons and your daughters shall prophesy, your old men shall dream dreams, your young men shall see visions." 2 Timothy 1:7, "For God hath not given us the spirit of fear; but of power, and of love, and of a sound mind." What am I really saying to God when I say 'I am afraid. I don't know if I can do that. What will people say. I might fail.'

Love looks like _____

My strength in this area _____

My weakness in this area _____

Dear God, You have promised _____

You have told me that it is in my best interest to _____

I praise Your name for helping me to _____

YT "Never give up" Yolanda Adams
YT "It wasn't easy" CeCe Winans YT "Only the strong survive" Jerry Butler

He wants me to be holy – whole and complete in Him. Leviticus 19:2, "Speak unto all the congregation of the children of Israel and say unto them, Ye shall be holy for I the Lord your God am holy." **Psalm 37:31, 37,** "The law of his God is in his heart: none of his steps shall slide. 37 Mark the perfect man, and behold the upright: for the end of that man is peace." **Matthew 5:48,** "Be ye therefore perfect as your Father which is in heaven is perfect."

Love wants me to do what is right and perfect.

Noah got drunk off wine and was naked in his tent. Yet God says in Genesis 6:9, "…Noah was a just man and perfect in his generations, and Noah walked with God." God said to Satan in a conversation they were having in Job 1:8, "…Hast thou considered my servant Job, that there is none like him in the earth, a perfect and an upright man, one that feareth God and escheweth evil?" Yet Job had doubts and questions. Hebrews 11:4, "By faith Abel offered unto God a more excellent sacrifice…by which he obtained witness that he was righteous, God testifying of his gifts…"

Hmmm! Why do I struggle with those words "holy" and "perfect?" Why do I hear so many people who go to church say no one is perfect – nobody can be perfect? Yet God calls Noah and Job perfect and Abel righteous– all men who walked this earth with flaws and faults just like I have. Why am I praying for victory over sin every day and struggling with whether God truly means what He says in 1John 5:3, 4-5, "For this is the love of God, that we keep his commandments… For whatsoever is born of God overcometh the world: and this is the victory that overcometh the world, even our faith. Who is he that overcometh the world, but he that believeth that Jesus is the Son of God." Love never asks me to do what is impossible for me to do because He has promised to be my strength and my power. Christ in me is what makes me holy. His righteousness clothes me and is what God sees when He looks at me, not my righteousness – or lack thereof.

The same Spirit available to Noah, Job, and Abel that enabled them to live perfect and righteous lives is the same Spirit dwelling in me with the intent to accomplish the same thing. Ephesians 1:3-4, "Blessed be the God and Father of our Lord Jesus Christ, who hath blessed us with all spiritual blessing…he hath chosen us in him before the foundation of the world, that we should be holy and without blame before him in love."

Love looks like _____

My strength in this area _____

My weakness in this area _____

Dear God, You have promised _____

You have told me that it is in my best interest to _____

I praise Your name for helping me to _____

YT "Victory" Yolanda Adams
YT "We're going all the way" Jeffrey Osborne
YT "The Potter's House" Tremaine Hawkins

HE WANTS ME TO BEAR FRUIT.

John 15:16, "Ye have not chosen me but I have chosen you, and ordained you, that ye should go and bring forth fruit, and that your fruit should remain: that whatsoever ye ask of the Father in my name, he may give it to you."

Love bears fruit, more love, over time. Fruit has two outcome goals: to produce seeds so that more fruit may be produced and to feed others. Orange trees produce more oranges. The cycle continues to produce more fruit by producing seeds. The seed, planted in soil that provides nourishment and water, has to first die. The fruit tree does not feed itself; it gets it's nourishment from the soil and its light from the sun. Notice how trees always grow upward towards the light. Light is needed for its life. A fruit tree matures amid storms, clouds, and darkness, as well as sunshine. In order to produce fruit, the branches must stay connected to the tree. The trees must be pruned in other to bear good quality fruit. Non-fruit producing branches must be cut off.

Fruit produces additional fruit for two primary purposes: to produce more seed to continue producing fruit and to provide food and nourishment for others. Love grows in the same way and has the same purpose. It gets its nourishment from the Bread of Life and the Everlasting water. It gets its light from the Light of the world. It matures in storms, clouds, and darkness, as well as sunshine. I must stay connected to the Source of Love to receive the nourishment I need for my love to grow. John 6:51, "I am the living, bread…if any man eat of this bread, he shall live forever…" John 7:37, "…If any man thirst, let him come unto me, and drink."

The seed of God's love planted in me first dies – I must die to self. Galatians 2:20, "I am crucified with Christ; nevertheless I live; yet not I, but Christ liveth in me…" Christ's Spirit in me implants Christ's character –love in me. Love grows over time to accomplish two things: produce additional seeds of love and as food for others. My fruit bearing is manifested in good works that I do in showing how I love others as I love myself.

Love looks like _____

My strength in this area _____

My weakness in this area _____

Dear God, You have promised _____

You have told me that it is in my best interest to _____

I praise Your name for helping me to_____

YT "The Love of God" Wintley Phipps
YT "This little light of Mine" Manfort YT "It's growing" Temptations

HE WANTS MY HEART.
Proverbs 23:26, "My son, give me thine heart, and let thine eyes observe my ways." Love wants me to give Him my heart – all my feelings. Love wants me to observe His ways – look at Him – to observe the thoughts and intents of His heart, to see His ways that show me that He loves me.

He wants all of me. Praise, adoration, happiness, joy, peace, tenderness, trust, sadness, anger, fear, frustration, hurts, pain. He wants them. My soul. He wants me to observe His ways to see what He does with them. He wants me to live for Him alone. He doesn't want anything or anybody to come between us. He wants me to want Him, just like He wants me.

He wants me to walk with Him. Talk to Him. Wait patiently for Him when He steps away. Search for Him when I think He's not around.

He wants me to delight myself in Him. Rejoice in Him. Praise Him. Pant after Him like a deer pants for water. To thirst for Him. Cry for Him. Hope in Him. Remember Him.

He wants me to be honest with Him. Tell Him when I have been unfaithful to Him, disappointed Him.

Psalms 63:1, "O God, thou art my God; early will I seek thee: my soul thirsteth for thee, my flesh longeth for thee in a dry and thirsty land, where no water is. 8 My soul followeth hard after thee: thy right hand upholdeth me." Psalms 86:11-12, "Teach me thy way, O Lord: I will walk in thy truth; unite my heart to fear thy name. I will praise thee, O Lord my God, with all my heart: and I will glorify thy name for evermore."

Love looks like _____

My strength in this area _____

My weakness in this area _____

Dear God, You have promised _____

You have told me that it is in my best interest to _____

I praise Your name for helping me to

YT "THIS IS MY DESIRE/I GIVE YOU MY HEART" THE CHRISTIAN LIFE
YT "I COULD NEVER LOVE ANOTHER" THE TEMPTATIONS
YT IF YOU'LL GIVE ME YOUR HEART" DOROTHY MOORE

HE WANTS ME TO KEEP AND OBEY THE LOVE LAWS.
John 14:21, "He that hath my commandments, and keepeth them, he it is that lovethe me: and he that loveth me shall be loved of my Father and I will love him, and will manifest myself to him." **Luke 6:46, 47,** "Why call ye me Lord, Lord and do not the things which I say?…heareth my sayings, and doeth them, I will shew you to whom he is like."

Love, knowing that the Lover knows me, tells me that it is in my best interest to keep and obey His commandments. Everything in God's created universe is governed by law. The planets stay on course because they obey gravitational law. The sun rises every morning in the east and sets in the west. Rain falls to the ground following the laws of gravity. Proverbs 15:1, "A soft answer turneth away wrath: but grievous words stir up anger." This command illustrates a social law. Proverbs 18:24, "A man that hath friends must shew himself friendly and there is a friend that sticketh closer than a brother. An excellent example of an emotional intelligence law." 2 Timothy 2:15, "Study to show thyself approved unto God…" deals with laws related to intelligence.

The outworking of the summarized laws to love God, self, and others is given in His ten commandments given to Moses on Mt. Nebo that are found in Exodus 20. The first four of those commandments tells me how God wants me to demonstrate my love for Him and the last six tells me how God wants me to demonstrate my love for myself and others.

I really like the third commandment in Exodus 20:5, "…have no other gods before me because I the Lord thy God am a jealous God." He is jealous when I love someone or something more than I love Him. He does not want me to give the affections that belong only to Him to anyone else. I also like the fourth commandment in Exodus 20:8-11, "Remember the Sabbath day to keep it holy. Six days shalt thou labor and do all thy work but the seventh day is the Sabbath of the Lord thy God…" In other words, I am giving you six days, but I want My day, My time with you, and I only want you to focus on Me. He wants me to spend a whole day with Him, so I can get to know Him! He will spend that time revealing Himself to me, so that I can know Him! I get a whole day every week just to spend with Him! The God who gave His only Son because He loved me so much wants to spend a whole day with me! The God who created me, created the universe, He is jealous of me! Me! He really knows how to make me feel special. He made love laws telling me that He wants to spend time with me and is jealous of my affections. What love!

Love looks like _____

My strength in this area _____

My weakness in this area _____

Dear God, You have promised _____

You have told me that it is in my best interest to _____

I praise Your name for helping me to _____

YT "Trust and obey" Big Daddy Weave
YT "Jealous kind of fella" Garland Green

He wants me to reason from cause to effect.
Isaiah 1:18-20, "Come now, and let us reason together, saith the Lord… If ye be willing and obedient, ye shall eat the good of the land. But if ye refuse and rebel, ye shall be devoured with the sword…

Love, based on law, acknowledges that choices and actions have consequences. Love is not blind to consequences. Nor is love headstrong, rash, unreasonable, or defiant of all restraint.

If I am going around a curve banked to be driven at 20 mph at 55 mph, a probable consequence is I am going to crash into that big tree next to the curve. If I drink wine, I am likely to get drunk. If I consistently take in more calories than I exercise to get rid of, I am going to gain weight. If I leave the door open on a cold day, the heat, following the first law of thermodynamics, is going to leave the room and go outside, leaving the room cold. Newton's law of motion, for every action, there is an equal and opposite reaction used in physics often applies to the laws of love, emotional, spiritual, physical, and intellectual.

When I am looking at love, I must consider the consequences of the choices that I make leading to the actions that result. Feelings signal the motivation to engage or not engage in certain behaviors. Actions based on feelings without consideration of the consequences of the actions can get me into a lot of trouble. There is where reason, rational thinking, plays an important role. Remember thoughts and feelings together make up character and character is the only thing I shall take from this world to heaven. My behaviors, based on those thoughts and feelings, are used to evaluate whether I spend eternity with God or not. Just because it makes me feel good doesn't mean that it is in my best interest to do it. Just because I want it doesn't mean that it is in my best interest or in the best interest of those that I must love as I love myself. The equal and opposite is also true. I don't "feel" like engaging, but it is in my best interest to do so. I don't "want" to do it, but it is in my best interest to do it. He has told me that believing in Him leads to eternal life. If I choose not to believe in Him, the equal and opposite choice that I am making is death. He has told me that if I love Him, I will keep His words in my heart and He will write His law on my heart. Those are the words that I will use to help guide in making choices.

Love looks like _____

My strength in this area _____

My weakness in this area _____

Dear God, You have promised_____

You have told me that it is in my best interest to_____

I praise Your name for helping me to_____

YT "Because He Lives I can face tomorrow"
YT "If you want a do right, home days woman... be a do right home nights man" Aretha Franklin
YT "The Closer I get to you" Roberta Flack/Donny Hathaway

He wants me to talk about Him.

Jeremiah 20:9, "Then I said I will not make mention of him, nor speak any more in his name. But his word was in mine heart as a burning fire shut up in my bones, and I was weary with forbearing, and I could not stay."

Love is like a fire burning in my bones. I just can't keep it to myself. I have to talk about Him.

I have seen multiple people with bone cancer. The description, "fire burning in my bones," is very real to those that have experienced it. The pain is so terrible that it affects every other system of the body and the person cries out in pain.

When I love Him, I can't keep it to myself. The desire to talk about Him is so overwhelming that I want to talk about Him to everybody I see. It is so hard to keep from talking about Him. I can't find words sufficient to express how good and kind He is to me, how He impacts my life. I find myself sharing the words He has spoken to me that have helped me to grow. I remember the words that He speaks to me and I keep them in my heart. Those words have changed my life for the better. I talk about how He helped me get through hard times. I talk about how good it feels to be in His arms. I talk about how He tells me when I am not acting in my best interest. I talk about how He influences me to make wiser choices when I am about to mess up. I talk about how He sacrificed His own feelings and desires to make sure I could have eternal life. I talk about how He was an emotional wreck in the Garden of Gethsemane when struggling with the decision to die for me or not. I talk about how intently He listens to me. I talk about Him to whoever will listen, my husband, my siblings, my friends, children, strangers. Love wants me to talk about Him because if they see how much He loves me, they realize that this kind of love is available to them as well, and perhaps they will choose to believe in Him, come to Him, and have eternal life as well. Matthew 28: 19-20, "Go ye therefore, and teach all nations, baptizing them in the name of the Father and of the Son, and of the Holy Ghost. Teaching them to observe all things whatsoever I have commanded you and lo, I am with you always, even unto the end of the world."

Love looks like _____

My strength in this area _____

My weakness in this area _____

Dear God, You have promised _____

You have told me that it is in my best interest to _____

I praise Your name for helping me to _____

YT " I will talk about my Saviour everywhere I go"
Ngobe Media
YT "Testify" Johnny Taylor

He knows the right time for me.

Galatians 4:4-5, "When the fullness of time was come, God sent forth His son…to redeem them that were under the law, that we might receive the adoption of sons. **Jeremiah 1:5,** "Before I formed thee in the belly, I knew thee and before thou camest forth out of the womb I sanctified thee, and I ordained…" **Jeremiah 29:11,** "For I know the thoughts that I think toward you…thoughts of peace and not of evil, to give you an expected end."

Love knows the right time for the purposed plans that He has with a designated, specific outcome.

When the time was right – perfect timing for the intended outcome. God sent forth His son – person designated to accomplish the plan. To redeem them that were under the law – designated, specific intended outcome. That we might receive the adoption of sons – designated specific outcome. I was on death row because of sin, God sent His son to die in my place, so I wouldn't have to die, I could live.

He thinks specific thoughts about me. Thoughts of peace and not of evil. Thoughts to bring me to a specific end – redemption from the law (my sins) and adoption as His son. He knew before He brought those forty-six chromosomes from my parents together to form me – chromosomes still filled with Adam's DNA – sin-prone chromosomes. He knew me as a fetus, when I took my first heartbeat, when my spinal cord and brain were developing, when I transitioned from one cell to many cells – in that nine months when I was a parasite in my mother's womb. Compromising her heart and blood supply. Taking her oxygen for myself. Putting her at risk at dying for me. He was there all the time. Watching over me. With plans for me already in place. Plans to bring me to an expected end. That plan continued after I was born. What is the narrative that goes with that plan? Who will He involve in moving that plan forward? What are the highlights along the way to bring me to an expected end? He knows. That's way He tells me to trust Him, ask Him, and obey Him. That's what His love looks like.

Love looks like _____

My strength in this area _____

My weakness in this area _____

Dear God, You have promised _____

You have told me that it is in my best interest to _____

I praise Your name for helping me to _____

YT "Lord help me to hold out" James Cleveland
YT "I found a love" Wilson Pickett

HE WANTS ME TO WAIT AND WATCH FOR HIS COMING.
Matthew 24:27, "For as the lightning cometh out of the east and shineth even unto the west; so also shall the coming of the Son of man be." **Revelation 22:12,** "And behold I come quickly and my reward is with me to give every man according as his work shall be **20**...even so, come Lord Jesus."

Love tells me how He is coming and wants me to look for His coming in anticipation. The sun rises every morning in the east and sets in the west in the evening – without fail. God has told me to look to the east from which direction the sun rises in anticipation of His coming. He tells me that it will be quick and He will bring my reward with Him.

How do I wait in anticipation of His coming? Knowing that He is bringing His reward with Him lets me know that at some point He has decided in His evaluation of me which reward I am going to get. He has also told me the criteria that He will use to evaluate that reward - the behaviors that indicate whether I love Him, love myself, and love others as He has commanded. Revelation 12, "…I saw the dead stand before God and the books were opened…the book of life; and the dead were judged out of those things that were written in the book. Revelation 3:5, "He that overcometh…I will not blot out his name out of the book of life." This and the time factor is shared in Revelation 14:6-7, "And I saw another angel fly in the midst of heaven, having the everlasting gospel to preach unto them that dwell on the earth…saying with a loud voice, Fear God and give glory to him for the hour of his judgment is come: and worship Him that made heaven, and earth, and the sea, and the foundation of waters." The hour of His judgment is now. He starts first with the dead, then He moves to the living and the only names in consideration are those whose names are written in the book of life. 1Peter 4:17, "…judgment must begin at the house of God: and if it first begin at us, what shall the end be of them that obey not the gospel of God?" While I wait for Him to return, I tell others how much He loves me, how much He loves them, how to get their name written in the book of life (by saying I love you Lord, I repent, and I believe in You). I love them by telling them that His judgment is going on now. I tell it with such love, passion, and emotion that they want to partake of His love and salvation. I remind myself of how much He loves me and what He has told me to do to show Him that I love Him and I love myself and others as He commanded. Even so, come, Lord. Jesus.

Love looks like _____

My strength in this area _____

My weakness in this area _____

Dear God, You have promised _____

You have told me that it is in my best interest to _____

I praise Your name for helping me to _____

YT "WE SHALL BEHOLD HIM" VICKIE WINANS
YT "WAIT FOR LOVE" LUTHER VANDROSS
YT "THE MIDNIGHT CRY" CENTRAL CHURCH OF GOD CHOIR NC

He will love me forever. I am His precious treasure. Jeremiah 31:3, "…Yeah, I have loved thee with an everlasting love: therefore with loving kindness have I drawn thee." **Malachi 3:17**, "And they shall be mine…in that day when I make up my jewels: and I will spare them as a man spareth his own son that serveth him."

Love keeps me forever. Love regards me as a jewel, a precious treasure.

He loves me with an everlasting love. He never forgets me. His loving kindness draws me to Him. Makes me want to be in His presence forever. Walk with Him. Follow Him wherever He goes. Hold His hand. Look into His eyes; what He sees, I see. What I feel, He feels. The two of us are one. Makes me long to be with Him, to feel His touch, see Him, hear His voice, His encouraging words, His words that explain how He feels, His thoughts about what is best for me, to know the power of His love and how it changes my life; know that I am never alone. He can be trusted to be there when I need Him. He never lets me down.

He considers me a jewel, a precious treasure. What do I do with precious treasures? I put them up on a shelf and I take care of them. They are on a pedestal. I bring them out on special occasions and show them off. I take extra special care of them, so that they maintain their value. I don't let just anybody touch or hold them. They are special. They are unique. That's what I am to Him, a jewel. Love will love me forever and keep me as a precious jewel.

Love looks like _____

My strength in this area _____

My weakness in this area _____

Dear God, You have promised _____

You have told me that it is in my best interest to _____

I praise Your name for helping me to _____

YT Jesus loves me" Whitney Houston
YT "Endless love" Diana Ross/Lionel Ritchie
YT "Jesus is Love" Commodores

♥

Chapter 2
What's in it for me?

AN INTENDED OUTCOME GOAL OF LOVE IS UNITY.
Ephesians 4:2-4, "With all lowliness and meekness, with longsuffering, forbearing one another in love; endeavoring to keep the unity of the Spirit in the bond of peace. There is one body, and one Spirit, even as ye are called in one hope of your calling."

Love brings unity, oneness.

When God made mankind, He knew the importance of oneness. God and His Son were united in the creation. Eve was created by using Adam's rib. By "one" man, sin entered the world. In the Father-Son love relationship, unity is recognized as one of the outcome measures. He said to His Father in John 17:23, "I in them and thou in me, that they may be made perfect in one…" The essential ingredient of unity in mankind is Christ in me, the hope of glory (Colossians 1:27), via the indwelling Holy Spirit.

He placed within man to help achieve this "oneness," the hormone, oxytocin, the "love hormone." Oxytocin is released with physical contact with another person – hugs, massages, holding hands, sexual intercourse. When I make eye contact or laugh, oxytocin is released. Listening to those love songs that produce a certain mood releases oxytocin. Looking at a picture of that man I love releases oxytocin.

Unity is often mistakenly viewed as uniformity. They are not the same. Unity focuses on purpose, goals, outcomes, and uses processes to accomplish those. Uniformity deals with the appearance – looking alike, thinking alike, doing things the same way. When I attempt to move a box of books that weighs 200 pounds, it is a whole lot easier if I have someone to help me than if I try to do it alone. In a marriage, the two become one. In church the central unifying goal is giving the gospel for the salvation of others.

Unity grows overtime when it is stretched, pressured, or threatened depending on how the gifts and talents of those involved are used. This is true whether I am talking about the oneness that occurs in a married couple, in a group, or in a church. Pride and self-interest are the modifiers that most interfere with unity. The gentleness and humility associated with love are the modifiers most closely associated with growing unity. When the central focus is lost, unity tends to fall apart. Love must keep in mind the central focus of the union, whether it is my marriage or the gospel story of Jesus in church.

Love looks like _____

My strength in this area _____

My weakness in this area _____

Dear God, You have promised _____

You have told me that it is in my best interest to _____

I praise Your name for helping me to _____

YT "MAKE US ONE" PHILIP BAILEY
YT "UNITED" PEACHES AND HERB

AN INTENDED OUTCOME GOAL OF LOVE IS GOOD HEALTH IN ALL DIMENSIONS.

3 John 1:2, "Beloved, I wish above all things that thou mayest prosper and be in health, even as they soul prospereth." I John 4:18, "There is no fear in love; but perfect love casteth out fear: because fear hath torment. He that feareth is not made perfect in love."

Love has no fear. Fear triggers the stress response, which if prolonged, can be harmful to the body. Health benefits of love are known to include: fewer doctor visits, less depression, increased alertness and knowledge, lower blood pressure, less anxiety, fewer colds, and better stress management.

God has made me so that when I think I am in danger, my body acts by releasing hormones that tell me to run or fight. Fear tells my sympathetic nervous system, which is in place to protect my body when it is threatened, to release several hormones that work with critical organs of my body to protect it. Cortisol increases the amount of sugar needed to fuel my muscular system, so I can fight or run. Epinephrine raises my heart rate and blood pressure to help me fight or run. These hormones also suppress my immune response (designed to keep disease away) and other body functions, so that all attention is given to protecting the body at the time it is in danger. When fear is present beyond the time needed to protect my body, these same hormones, intended to protect me when I am in trouble, have negative effects on my body. Long time presence of cortisol increases my blood sugar levels, works to weaken my bones, decreases my ability to respond to infections, and has other negative effects on my body.

When I love and am loved, the love hormones, oxytocin and endorphins, are released to cooperate with the organs of my body to produce my best health outcomes. When the stress hormones are present, the love hormones are overshadowed. With love hormones, learning is easier. I am friendlier and easier to get along with. I work better on a team. My blood pressure is kept under control.

One of the outcomes of sin was the onset of fear. Look at the interaction between Adam and God after Adam sinned "...God called unto Adam...Where art thou? And I heard thy voice in the garden, and I was afraid...and I hid myself," Genesis 3: 10. Adam ran, a typical fear response. God's message, "fear not," is found over and over again in His word. When I fear, I run, I hide from God, from you, from myself. God is love. His nature is love. That love has placed within me the ability to give and receive love knowing that my best health outcomes are achieved when I love and I receive love in return.

Love looks like _____

My strength in this area _____

My weakness in this area _____

Dear God, You have promised _____

You have told me that it is in my best interest to _____

I praise Your name for helping me to _____

YT "Love casts out fear" Phil King
YT "I will survive" Gloria Gaynor

AN INTENDED OUTCOME GOAL OF LOVE IS TO TRANSFORM CHARACTER
Romans 8:29, "For whom he did foreknow, he also did predestinate to be conformed to the image of his Son, that he might be the firstborn among many brethren."

Love transforms my character. Character, thoughts, and feelings that motivate to engage in behaviors, is transformed by love. My thoughts change. My feelings change. The change in feelings motivates me to change my behaviors to conform to the image of Love. Psalm 51:7, "Purge me …I shall be clean. Wash me… I shall be whiter than snow."

Romans 12: 1-2, "…present your bodies a living sacrifice, holy, acceptable unto God…be ye transformed by the renewing of your mind…" In the bible, when a lamb was offered as a sacrifice representing the future death of Jesus on the cross, the lamb had to be without spot or blemish. It had to be the best in the flock. This represented Jesus' death for my sins. Life is in the blood. The oxygen and nutrients needed to sustain life are carried in the blood to the organs that need them. The waste products needing to be removed from the body are carried by the blood to the kidneys where they are excreted in urine. If I were that sinner, of my own voluntary will, I would have to lay my hand on the head of the lamb and kill the lamb myself. I would watch the blood of the lamb run down the altar, and I would be reminded that it was because of the things I had thought, said, felt, done was why I was shedding the blood of this lamb.

The lamb didn't die right away. I would have to look at his eyes shift as the blood that gives life was draining onto the ground. I would have to watch as his body went limp when there was no more oxygen and fuel to the muscles. I had to keep his feet tied, so he wouldn't be able to run away. I would have to feel the cold, non-moving body when there was no longer blood circulating through it to keep it warm. I was responsible for taking life that only God can give. I witnessed the love that God has for me in my slaying of that lamb. I walked away from that site a changed person. Determined to never have to shed the blood of another lamb, determined to love as God commands only to fall short a little while later because I thought I could do it on my own and I couldn't. 2 Corinthians 12:9, "And he said unto me, My grace is sufficient for thee; for my strength is made perfect in weakness." Come Lord, live in me, so that it is You I breathe. What You see, I see. What You think, I think. What You feel, I feel. Love, Christ, the hope of glory in me, provides strength to accomplish the transformation of my character into His image.

Love looks like _____

My strength in this area _____

My weakness in this area _____

Dear God, You have promised _____

You have told me that it is in my best interest to _____

I praise Your name for helping me to _____

YT "Christ in Me" Jeremy Camp
YT "I must go on" Shirley Miller" YT "I feel like going on" Five Stairsteps

AN INTENDED OUTCOME GOAL OF LOVE IS TO BLESS OTHERS. **Matthew 5:43,** "…love your enemies, bless them that curse you, do good to them that hate you, and pray for them which despitefully use you, and persecute you."

Love flows out to bless others. Loving the enemy benefits the lover, as well as the enemy.

The needs of being loved include recognition, respect, and acknowledgment by others. I often tell nursing students when interacting with a patient that is cursing and screaming at them to step back, put their own need to be acknowledged on hold, and enter the framework of the patient cursing them out. I point out to them that the cursing and screaming has nothing to do with them but has more to do with what is going on with the patient screaming at them.

Most of the time, when a person is mistreating me, they are in some way seeking to have their own inner heart needs met. If I can suspend my own pride and needs and enter into what is going on with the person hating on me, I grow, as well as helping the hater to grow. Every person has something inside them that can benefit me and help me grow to be a better person. God has also placed that "inner" something within me. It is the "valued" something that Christ in me has placed there that I give to others that benefits both of us. Acts 20:35, "…it is more blessed to give than to receive."

Titus 2:11, "For the grace of God that bringeth salvation hath appeared to all men." God's grace is the hallmark that illustrates this example for us. Grace, God giving me something that I don't deserve because He loves me, benefits me; it brings salvation. It is my choice to receive it just as it is the choice of the person cursing me out to receive what I offer in love. Both of us grow when the love is offered and received. If the person mistreating me fails to receive the love, I still have benefited, I have grown.

A fifteen-year-old male student at a Christian school bought a jacket online that had this message, "Forgive me as God has forgiven you." I was totally impressed that a fifteen-year-old had already accepted the message of love that God wants us to display to others. An intended outcome goal of love is the blessing of others, including my enemies, that also blesses me in the process.

Love looks like _____

My strength in this area _____

My weakness in this area _____

Dear God, You have promised _____

You have told me that it is in my best interest to _____

I praise Your name for helping me to _____

YT "Your grace and Mercy" Mississippi Mass Choir
YT "Willing to Forgive" Aretha Franklin

LOVE MAKES ME SAFE AND FEARLESS.
Psalm 27:1, "The Lord is my light and my salvation; whom shall I fear: The Lord is the strength of my life; of whom shall I be afraid?"

Love provides a safe place for the loved. Love makes the loved strong and fearless.

Psalm 91:11, "For He shall give His angels charge over thee, to keep thee in all thy ways." Psalm 121:4, "…He that keepeth Israel shall neither slumber nor sleep." Physical and emotional safety are concerns for most people. Many people are afraid of the dark. God provides safety, and there is no reason to fear for either my physical or emotional safety. Jesus is the light. Light must be present for life to exist. Light provides the means for me to be able to see, so that I can move forward safely. It provides me safety in His presence.

I want to feel safe in my relationships. I fear being alone. I fear being criticized. I don't want to be rejected. I want to be wanted. I want to feel warmth and closeness. I want to feel like I am good enough. God tells me in 1 John 4:18, "…There is no fear in love. Perfect love casteth out fear." In my relationship with God, I have unconditional acceptance. My trust and belief in Him provides the confidence that I need to be strong and fearless. I know who I am in Him – His child, an heir to His throne. I don't have to worry that God has a fragile ego that feels attacked when I ask Him "why" questions. I have the assurance that He will be around for a long time because He has promised to never leave or forsake me. I can ask Him for what I want because He has told me that He will "supply all my needs." I can tell Him anything I want, and He talks back.

Others want to feel safe in my presence. I will say to them, "I will never hurt or disappoint you." I will offer words of encouragement. I will talk about their strengths, their accomplishments. I will share my inner self with them, so that they can get to know me. They can ask me questions and I will answer to the best of my ability. I will treat them like they are "one in a million" because they are.

When I provide safety and assurance for others, it enhances their own ability to be safe and trustworthy. We both realize the intended outcome of fearlessness and safety, similar to what God offers us.

Love looks like _____

My strength in this area _____

My weakness in this area _____

Dear God, You have promised_____

You have told me that it is in my best interest to_____

I praise Your name for helping me to_____

YT "SAFE IN HIS ARMS" MILTON BRUNSON
YT "YOU DON'T HAVE TO BE A STAR TO BE IN MY SHOW" MARILYN MCCOO/BILLY DAVIS

LOVE MAKES ME WHOLE, COMPLETE.
Colossians 2:10, "And ye are complete in him, which is the head of all principality and power." **Corinthians 3:18,** "But we all with open face beholding as in a glass the glory of the Lord, are changed into the same image from glory to glory, even as by the Spirit of the Lord."

Love makes me whole and complete. Wholeness, an integration of thoughts, feelings, and behaviors. God has placed within us the ability to co-operate with Him to achieve wholeness by making it possible to integrate our physical, emotional, spiritual, and mental compartments. Electrical pathways are laid down in the brain that enhance the ability to think. Hormones are released into the blood that bind to cells in various organs to produce outcomes that impact our physical, emotional, mental, and spiritual health.

Love has promised me that I will be changed into the same image as Jesus. When God created Adam, he was created in the image of God, perfect – with feelings, with a physical body, with God's nature, love. Just as my physical health varies right now, so does my emotional, mental, and spiritual health. God has promised to restore that "wholeness" image in me. John 17:17, "Sanctify them through thy truth; thy word is truth." Sanctification is the process through which God is restoring that "wholeness," through the indwelling of His Spirit, in me. When He comes, He has told me, I will be like Him, again. I John3:2

My emotional health is at varying degrees of wholeness. Galatians 5:22 assures me that the fruit of the Spirit dwelling in me is "…love, joy, peace, kindness, goodness, faithfulness, gentleness, self-control." In Psalms 51:10, David asks God to "Create in me a clean heart…renew a right spirit within me." Spiritual intelligence is enhanced by the "renewing of my mind." Romans 12: 2 Mental health is impacted by my spiritual perceptions of whether I am "good enough" or "capable" of doing something. If I believe what God says when He says I am His child, created in His image, an heir to His throne, it will impact my mental health and my perceptions of whether I am capable of achieving His plan for my life. My emotional state is impacted by these as well. If I feel good about myself, if I am not controlled by fear, anxiety, anger, and other negative emotions, my ability to cooperate with God in carrying out His plan for my life is unlimited. When I believe and accept that God has told me an outcome of His love is that I will be changed back into that "whole" image that He gave me, the integration of thoughts, feelings, and behaviors will occur in recognition of that love. Wholeness is an intended outcome goal of love.

Love looks like _____

My strength in this area _____

My weakness in this area _____

Dear God, You have promised _____

You have told me that it is in my best interest to _____

I praise Your name for helping me to _____

YT "Make me whole" Beau Williams
YT "Whole Again" Atomic Kitten

AN INTENDED OUTCOME GOAL OF LOVE IS TRANSFORMATION.
2 Corinthians 3:18, "But we all, with open face beholding as in a glass the glory of the Lord, are changed into the same image from glory to glory, even as the by Spirit of the Lord."

An expected outcome goal of love is transformation of the loved. I change from hating myself and others to loving myself and others. From being fearful to being courageous. From being weak to being strong. From being angry to being filled with joy. From being down and depressed to being happy. From feeling insecure to feeling secure. From doing things that are not in my best interest to doing those things that are in my best interest.

David saw a beautiful woman – Bathsheba- wanted her, slept with her, impregnated her, and then had her husband killed, so he could have her. The child that was born as a result of his choices and behaviors did not live. Yet God said that David was a man after His own heart. David attempted to cover up his behavior, but everyone around him knew what he had done.

Can you imagine the pain in Bathsheba's heart when she was told that her newborn was not going to live because of what David had done? Can you imagine what that conversation was like with him as she cried uncontrollably at realizing the impact of poor choices when holding the cold, lifeless form in her arms that had lived in her womb for nine months? He did marry her to make it legitimate. But the damage that had been done would be there for a lifetime for both he and Bathsheba to think about.

David was finally confronted by the prophet Nathan when God, loving him and knowing David's potential as well as his strengths and weaknesses, sent him to talk to him. Psalm 51 shares David's response after that visit from Nathan and reflection on his disappointment in letting God down by the poor choices he had made. "Have mercy upon me, O God, according to thy lovingkindness; according unto the multitude of thy tender mercies blot out my transgressions. Wash me thoroughly from mine iniquity, and cleanse me from my sin. For I acknowledge my transgressions: and my sin is ever before me. Against thee, thee only, have I sinned, and done this evil in thy sight... Create in me a clean heart, O God, and renew a right spirit within me. Cast me not away from thy presence: and take not thy holy spirit from me. Restore unto me the joy of thy salvation; and uphold me with thy free spirit. The sacrifices of God are a broken spirit: a broken and a contrite heart, O God, thou wilt not despise..." David was transformed. God answered his prayer. David was not cast away. God's Holy Spirit continued to work in him to restore to David the joy of salvation. Love changes the loved. When I am loved and I love myself and others as God has said is in my best interest, I am transformed. Those that I love are transformed.

Love looks like _____

My strength in this area _____

My weakness in this area _____

Dear God, You have promised_____

You have told me that it is in my best interest to_____

I praise Your name for helping me to_____

YT "Changed" Tremaine Hawkins
YT I know I've been changed" LaShun Pace
YT A Change is gonna come" Sam Cooke

AN EXPECTED OUTCOME GOAL OF LOVE IS FRIENDSHIP THAT INFLUENCES OTHERS.

Proverbs 18:24, "A man that hath friends must shew himself friendly; and there is a friend that sticketh closer than a brother."

Love makes friends and has influence on the lives of the loved. Friends stick closer than brothers. James 2:23, "…Abraham believed God, and it was imputed unto him for righteousness: and he was called the Friend of God." God is my friend.

Friends provide ongoing support. They celebrate each other's successes. They laugh together, releasing oxytocin and endorphins to bind them closer together. Physical distance doesn't eliminate the friendship. Friends are honest with each other. Friends forgive each other. Friends recognize and respect boundaries. Friends trust each other. Friends depend on each other and are loyal to one another. Friends listen to each other. Friends do not judge each other. Friends are fun to be around. Friends influence and change behaviors.

Love's influence can increase my self-control. Those with loving friends are likely to live longer. Friendships lower the risk of disease. They provide moral support to help resist temptation. People that are friends often start acting like their friends. The influence of friends increases my self-esteem, my ability to love myself as God intends. Friends keep me active, supporting long term health outcomes.

Influence is important. I influence others. They also influence me. Choice is an important factor in influence. Proverbs 18:21, "Death and life are in the power of the tongue: and they that love it shall eat the fruit thereof." Words are powerful. God has given me the ability to speak words of life or speak words of death. Which am I choosing to speak to influence those that I love? What I speak to others, I hear, so those words also speak back to me. What words am I speaking to myself, words of life or words of death?

Love looks like _____

My strength in this area _____

My weakness in this area _____

Dear God, You have promised_____

You have told me that it is in my best interest to_____

I praise Your name for helping me to_____

YT "There is not a friend like Jesus" Cloverdale Bibleway
YT "Lean on me" Bill Withers

LOVE BRINGS THE EXPECTED OUTCOME OF JOY.
Nehemiah 8:10, "...Go your way, eat the fat, and drink the sweet, and send portions unto them for whom nothing is prepared: for this day is holy unto our Lord: neither be ye sorry: for the joy of the Lord is your strength."

An expected outcome goal of love is joy, a feeling of being truly happy with what I have, who I am, and the world around me. Joy provides me with endurance and strength. Joy helps me persevere through dark times. Joy is a gift from the indwelling Christ in me. Galatians 5:22, "...fruit of the Spirit is joy..."

Philippians 4:4, "Rejoice in the Lord always and again I say rejoice." Rejoicing, joy, stimulates the release of endorphins producing multiple benefits – healthier heart, relief from depression, reduction in prostate cancer, pain relief, and many other wholesome benefits. Joy produces my best outcomes versus sadness, which releases hormones in the body that increase depression and long term, can have negative impacts on the body.

The joy of the Lord is my strength. God experiences joy and His joy is my strength. In Luke 15:10, angels experience joy, "...there is joy in the presence of the angels of God over one sinner that repenteth." I wonder how God expresses His joy. Can you see it in His eyes? Do His pupils dilate at the mention of my name like mine do when you mention the name of someone I love? Does He jump up and down like I did when I heard that two children that were in foster care were going to be returned to their mother after their caseworker had moved to have them permanently taken away from her because the mother called her a b****? And how about the angels? Do they start dancing like I do when I hear "Just One Look," a song that reminds me of someone I love? Can they find words to express their joy when it comes to talking about how much God loves them like I am when trying to describe someone that I love dearly? Did they hug each other when overcome with those feelings of joy when I made that decision to give my life to Jesus and be baptized? Did they cry tears of joy like my daughter, who was dying from cancer, when she saw God had answered her prayer, to let her live until her youngest son graduated, as she watched him receive that high school diploma? Do they sing songs and dance like Hezekiah Walker and his praise team on that video "Every Praise is to our God?" How do God and the angels rejoice? I look forward to that day soon when I will see it for myself and rejoice with them on the streets of gold. Rejoice I say, and again I say rejoice. Love brings joy as an intended outcome.

Love looks like _____

My strength in this area _____

My weakness in this area _____

Dear God, You have promised _____

You have told me that it is in my best interest to _____

I praise Your name for helping me to _____

YT "Every Praise" Hezekiah Walker
YT "You bring me joy" Anita Baker

LOVE BRINGS PEACE, CALMNESS, COMPOSURE, AND CONFIDENCE. Psalm 119:165, "Great peace have they which love thy law and nothing shall offend them."

Expected outcome goals of love include peace, calmness, composure, and confidence.

Peace is thought of as friendship and togetherness in the absence of violence and angry behavior, a lack of conflict. Peace, for me, is not the absence of strife but rather the presence of Jesus during strife.

Christ in me, the hope of glory, brings peace, a fruit of the Spirit. Mark 4:39, "Peace be still." During a great storm where the disciples feared for their very lives, Jesus, who was on the ship with them, was asleep. They woke him in great fear saying, "Master, carest thou not that we perish?' He got up, spoke to the storm, the wind ceased, and there was calm. Isaiah 32:17, "And the work of righteousness shall be peace: and the effect of righteousness quietness and assurance forever." The presence of love in our midst brings peace.

I John 4:17, "Herein is our love made perfect, that we may have boldness in the day of judgment, because as he is, so are we in this world." Ephesians 3:12, "In whom we have boldness and access with confidence by the faith of Him." Hebrews 4:16, "Let us come boldly unto the throne of grace…"

When David approached Goliath, he said, "I come to you in the name of the Lord." The Hebrew boys, Shadrach, Meshach, Abednego, walked upright in a fiery furnace and Nebuchadnezzar saw a "fourth" person walking with them, the Son of God. God is love. Colossians 3:15, "And let the peace of God rule in your hearts…" Hebrews 12:14, "Follow peace with all men, and holiness, without which no man shall see the Lord." Peace – friendship, togetherness in the absence of violence, needed in our relationships with each other, is accomplished only in the presence of love. The presence of love brings peace, calmness, composure, and confidence.

Love looks like _____

My strength in this area _____

My weakness in this area _____

Dear God, You have promised _____

You have told me that it is in my best interest to_____

I praise Your name for helping me to_____

YT "Peace be still" James Cleveland
YT "The Lord is my light" Andre Crouch

LOVE PRESERVES RESPECT FOR SELF AND OTHERS.
Phillipians 2:2-3, "Fulfill my joy, that ye be likeminded, having the same love, being of one accord, of one mind. Let nothing be done through strife or vainglory; but in lowliness of mind let each esteem other better than themselves."

Respect, due regard for the feelings, wishes, and rights of other, provides a sense of worth or personal value that I attach to myself and others. Love has outcome goals of respect for self and respect for others. Accrediting bodies for nursing programs to train registered nurses require nursing schools to evaluate whether nursing students know how to care for themselves. The underlying assumption is consistent with the command to "love others as you love yourself." The implication is that if a nursing student does not know how to care for him/herself, the student will not be able to care for patients.

Genesis 4:4-5, "…And the Lord had respect unto Abel and to his offering… But unto Cain and to his offering he had not respect…" God, in giving respect, evaluated Abel and Cain's feelings and the behaviors that resulted from those feelings. Both knew what God had asked them to do, but Abel respected and honored God by doing as God said. Cain was angry and decided that what he felt was more important than what God had asked them to do.

Respect is an evaluation I make based on many things: what I am doing with my life, how I treat others and myself, whether I am honest, whether I consistently do good things for others. Am I an effective listener? What about acceptable manners and proper conduct? Do I accept responsibility for my behavior, or do I have a need to blame others? Am I comfortable with apologizing when I am wrong? Do I have a mission, a focus for my life? How do I use my influence? Do I understand that respect does not have to be earned, it is deserved as it is an outcome of love. If I love myself, I will respect myself as a child of God, heir to His throne. If I don't respect myself, it is likely that I don't how to respect others.

Life's experiences with myself and others will always be a background reference for how I respect myself and others. In other words, each person brings "baggage of experience" to any interaction with self and others. When looking at my self-respect and respect of others, I have to be aware of past experiences that may be affecting current feelings and behaviors for both parties. If I love others as I love myself, I will respect them. If I love God, I will show Him respect in the way He has told me in His word.

Love looks like _____

My strength in this area _____

My weakness in this area _____

Dear God, You have promised _____

You have told me that it is in my best interest to _____

I praise Your name for helping me to _____

YT "Respect" Aretha Franklin

To love you is to know you.
Jeremiah 31:33-34, "…I will put my law in their inward parts, and write it in their hearts… for they shall all know me…" **Hebrews 10:24**, "And let us consider one another to provoke unto love and to good works." **Haggai 1:5**, "Now therefore thus saith the Lord of hosts: Consider your ways."

An outcome of love is that the lover knows the loved. When I know myself, that knowledge will determine how I interact with myself and that knowledge will produce my best outcomes. In order to know myself, I must talk to myself about myself. I must be willing to go beyond the superficial and get to the deep parts and be honest with myself. Time and presence are essential requirements of knowing.

Loving me means that God knows me. I said, "God, it hurts." And God said, "I know." He knew me then and He knows me now. He knows the plans that He has for my life, plans to prosper me and not to harm me. Jeremiah 29:11-13

Knowing about someone is not the same as knowing someone. The depth of knowing someone increases from knowing about you- I know your name, where you live; to knowing your concerns- what you want, what your plans are; to knowing your identity- who do you say that you are. Understanding you deeply requires experiential observation, testing, questions, and analysis of results much like learning in a science lab and similar to the way in which God tells us to test and prove Him.

Jeremiah 9:24, "…that he understandeth and knoweth me, that I am the Lord which exercise lovingkindness, judgment, and righteousness, in the earth; for in these things I delight, saith the Lord." John 17:3, "…this is life eternal… know thee, the only true God and Jesus Christ whom He has sent." God reveals Himself to me in His word. He delights in exercising kindness, judgment, righteousness. How does God express that delight? I see His joy when the birds are eating. I see that smile on His face when He sends rain to drought areas and the people are able to eat. I hear the excitement and joy in His voice when I talk to Him when I am lying in my bed at night. I see the joy on my angel's face as she writes in the Book of Life that I have been victorious over sin today.

Loving "me" requires that I know myself. Psalm 4:4, "…commune with your own heart upon your bed, and be still." Heart – feelings. Why am I angry? Why am I happy? Loving you requires that I know you and am willing to reveal those heart-feelings to you in the time I spend with you.

Love looks like _____

My strength in this area _____

My weakness in this area _____

Dear God, You have promised _____

You have told me that it is in my best interest to _____

I praise Your name for helping me to _____

YT "HE KNEW ME THEN" DALLAS HOLM
YT "I WANT TO KNOW WHAT LOVE IS" FOREIGNER
YT "CHERISH"   KOOL & THE GANG

Love is faithful. It can be tested and proven to be trustworthy.
Malachi 3:10, "…prove me now herewith saith the Lord of hosts, if I will not open you the windows of heaven and pour you out a blessing, that there shall not be room enough to receive it. **Hebrews 4:16,** "…come boldly to the throne of grace, that we may obtain mercy, and find grace to help in time of need."

Love is faithful. Love can be tested and proven. The proving requires a standard for evaluation. Jeremiah 31:33 identifies the standard by which love is tested, evaluated, and proven. "…I will put my law in their inward parts, and write it in their hearts." The evaluation has to look for consistency in the application of the standard and the lover knows that there is a time period in which that evaluation occurs. This probation period is for both the lover and the loved.

God tells me to pay tithe and prove Him. Every time I give Him the ten percent of my goods, whatever they are, I am testing and proving God's love. When my husband worked for General Motors in Michigan, we lived in a very nice house and sent all of our five children to a private church school. Several of his coworkers would drive past our house and make comments like, "No one with your salary could live like you do." God was proving His love by honoring His promise to pour out blessings that others could not understand.

One day driving from Detroit, Michigan where my children were in church school to Fenton, Michigan where we lived, a car came from nowhere and was about to hit us when out of my daughter's mouth in less than ten seconds came the words, "Preserve me O God for in thee do I put my trust." This is a bible promise in Psalm 16:1 that we claimed at every morning and evening worship time. Time has proven that God's love promises can be trusted. He is faithful and honors His promises. Am I consistent over the time with the promises that I make to myself? The promises that I make to you? Can I be trusted to do what I say I am going to do? Can you trust that when I say, "I love you" that I really do love you?

God gives me a probation time to develop and show that love. He wants to know that I love Him and love others as I love myself as He has told me it is in my best interest to do. He uses the same law, in place before creation of the world, put in my thoughts and written on my feelings, to evaluate my behaviors that show whether I love Him, myself, and others. His law reflects His love, loving kindness, judgment, and righteousness. When tested and evaluated by His law, love will be shown to be faithful.

Love looks like _____

My strength in this area _____

My weakness in this area _____

Dear God, You have promised _____

You have told me that it is in my best interest to _____

I praise Your name for helping me to _____

YT "Great is thy faithfulness" CeCe Winans
YT "Testify – I just wanna testify" Johnny Taylor

LOVE IS EXPECTED TO MAKE LIFE'S JOURNEY EASIER.
Romans 13:10, "Love worketh no ill to his neighbor: therefore love is the fulfilling of the law."

An outcome measure of love is that life's journey is made easier. Matthew 11:29-30, "Take my yoke upon you, and learn of me…my yoke is easy and my burden is light."

"Christ came to the earth…with the unhoarded love of eternity, and this is the treasure that through connection with Him, we are to receive, to reveal, and to impart." *God's Amazing Grace p. 16* White, Ellen G. 1973

When Adam sinned, all that was supposed to occur in life was fear, pain, suffering, and death. God's grace and mercy intervened to provide blessings to minimize that fear, pain, and suffering, so that as I travel my life's journey, God minimizes, to some extent, those intended outcomes resulting from sin. Love is the mechanism which God, from the very beginning, has had in place to counter those negative outcomes from sin.

To receive the "unhoarded love" that Christ offers, I must open the door to my heart (feelings) and let Him in. Rev 3:20. To reveal that "unhoarded love," Christ must dwell within my heart. I can't do it on my own. Christ places His Spirit in me as His dwelling place, which empowers me to reveal that love that makes life's journey easier for me and for those that I love.

Love works no ill to my neighbor. Love works no ill to myself. Love works no ill to my God, who loves me so much He watched men who His Son created, nail Him to the cross, and did nothing. He loved those men, too. I make choices based on what God has shared with me in His word and what He reveals to me in our talks with each other. The influence from how I live out those choices changes my life and the lives of those I love.

I will tell you the truth. I will help you with that broken heart. I will encourage you to go forward. I won't do anything to make it harder for you. I know that when I hurt you, I am hurting myself. I will not cheat you or myself. Love works no ill to the loved. By God's grace, I will make your pathway in life easier. I will love you as I love myself with the help of the indwelling Holy Spirit.

Love looks like _____

My strength in this area _____

My weakness in this area _____

Dear God, You have promised_____

You have told me that it is in my best interest to_____

I praise Your name for helping me to_____

YT "This too shall pass" Dallas Holmes
YT "I've been good to you" Smokey Robinson

LOVE LASTS FOREVER, GROWS OVERTIME, CANNOT BE MEASURED, AND DRAWS THE LOVED CLOSER.
Isaiah 54:10, "For the mountains shall depart, and the hills be removed, but my kindness shall not depart from thee, neither shall the covenant of my peace be removed… " **Jeremiah 31:3,** "…Yea, I have loved thee with an everlasting love: therefore with lovingkindness have I drawn thee."

Expected outcomes of love are that it lasts forever, grows overtime, and draws the loved closer and closer. This is consistent with knowing the loved. I will spend eternity getting to know God (John 17:3) and God promises to love me with an everlasting love.

Forever is a long time. Everlasting is even longer. A symbol is used in math to demonstrate infinity, no known beginning and no known ending on a number line. The line extends forever. I can identify points on the line by using various math formulas, but the line extends forever in two directions. Love is pretty much the same way. I identify points in time on a continuous time pattern, but I cannot identify the moment of its origin and I know that it will never end. I cannot measure love. There are no units of measurement that could quantify how much God loves me. I cannot put a quantified number to measure Jesus' death on the cross for me.

What joy and peace that brings! To know that God's love for me will last forever! To know that His lovingkindness will extend to me forever and draw me closer and closer to Him! To know that everything He does and says will always be for my best outcomes, my best good!

His love will draw me closer. I will feel more and more the love and warmth that being close to Him brings. I will feel more joy and happiness as He draws me closer and closer. He will reveal more and more of Himself to me, so that I can know and trust Him at an even deeper level. My love for Him will grow overtime. The more I know Him experientially, God my Savior, God my deliverer, God my provider, God my healer, God my friend, God my Lover, God my peace, God my joy, God my happiness, the more I will love and trust Him. Love lasts for eternity.

Love looks like _____

My strength in this area _____

My weakness in this area _____

Dear God, You have promised _____

You have told me that it is in my best interest to_____

I praise Your name for helping me to_____

YT "The Love of God" Wintley Phipps
YT "It's growing" Temptations
YT "I guess I'll always love you" Isley Brothers

LOVE MEETS ALL NEEDS.
Phillippians 4:19, " But my God shall supply all your need according to His riches in glory by Christ Jesus."

Love meets the needs of the loved. Knowing the loved is required to identify the needs of the loved. Need is different than want. Need is required for survival, wants are desired, but I can survive without them. Because I am made in God's image and He made me, He knows what those needs are and promises to meet them. Often He works through others to meet those needs, but many times in life, I look to man to find only the need that God can fulfill. When I see the pattern of Him honoring His promise to meet my needs, my trust, another expected outcome of love, in Him grows. In my life's journey, in my regular communication with Him, God helps me differentiate those needs that only He can meet and those that He will work through others to meet.

God meets my physical needs. When I eat that apple, it reinforces that God is honoring that promise to supply all my need. He sends the rain to make sure I have a continuous supply to meet the sixty percent water that my body needs. He uses photosynthesis to make sure the plants release oxygen for me to breathe. He regulates the hours of day and night, so that I can get the sleep that I need for the release of hormones needed for my body to function.

He meets my emotional needs. When I am sad, He reminds me that He loves me to cheer me up. When I get tired of trying to meet expectations and deadlines, He gives me a picture of the mansion He has waiting for me in heaven. When I am angry, He reminds me to be careful and sin not. He sends that special someone to hold me, touch me to release the hormones that increase my bonding and trust, not only with the person He sends but with Him as well.

He meets my intellectual needs by reminding me to "study to show myself approved" and tells me to "search the scriptures" to see if these things are so. He makes me aware that addition and subtraction, number theory, and all that goes with math is under His control and that if I lack wisdom, I can ask Him and He will give it to me liberally, without blaming me for asking.

He dwells within me to meet my spiritual needs. He integrates my physical, emotional, and intellectual needs to produce the unity, the oneness, that I need with Him and others for survival. An expected outcome of love is that my needs shall be met.

Love looks like _____

My strength in this area _____

My weakness in this area _____

Dear God, You have promised _____

You have told me that it is in my best interest to _____

I praise Your name for helping me to _____

YT "My God is awesome" Charles Jenkins
YT "Baby, I need your loving" Four Tops

LOVE BRINGS BONDING, TRUST, AND OBEDIENCE.
Colossians 2:2, "That their hearts might be comforted, being knit together in love, and unto all riches of the full assurance of understanding, to the acknowledgement of the mystery of God, and of the Father and of Christ."

Love brings the trust and bonding needed for obedience to His commands. Oxytocin, released by the posterior pituitary gland, is a hormone that God has placed to work in the brain that influences social interaction. It is known to increase bonding and attachment in the newborn-mother relationship. Its release increases trust and reduces fear in the bonding of couples. It is known to increase generosity by increasing empathy. Oxytocin levels increase during sex, kissing, hugging, holding hands, laughing, exercising, touching, looking at pictures of my lover, hearing his voice, hearing songs that bring him to mind, and other situations where people are in close proximity with each other. It underlies individual and social trust and is used as an antidote to depression. It produces warm and fuzzy feelings during moments of intimacy. It supports monogamy and decreases the likelihood of unfaithfulness in marriage.

Genesis 2:18, "... God said It is not good that the man should be alone. I will make him an help meet for him." My Creator knew exactly what He had placed in man and how it would work. Look at what He has told me to do to increase the oxytocin levels that He knew would enhance my ability to produce my best outcomes of bonding and trust, which is essential to obeying His commands. Genesis 2:24, "...the two shall become one flesh." Philippians 4:4, "...rejoice always. 2 Corinithians 12:12, "Greet one another with a holy kiss." 1Samuel 20:41, "...and they kissed one another and wept…"

The woman with the issue of blood said, "If I may touch the hem of His garment…" Jesus healed a blind man's blindness by "touching his eyes." Jairus asked Jesus to "come and lay your hand" on his daughter, so she would live. When Jacob was about to die, he asked Joseph to "put your hand under my thigh and promise to deal kindly with me." When David was cold and dying, they found a young, beautiful woman to "lie in his bosom" that he might get heat.

Proverbs 3:5-6, "Trust in the Lord with all thine heart and lean not to thine own understanding…He will direct thy paths." John 14:15, "If ye love me, keep my commandments." Trusting God's judgment better than my own is crucial to my ability to obey His commands. Love brings bonding and trust needed for obedience to God's commands.

Love looks like _____

My strength in this area _____

My weakness in this area _____

Dear God, You have promised_____

You have told me that it is in my best interest to_____

I praise Your name for helping me to_____

YT "Trust in You" Anthony Brown
YT "The Hem of His Garment" Sam Cooke

Love speaks powerful words.

Proverbs 18:21, "Death and life (are) in the power of the tongue: and they that love it shall eat the fruit thereof."

Love speaks powerful words, words of life or words of death. Words spoken to others. Words that I speak to myself. In the creation of the world, God spoke and it was done. Psalm 33:9, "For He spake, and it was done; He commanded, and it stood fast.

Words provide an affirmation of my thoughts. They confirm how I see others, as well as how I see myself. Without words my thoughts never become reality. I have the power in my words to bring joy or create despair, to put a smile on a face or cause tears to flow. Long after I am gone, my words will have power on those with whom I have spoken.

Words create desire. Words affirm to myself and to others who I am, my dreams, hopes, successes. "I am…" very powerful, state of being words. I am fat. I am beautiful. I am dumb. I am smart. Words spoken to others impact their desires as well. I love you. I want you. You are beautiful. You are different. You are smart.

I must keep in mind that whatever I am saying influences myself and others, to life or to death. There is no middle ground. What kind of words am I speaking? If I start with the desired outcome that I would like to have as a result of the words that I speak, I can make better choices as to the words that I say. Then I choose those words carefully, having an idea of the potential emotions that can be triggered by certain words. What comes to my mind when I hear the words calm, grateful, sincere, confident, unique, dynamic, optimistic, energetic, thrilled?

The words that I speak to others, I hear myself. Those words also impact me. Ephesians 4:29, "Let no corrupt communication proceed out of your mouth, but that which is good to the use of edifying…" Proverbs 12:18, "…the tongue of the wise is health." Proverbs 15:1, " A soft answer turneth away wrath: but grievous words stir up anger." Matthew 12:37, "For by thy words thou shalt be justified, and by thy words thou shall tbe condemned." Love speaks words of encouragement. Words that edify and build up. Words that give hope. Words that inspire. Love speaks powerful words that lead to life.

Love looks like _____

My strength in this area _____

My weakness in this area _____

Dear God, You have promised _____

You have told me that it is in my best interest to _____

I praise Your name for helping me to _____

YT "Speak to me Lord" Robert Morgan The Color Purple
YT "Talk to me" Little Willie John

Love can be seen in the countenance of the lover and the loved.
Song of Solomon 1:15-16, "How beautiful you are, my love. Your eyes glow with love for me. How handsome you are, my dear. You delight me with your strong presence… "

Love is reflected in the countenance of the lover and the loved.

Zephaniah 3:17, "The Lord your God is with you… He will take great delight in you; in his love he will no longer rebuke you, but will rejoice over you with singing." God is with me. He takes great delight in me. He quiets me with His love. He calms all my fears and the peace and joy show on my face. He exults over me with joy. He sings songs of rejoicing over me. Isaiah 62:5, "…as a groom rejoices over his bride, so your God will rejoice over you." I have seen that look on a groom's face when He looks at his bride. God's love for me looks like that groom's face. Love shows in His countenance, and when I am in His presence and feel the comfort of that love, it shows on my face. I keep His words in my heart. I remember them and say them over and over. It makes me want to do everything I can to please Him and make Him happy. Psalm 40:8, "I delight to do thy will, O my God: yea thy law is within my heart." My countenance is changed and people say, "There is something different about you."

Love's reflection in the body often shows up first in my eyes. My pupils dilate when I am looking in his eyes. My eyebrows are raised. I lean forward to make eye contact. He looks back and smiles. Then a smile crosses my face and it is a different smile than I smile at others. The happiness and joy show on my face. I notice the glow on his face. He touches my hair. He starts to hum love songs. I want to hear and sing songs of love. He pulls me close to hug me. He kisses me on my forehead. He keeps getting up to get things he thinks I need. He does everything possible to make me comfortable. I reach for his hand to hold. My countenance remains changed, even when I am not in his presence. My face lights up at the mention of his name. People notice the change and make comments like, "You are different." Love is reflected in the countenance of the lover and the loved.

Love looks like _____

My strength in this area _____

My weakness in this area _____

Dear God, You have promised _____

You have told me that it is in my best interest to _____

I praise Your name for helping me to _____

YT "God has smiled on me" James Cleveland
YT "The look of love" Dionne Warwick

LOVE MOVES ME FROM DEATH TO LIFE.
I John 3:14, "We know that we have passed from death unto life, because we love the brethren."

God never intended for me to die. I often hear people say, "Let him/her die with dignity." There is no dignity in death! It was never God's intention that anyone should die. The most important outcome goal of love is that I live, that I live eternally in the presence of the God who made me, knows me, and sent His Son to die for me, so that I could be reconciled to Him so that I could live forever in His presence. Loving and knowing God provides the basis for eternal life. John 17:3. Loving others is my assurance that I have passed from death unto life.

Death here is not referencing the end of the physical life; my heart stops beating, I stop breathing. God here is talking about the second death, which in essence is eternal separation from God who loves me. I have never experienced the second death, so it is hard to grasp what eternal separation from God feels like. However, the loss of my parents and the death of my daughter references some of the despair and sadness that I will feel if I am eternally separated from God via the second death. Forever separated from the One that loves me totally, completely, just as I am. That's the second death. It is unimaginable because we have not experienced it. Jesus experienced that separation on the cross. He died the death that I was supposed to die because of my sin.

How do I know that I love my brother? 1 John 3:16-18, 24, "We know that God loves us because He sent His Son to die for us; therefore, we ought to be willing to die for our brothers and sisters. When you who have possessions see a brother or sister in need, but you don't help him, how can you say that you love God? My dear children, to love someone doesn't mean just saying so or being fond of them. It means helping them, whether we feel loving toward them or not... The person who lives by God's law of love is living out Christ's spirit in his own life. We know that God is living in us by the kind of spirit we have." Love, though influenced by feeling, is a principle from which behaviors are chosen that benefit the loved, even when I do not "feel" like doing it. I show my love for others by helping them when they need help. By speaking words of life to them, encouraging words, uplifting words, inspiring words. I feel pain when they hurt. I cry with them when they cry. I laugh with them when they laugh. I rejoice with them over their successes. I show my love for God and others reflected in Matthew 25:40, "…Inasmuch as ye have done it unto one of the least of these my brethren, ye have done it unto me."

Love looks like _____

My strength in this area _____

My weakness in this area _____

Dear God, You have promised _____

You have told me that it is in my best interest to _____

I praise Your name for helping me to _____

YT "Eternal Life" Walter Hawkins
YT "My whole world ended" Temptations
YT "Days of Elijah" Brooklyn Tabernacle Choir

LOVE BRINGS COMFORT.
2 Corinthians 1:3-4, "Blessed be God…the God of all comfort; who comforteth us in all our tribulation, that we may be able to comfort them which are in any trouble, by the comfort wherewith we ourselves are comforted of God."

An expected outcome goal of love is comfort. Comfort, physical, emotional, spiritual, is mediated physiologically through decreasing stress hormones and increasing hormones that impact mood. Dopamine works in the brain's reward system. Praise and pleasure are mediated through dopamine release. Serotonin elevates my mood. Physical exercise is the most natural way to increase serotonin, a daily walk makes me feel good. Oxytocin increases trust and bonding. Spending time with a loved one, touching, kissing, hugging, releases oxytocin. Estrogen and progesterone, two other hormones, work with serotonin to help protect from irritability and anxiety, keeping my mood steady. Eating right is the first defense for balancing these hormones.

Fear is the most common initiator of discomfort. Getting rid of fear is a very appropriate way to decrease the stress hormones associated with discomfort.

If someone feels close to me, they want to be close to me. Leaning in and moving closer, face to face interactions increases my comfort. My head rested on my hand shows comfort. Sitting with my arms open and unfolded increases my comfort and the person that I may be talking to. When I smile and others smile back, they display comfort. If someone is touching me or allowing me to touch them, there is comfort between the two of us.

John 14:27, "Peace I leave with you…do not let your heart be troubled… nor let it be afraid." Psalm 34:18, "The Lord is near to the brokenhearted…" Matthew 5:4, "Blessed are those who mourn, for they shall be comforted." 1 Peter 5:7, "Casting all anxiety on Him, because He cares for you." Philippians 4:6, "Be anxious for nothing…" Psalm 34:4, "…and delivered me from all my fears." Love decreases fear and brings comfort.

Love looks like _____

My strength in this area _____

My weakness in this area _____

Dear God, You have promised _____

You have told me that it is in my best interest to_____

I praise Your name for helping me to_____

YT "Comforter" CeCe Winans
YT "When you cry" Winans

Jealousy is an Expected Outcome of Love

2 Corinthians 11:2, "For I am jealous over you with godly jealousy; for I have espoused you to one husband, that I may present you as a chaste virgin to Christ."

Jealousy is an expected outcome of love. Exodus 20:5, "You shall not bow down to them or worship them; for I, the Lord your God, am a jealous God..." God is possessive of me. He doesn't want anybody or anything to come before Him. He tells me that He is jealous and wants my attention and affections first and foremost for Him. Understanding that He loves me and tells me only what is for my best outcomes. I understand His jealousy and I make sure that I don't put anyone else before Him.

Jealousy suggests someone is competing for my affections and that I might leave for someone else. Satan is real, and he seeks to pull me from the God who loves me. A third of the angels loved Satan more than they loved God and they walked away from God for Satan. Any of my attention or affection that I give to him robs God of the attention and affection due to Him only. God's jealousy suggests that my relationship with Him is in danger and serves as a wake-up call to me to watch what I am doing that makes Him upset with me. The danger is not that He will leave me but that I will leave Him. Jealousy is a necessary emotion that preserves bonds and trust and motivates me to engage in behavior that maintains my loving, trusting relationship with God.

Knowing that God is jealous of my affections strengthens my relationship. I will reflect on what I am doing that produces that emotional response in Him and cooperate with Him to repair the bond. I tell Him that I love Him. I avoid situations and temptations that Satan attempts to engage me in that pulls me away from the time, talks, praise, and devotion that I give to Him. I monitor His word, so that I know the things that please Him and make Him happy. I work on communicating with Him, listening to Him, telling Him my feelings. I am direct in asking Him how to resolve the situation. I ask Him how I have betrayed His trust and what I need to do avoid such situations in the future. My love response with myself and others is going to follow similar patterns. Jealousy, when used to strengthen my relationship, is a potent emotion that is in my best interest and produces my best outcomes.

Love looks like _____

My strength in this area _____

My weakness in this area _____

Dear God, You have promised_____

You have told me that it is in my best interest to_____

I praise Your name for helping me to_____

YT "Jesus love me" Whitney Houston
YT "A Woman's love" Carla Thomas
YT "Jealous kind of lover" Garland Green

LOVE IS TENDER, KIND, AND FORGIVING.

Ephesians 4:32, "And be ye kind one to another, tenderhearted, forgiving one another, even as God for Christ's sake hath forgiven you."

Love's outcomes are tender, kind, and forgiving. God saw a hurt, brokenness, and despair. He saw that I would be without hope of breaking from pain and suffering. So He sent His Son to rescue me. That's kindness. Kindness is a fruit of the Spirit. Fruit is produced by staying attached to the fruit tree, getting the nourishment and water needed from the ground in which the tree is planted. Kindness, not just in deeds but in words and how I say them, is an outcome goal of love.

Genesis 34:3,"…and he loved the girl and spoke tenderly to her." 2 Samuel 1:26, "…You have been very pleasant to me. Your love to me was more wonderful than the love of women." Luke 1:78, "Because of the tender mercy of our God, with which the sunrise from on high will visit us." Deuteronomy 32:10-14, "He found him in a desert land…in the howling waste of a wilderness. He encircled him…cared for him…guarded him as the pupil of His eye…spread His wings and caught them. Hosea 2:14, "…I will allure her. Bring her into the wilderness. And speak kindly to her."

I feel comfortable in your presence. I feel safe in your presence. You are so calm and gentle. I want to feel your touch. I know what love is because of you. You don't love me because I am beautiful, I am beautiful because you love me. I feel like I am in paradise when I am with you. You have never spoken an unkind word to me. You have always been so gentle and tender.

Love is forgiving. 1 John 1:9-10, "If we confess…He is faithful and just to forgive…" Hebrews 8:12, "…their iniquities will I remember no more." Someone has wronged me. I want revenge, justice, but forgiveness is in my best interest. The stress relief that I get from forgiving others benefits me more than it benefits the person that has wronged me. Forgiveness is an act of my will. It does not mean that I forget, it means that I don't let the negative feelings associated with the wrong infect my being. I make a conscious choice and take deliberate actions not to continue dwelling on the wrong. I don't excuse the wrong. Excusing the wrong doesn't help the person doing the wrong to grow. I simply keep no record of the wrong. Outcome goals of love include tenderness, kindness, and forgiveness for myself and others.

Love looks like _____

My strength in this area _____

My weakness in this area _____

Dear God, You have promised _____

You have told me that it is in my best interest to _____

I praise Your name for helping me to _____

YT "He giveth more grace" Aneisa Simon
YT "The greatest love of all" Whitney Houston
YT "God favored me" Hezekiah Walker
YT "Man in the Mirror" Michael Jackson

Love brings humility, meekness, longsuffering, and patience. **Ephesians 4:2,** "With all lowliness and meekness, with longsuffering, forbearing one another in love."

Love has as outcome measures humility, meekness, longsuffering, and patience.

Humility and meekness stem from acknowledging who God is and who I am in comparison to Him. I know that God is the Creator. I know that He is in charge of all things. I know that He knows the end from the beginning. I accept His position of authority because of who He is. I am created in His image, a little lower than the angels. I am an heir to His throne, a priest in His kingdom. God saves me because I am lowly. Job 22:29. Psalm 22:6, "I am a worm…" Because I know that I am God's child, I follow Philippians 2:3 in my treatment of others. "Do nothing from selfish ambition or conceit." I put my confidence in my Savior, not myself. I complain about my heart, not my circumstances, and I say, like Paul, "Wretched man that I am" and cry out for more of God's grace. I uplift Christ and accept His reproof for my wrong doing. I don't need to be out-front and recognized by man; my need is to magnify God. I am content in whatever place God puts me. I have no problem picking up the garbage because it needs to be picked up and the environment will be a better place because I have picked it up and I will have grown in God's grace.

God operates on a much longer time frame than I do. One day is like a year to Him. Longsuffering and patience are traits I need to develop. Longsuffering allows me to bear and allow for the weakness of others while patience is used to bear with things concerning myself and enduring my personal struggles. God is longsuffering toward me (Psalm 86:15) and knows that it is in my best interest for me to be longsuffering with others. Longsuffering removes pride and is needed, so I can help and comfort others. Factors that interfere with my longsuffering and patience include lack of sleep, stress, health problems, as well as things that increase those stress hormones: anger, sadness, bitterness. Patience allows for peace, flexibility, and support when I am having a bad day or when I am not at my best. Adjusting to the ups and downs of life, the mood swings of life, helps to support the feeling of being unconditionally loved. Christ in me produces the meekness, humility, longsuffering, and patience that are outcome goals of love.

Love looks like _____

My strength in this area _____

My weakness in this area _____

Dear God, You have promised _____

You have told me that it is in my best interest to _____

I praise Your name for helping me to _____

YT "Herbert the Snail" Music Machine
YT "Wait for love" Luther Vandross

Love rejoices in truth.

1 Corinthians 13:6, "Rejoice not in iniquity, but rejoiceth in the truth."

Love rejoices in truth. Pilate asked Jesus in John 18:37, "What is truth?" A question I continue to ask, and as I read God's word daily, He shares with me on an ongoing basis what truth is.

Jesus says I am, the way, the truth, the life. I like this verse stated in the appositive. I AM, the truth. This is consistent with knowing Jesus, I know the truth. Apart from Him, there is no truth. Ye shall know the truth and it shall make you free. Knowing truth brings joy and rejoicing. I grasp the truth because I know Him in my heart. My conscious experience is the only way I have of knowing that I am in contact with truth. Truth is firm, solid, steadfast, and provides a foundation to stand on. It represents who I am in character.

Believing that something is true doesn't make it true. My beliefs don't determine truth, but they do determine my outcomes. People in the olden days believed that the world was flat. It kept them from experiencing a whole new round world. Beliefs about what is truth obviously impact behavior. Numbers 23:19, "God is not a man that he should lie." The trust needed to obey what He tells me to do is based on knowing that He does not lie to me. I can depend on what He says. That brings joy and peace. When I tell lies, my health is affected; my heart rate increases, my respiratory rate goes up. The stress response, based on fear, is triggered. If I don't completely trust God, I can't possibly love Him.

The same is true with my relationship with myself and others. If I lie to myself, I can't possibly truly love myself. If I lie to others with whom I am in a relationship, trust is broken, and it is very difficult to repair. My relationship will be confused, suffer, and breakdown. Honesty is the most important part of any relationship. It is the foundation of trust. Telling the truth empowers me and those around me to change and grow. It creates deeper connections in my relationships. It increases respect and allows me to grow progressively better in love. It is an ultimate sign of love and brings joy and rejoicing.

Love looks like _____

My strength in this area _____

My weakness in this area _____

Dear God, You have promised _____

You have told me that it is in my best interest to _____

I praise Your name for helping me to _____

YT "Truth and Honesty" Aretha Franklin
YT "Just be true" Jerry Butler

Love restores hope, belief, perseverance, and endurance – outcome measures of love.

I Corthians 13: 7, "Beareth all things, believeth all things, hopeth all things, endureth all things."

Bears all things. Love protects me, like a roof protects a house and his banner over me *was* love." It protects me from things outside that would harm me. Sometimes He has to protect me from choices that I made that were not in my best interest. Sometimes He has to protect me from the cold. From the heat. From others that would abuse me.

Love believes all things. Love is not blind or stupid, but it fills me with hope, so that I see beyond the negative to the potential for what will be. God doesn't see me as I am but what I will be through His love and the power of His Spirit. I will look like Him when He appears. I don't get discouraged by "what is" because I know what can be. My friend lied to me, but I can see beyond the lies, so see the potential in the relationship once we have handled the impact of the lie and decided to deal with the outcomes.

Love hopes all things. I see the worst, but I hope and anticipate the best in myself and in others. I expect the best. A mother sees her son addicted to drugs. She knows the gifts and talents that he has and looks forward to what his life will be like when he is no longer using drugs.

Love endures all things. I refuse to surrender or give up in defeat. I am committed to being here to stay. I patiently cooperate with God to make the changes I need to move forward to where He wants me to be. I didn't pass the test the first time, but I don't drop the class. I am longsuffering with you as I wait for you to get to where God wants you to be. You didn't get the job that would have made it easier for all of us, but I am not walking out the door because we are struggling. Love bears, believes, hopes, and endures all things.

Love looks like _____

My strength in this area _____

My weakness in this area _____

Dear God, You have promised _____

You have told me that it is in my best interest to_____

I praise Your name for helping me to_____

YT "Victory" Yolanda Adams
YT "One moment in time" Whitney Houston

Chapter 3
I just want to feel good!

I Just Want to Feel Good
Ecclesiastes 2:3, "I tried cheering myself with wine and embracing folly—my mind still guiding me with wisdom. I wanted to see what was good for people to do under the heavens during the few days of their lives."

Whether in utero, in any state of thriving after the birth experience, or minimally responsive in a persistent vegetative state, responses to stimuli can be detected. Today's text was written almost 3,000 years ago as musings of the wisest ruler of all time. If knowledge is power and power is characteristic of earthly kings and rulers, then when confronted by internal insecurity and external inequities, feelings of inadequacy retains dominion. That is to say, when I do not experience love and feel good, I will be dominated by feelings of inadequacy. Why? Because God made me to feel good.

Four decades ago, in an effort to remediate this persistent longing, a composer wrote, "Try not to hide what you feel deep inside. If you care, you must dare to be free as the air." Earth, Wind and Fire sang the song.

Another prolific and articulate social commentator of the same era rhythmically shouted, "Whoa! I feel good like I knew that I would now. I feel good like I knew that I would now. So good, so good, I got you." James Brown

God made us in such a way that we respond to stimuli. Stimulation, either easily or minimally discernible, causes proportional nervous system arousal, musculoskeletal response. and experiential awareness that is categorized then stored as feelings. If the stimulus is perceived as challenging (pain, hunger, threat to bodily integrity, loss or inadequacy) energy stores will be expended. If the stimulus is perceived as comforting, the energy stores to indulge and sustain smooth and striated muscle activity will be replenished. These feelings in our bodies are supported through the sympathetic and parasympathetic nervous systems, as well as chemicals that are released that trigger either storage or expenditure of energy.

Categories of feelings can be considered emotions. The awareness and management of these feelings within, as well as their effects on others, is considered emotional intelligence. Empathy is one of many measures of emotional intelligence and is essential in the health care professions.

Stimuli, whether or not consciously perceived, through various hormones released effects dilation or constriction of the body's blood vessels, veins, arteries, and capillaries. Along the almost thirty feet of digestive tract and the thirty square centimeters of protective membrane covering it, circulatory variances register in the rich supply of nerves and actively engage immunologic monitoring mechanisms. This composite awareness has been known as "gut feeling, intuition, discernment, common sense, mother -wit, even as the question, "Have you lost your mind?!"

After the completion of the extensive clinical trials conducted widely by the wisest of kings to rule in this world, Solomon, a nonbiased universal literature review, referred to an effective remedy proposed by his father, David, almost four decades earlier and actively practiced by those immune to unrequited feelings. "Take delight in the Lord, and he will give you your heart's desires," Psalms 37:4.

YT "I FEEL GOOD" JAMES BROWN

I WAS CREATED TO FEEL GOOD.
Genesis 1:26-27, "And God said "Let us make man in our image, after our likeness… So God created man in his own image, in the image of God created he him; male and female created he them."

I am created in the image of God. Physical, mental, emotional, spiritual, and intellectual aspects of who I am are in the image of God. I desire to be known. I desire acceptance, acknowledgement, recognition. Just as God has feelings, I have feelings. I want to belong. I want to feel warmth, tenderness, compassion. I want to hear words of love. His Spirit in me gives me the desire to be safe and free. I want to trust and be trusted. I want to be safe. Just as God wants to be with me and wants me to be with Him, I want to be with someone and someone to be with me. The physical aspect of my being desires to be touched. I want to engage in sex to experience that feeling of the two becoming one.

The deeper longing that I have underneath every desire, dream, or want is to feel good, to feel joy, to feel peace, to feel contentment, to be free of pain, physical or emotional. Feeling good is more than an emotion. Feeling good is God's way of telling me that I am on the right track. The physical aspects of my being include chemicals, hormones, electrical pathways, and other mechanisms that He has placed within my body to help to integrate all of these aspects of who I am. It is not the responsibility of others to make me feel good. It is an internal process, triggered by the workings of Christ in me mediated by chemicals and processes that He has put within me to cooperate with Him in achieving His plan for me, plans to prosper me and not to harm me, plans to bring me to a good end, to give me hope and a future. Jeremiah 29:11, Note the inflammatory process within me that demonstrates one of those processes. When I scratch myself, chemicals that cause pain, swelling, and redness are released to let me know that I have been injured. My body is not on the right track. Within nanoseconds of scratching myself, the inflammatory process, the first stage of wound healing, is initiated that eventually heals the scratch, putting my body back on the right track. Ibuprofen, a known anti-inflammatory medicine, interferes with the process by reducing the swelling and pain that results. A scar remains as a reminder of injury.

While others can help me to feel good, loving myself as God has commanded is a necessity. I encourage and compliment myself, but I feel good when I am encouraged and complimented by you. I know and love who I am, but I feel good when I am accepted as I am by you. I acknowledge my strengths and weaknesses, but I feel so good when you recognize and acknowledge them. When you smile at me, I feel good. When you praise some good thing that I have done, I feel good. When you listen to me I feel good. When I know for sure that you love me, I feel good. Love makes me feel good.

Love looks like _____

My strength in this area _____

My weakness in this area _____

Dear God, You have promised _____

You have told me that it is in my best interest to _____

I praise Your name for helping me to _____

YT "Heaven must have sent you" Elgins
YT "I feel good all over" Stephanie Mills

I want you to know me.
Psalm 103:14, "For he knoweth our frame; he remembereth that we are dust.
Exodus 3:13-14 "And Moses said unto God, Behold, when I come unto the children of Israel, and shall say unto them, the God of your fathers hath sent me unto you; and they shall say to me, what is his name? What shall I say unto them? …and he said…say unto the children of Israel, I AM hath sent me…"
Proverbs 20:11, Even a child is known by his doings, whether his work be pure, and whether it be right.

My eternal life is based on who I know. John 17:3, "And this is life eternal, that they might know thee the only true God, and Jesus Christ, whom thou hast sent." The desire to be known is inherent in my nature as I am created in the image of God. Although your eternal life does not depend on you knowing me, just being "me" wants you to know me. I know me, and this is why I want you to know me. It makes me happier. It makes me feel good. It helps you make better choices and decisions about interacting and trusting me. You will have insight as to what motivates me to resist bad habits and develop good ones. When you know my values, you will have a better understanding of when to say yes or no to my requests. When you know me, you will better understand how to empathize with me. When you know me, it better enables us to have a richer, fuller relationship.

I know my values. I like to help others. I trust in God. I value my health. I want justice for all people. My values help me stay rooted and grounded. I know my interests, my passions, my hobbies, those things that catch my attention in an ongoing manner. I like my family. I like the outdoors, living in the country, and being in nature. Know my temperament. I am choleric. There are strengths and weaknesses in being choleric, and one of those strengths is I am more of a doer than a talker. Knowing my temperament can help me to know how I will function in groups, why I tend to act in certain ways. I know my body biological rhythms. I am a morning person. Knowing my rhythms help us both to use our energy efficiently. Do you know my life's mission and goals? My mission and goals are centered in Jesus' main goals for me and His creation, to spend eternity with Him and have His image fully reflected in me so that when He comes back, I will be like Him. His missions on this earth included pulling me from death to life, making His Spirit available to dwell with me to establish my holiness, show the immutability of God's law to the universe, and to reveal the love, grace, mercy, and justice of His Father to the universe. Do you know my strengths and weaknesses? Am I creative? Am I brave? Am I kind? Do I persevere under trial? I need you to know me. Please take the time to get to know me.

Love looks like _____

My strength in this area _____

My weakness in this area _____

Dear God, You have promised _____

You have told me that it is in my best interest to _____

I praise Your name for helping me to _____

YT " Who Am I?" Casting Crowns

I want you to accept me as I am and help me to change if I need to.
Romans 15: 5, 7, "Now the God of patience and consolation grant you to be likeminded one toward another according to Christ Jesus: Wherefore receive ye one another, as Christ also received us to the glory of God."

Acceptance means an awareness of my feelings with the understanding that feelings change and fluctuate, but at this time and space, this is who I am. Accept my reality. I want you to allow me to be who I am without trying to change me. I want you to allow me to have my feelings without trying to make me feel guilty or ashamed. I know it will take time and practice for you to get to the point where you can accept me as I am, but that is what I want from you. I know that you will go back and forth in getting to the point where you can accept me and that it will be frustrating for both of us at times. Your acceptance of me does not mean that I will never change, but the change has to come as a result of my choice and in my time frame. You can help me get to that point by accepting me as I am right now.

When I came to Jesus, He took me with all my baggage. He did the same for You. His focus was on me as He found me, although He knew what I would be like in the future. He works with me over time knowing that I can change. Your acceptance of me is a choice. Accepting things that you cannot change and allowing me the chance to grow will produce a happier, peaceful environment for both of us. I live in a world that is constantly changing. Your acceptance of me is not weakness, it is a realistic way of dealing with the here and now. If I am an alcoholic and I am trying to stop drinking, my body has to adjust overtime to change. When I stop drinking alcohol all at once, I will go into withdrawals that could lead to seizures and death. The same transition timing applies to other areas of who I am.

Timing is important. Ask me questions, so that you are clear on where I am. Help me by helping to list all the potential possibilities if I change. Give me hope for a future. Help me by helping me to understand why I am like I am and why I do the things that I do rather than judging me. Help me to be honest with myself and take responsibility for my choices. Help me to be realistic about what can and cannot be changed. Let me gently know if I am blaming others. Help me to make a plan for change. Accept me as I am.

Love looks like _____

My strength in this area _____

My weakness in this area _____

Dear God, You have promised _____

You have told me that it is in my best interest to _____

I praise Your name for helping me to _____

YT "Please accept me for who I am" Lloyd
YT "Just as I am" Whitley Phipps

I WANT YOU TO ACKNOWLEDGE AND RECOGNIZE ME.
Proverbs 3:6, "In all your ways acknowledge Him (God), and He will make your path straight."

God wants me to acknowledge Him. He promises that if I do, He will make my paths straight. When you call me by my name, when you say hello to me, when you congratulate me on my successes, when you tell me thank you for being kind and thoughtful, you are helping to meet my need to be acknowledged and recognized. I will not forget your recognition and how you made me feel. Thank you.

One way that I acknowledge God is that I understand my accomplishments come from the gifts He has blessed me with. I was born with tremendous gifts given to me by God, and they are used to guide me in the ways He wants me to go. Sometimes my best laid plans do not go like I want them to. So I ask myself, why is that? When I lean on my own understanding, I tend to stray away from the path that is meant for me. Life takes on many twists and turns in my own understanding. But He continually honors His promise to make my path straight when I recognize and acknowledge Him.

Jeremiah 10:23 states, "I know, O LORD, that a man's way is not his own; no one who walks directs his own steps." In high school, I knew my calling was to help others. I knew this was my calling, but the acknowledgement and recognition I received along this path were due to plans laid out by God. He put many people in my path that helped provide direction. He opened all the doors I needed to have opened and provided the resources I needed to move me to that calling. Looking at the calling that He gave me as a teenager. I am reminded that Jesus knew when He was twelve-years-old what His calling was. He chose to allow the Holy Spirit to work in Him to move Him to that calling. I wanted the acknowledgement and recognition that comes from attaining higher education but without the Holy Spirit and gifts given to me by God, I would have never heard or moved to act on my calling.

Psalms 37:23, "The steps of a man are established by the LORD, when he delights in his way." In my endeavors to achieve great things, acknowledgement and recognition by others has come with great success. My success and achievements are not my own but ordered out of the steps of God. Many times I wonder if I am on the right path. That is when I ask myself, have I given thanks to the Lord for my successes and accomplishments so far? Have I acknowledged Him in all things? Your acknowledgment and recognition of my accomplishments make me feel really good, but even better is the acknowledgment and recognition by My God that I am His child and that my equal acknowledgment of Him guarantees that He will make my paths straight.

Love looks like _____

My strength in this area _____

My weakness in this area _____

Dear God, You have promised _____

You have told me that it is in my best interest to _____

I praise Your name for helping me to _____

YT "He's that kind of Friend" Walter Hawkins

I WANT YOU TO BE FAITHFUL TO ME.
Proverbs 20:6, "Most men will proclaim everyone his own goodness: but a faithful man who can find?"

Faithful – constant, true, unswerving in your affections, devoted, steadfast. That is what I am needing from you. I need you to keep your promises to me no matter the circumstance." Deuteronomy 7:9, "Know therefore that the Lord thy God, he is God, the faithful God, which keepeth covenant and mercy with them that love him and keep his commands to a thousand generations." 2 Timothy 2:13, "If we turn against Him, He'll still love us because that's the kind of person that He is. His attitude toward us is not dependent on our attitude toward Him. <u>He will always love us because we are part of His body and He can't disown Himself.</u>" 1 Thessalonians 5:24, "Faithful is He who calls you, and He also will bring it to pass." God is faithful to His word, His promises, to the laws He put in place, to me, whom He created a little lower than the angels. I am created in His image, I am to be an imitator of God as His dear child. Ephesians 5:1, "By His power I can be faithful in thought, word, and deed."

Job demonstrated his faithfulness to his friends that had questioned his relationship with God after God rebuked them and sent them to Job to pray for them. Job 42:7-9, "God said to Miriam and Aaron when they questioned Moses authority, 'Not so with my servant Moses. He is faithful in all my house.'" Numbers 12:5-9 Jonathan showed his faithfulness to David when he shot the warning arrow telling David that his father, Saul, indeed was trying to kill him. John was placed in a pot of boiling oil because of his faithfulness to Jesus. In contrast Judas betrayed Jesus with a kiss; Peter denied Jesus three times, and David had sex with Uriah's wife and had him killed when it became known that she was pregnant.

Faithfulness is often associated with the marital relationship. Infidelity has a larger scope than sleeping with someone that you are not married to. Being faithful is more than never letting another person into your bed. Being faithful means you never let another person in your heart.

I need you, can I call you? I want you, can I send for you? Don't wait too long. I'll always love you. I'm always thinking of you. I have entrusted you with the secrets of my heart. Please don't use them to hurt me. I rely on you to do what you have said you will do. I count on you to tell me the truth. I need you to be the faithful envoy of Proverbs 13:17 and bring healing. I need you to be the like the cold of snow in the time of harvest, the faithful messenger described in Proverbs 25:13. Please be faithful to me.

Love looks like _____

My strength in this area _____

My weakness in this area _____

Dear God, You have promised _____

You have told me that it is in my best interest to _____

I praise Your name for helping me to _____

YT "He's so faithful" Brooklyn Tabernacle Choir
YT "Jesus is love" Commodores YT "If you need me" Solomon Burke

I want you to treat me like a priceless treasure.
Matthew 6:21, "For where your treasure is, there will your heart be also." **1 Samuel 24:10,** "Behold, this day thine eyes have seen how that the LORD had delivered thee to day into mine hand in the cave: and some bade me kill thee: but mine eye spared thee; and I said, I will not put forth mine hand against my lord; for he is the LORD's anointed." **Luke 12:7,** "But even the very hairs of your head are all numbered. Fear not therefore: ye are of more value than many sparrows"

My value cannot be estimated or determined. Jesus died on the cross for me. I need you to cherish me, to value me. I am expensive, the price that Jesus paid for me, He gave up everything for me, heaven, His life. I cannot be bought and I will not be sold.

I put priceless treasures in a special place. In that special place, the priceless treasure can be seen and admired but is kept safe, so that it won't be damaged or broken. The priceless treasures are made of different kinds of material that varies their worth but are nonetheless priceless. Some are made of gold, some of glass. Some are gifts from my children or my husband. Others are treasures that belonged to my parents or deceased siblings. I wash and polish them every now and then to keep them clean and help them retain their value. I am careful who I let touch them because I want to preserve them.

I want you to recognize my worth and treat me like the priceless treasure that Jesus has declared me to be. Keep me in that special place in your heart for where your treasure is, your heart will be also. Talk to me gently and with a kind tone of voice, so that I am not broken. Hold me up, so that others can see the value that Jesus places on me. Do not sell me down the river. Don't try to buy me. Keep me on that pedestal and don't let me off. Jesus paid an awfully high price for me.

Love looks like _____

My strength in this area _____

My weakness in this area _____

Dear God, You have promised _____

You have told me that it is in my best interest to_____

I praise Your name for helping me to_____

YT "Jesus paid it all" Mississippi Mass Choir

I WANT YOU TO UNDERSTAND ME.
Psalm 139:1-17, "O Lord, You have searched me and known me. You know my sitting down and my rising up; You understand my thoughts afar off. You comprehend my path and my lying down, And are acquainted with all my ways. For there is not a word on my tongue, but behold, O Lord, You know it altogether… Where can I go from your Spirit: Or where can I flee from your presence? If I ascend into heaven, You are there; If I make my bed in hell, behold, You are there…How precious are your thoughts to me, O God! How great is the sum of them."

I want you to know why I do what I do. I want you to understand me. Understanding my unmet needs and goals is a key to understanding me. We are not all the same. I see the world differently than you do. To understand me, you must feel and know my feelings. Can you put yourself in my shoes for just a little while, so that you can better understand where I am coming from? Why do you have a need to use that label "stupid" when you talk about me? I think it is because you don't understand me and you have a need to put me in a category, so that you will feel comfortable dealing with me. It could also be because you lack self-confidence and are jealous of me. Labels serve your needs, but they don't tell the truth about who I am. When you rush to label me, it is based on the baggage that you bring to the table. To understand me, you need to feel what I feel, live my past, and think like I think. I need you to put aside your belief system and try to enter mine. Please step outside of who you are and enter into who I am.

Do you understand what it going on with me when I cross my arms when we are talking? What does my tone of voice say to you? How do you interpret what I am saying when I sit with my legs crossed with my hands behind my head? How about when I am fidgeting or can't look you in the eyes? What does the look on my face say to you about me? Where am I in my stage of development? Am I a rational person, or do I operate more on my feelings? Am I process oriented, or are goals more important to me than the process? Am I introverted, get my energy and support from myself or an extrovert, do I need external reinforcement to feel good about myself? Am I thought oriented or action oriented? I need empathy from you, put yourself in my shoes. Look past those first impressions, find out what's in my heart. Know that I am afraid you are not going to like me when you really look deep and see who I am. Your understanding makes me feel so good. Please understand me.

Love looks like _____

My strength in this area _____

My weakness in this area _____

Dear God, You have promised _____

You have told me that it is in my best interest to _____

I praise Your name for helping me to _____

YT "He'll understand and say well done" **Yvette Flunder**
YT "God understands" **Clark Sisters**
YT "Don't let me be misunderstood" **Nina Simone**

I want you to respect me.
Leviticus 19:32, "Stand up in the presence of the aged, show respect for the elderly and revere your God. I am the LORD."

"Never take a person's dignity: it is worth everything to them, and nothing to you," Frank Barron. Give respect where it is due. Your respect helps me feel safe. It frees me to express myself to you. It helps me to know that you accept me as I am even if I am different from you.

R-E-S-P-E-C-T, find out of what it means to me, famous words from an Aretha Franklin song. But what do those words mean to you? For individuals of advanced age, respect is a concept that is rooted in the dignity of a person who has lived long enough to deserve it and have earned it. 1 Timothy 5:1, "Do not rebuke an older man, but appeal to him as to a father." In most cases, a father figure is someone I admire and learn from. My elders house a knowledge that only comes from living long enough to have navigated life and learned from its lessons. Elders are not revered as they once were. The knowledge they possess by being blessed with long life is often overlooked or dismissed due to their advanced age. 1 Peter 5:5, "Likewise, you who are younger, be subject to the elders. Clothe yourselves, all of you, with humility toward one another, for God opposes the proud but gives grace to the humble."

Life lessons are put along my path because God is trying to tell me something. I am supposed to learn from my successes and failures. I must respect that He has infinite wisdom, and His way is the only way I am to go. Romans 13:2, "Therefore whoever resists the authorities resists what God has appointed, and those who resist will incur judgment." The reading of the word of God helps me to understand what He wants from me. Respect for those words are proven in my actions with you. Deuteronomy 6:4-5, "Hear, O Israel: The LORD our God, the LORD is one. You shall love the LORD your God with all your heart and with all your soul and with all your might." I have to ask myself, am I too proud to listen to the words of my elders, a wisdom given by the grace of God? If I love God and have respect for His word, I will respect my elders as He has told me to knowing that is in my best interest to do so. I will also respect myself and you because I love you, and it is in both of our best interest to do so. I recall the words of a young man in a movie, "If you want respect, you have to earn it." Tell me what I need to do to respect you.

You show me respect by listening to what I say. I need you to have the courage to say to me things you might say to others about me, but it won't do me any good if I don't hear it from you. If you say it to them and I find out later, I feel violated and will be less willing to express myself to you. Do not violate my confidentiality. Please don't compare me with others. Know that opinions are like noses, everybody has one. Please respect mine. We come from different backgrounds, and no two people are alike. Instead of being sarcastic, I need you to speak gently to me. Please know what it means to respect me.

Love looks like _____

My strength in this area _____

My weakness in this area _____

Dear God, You have promised _____

You have told me that it is in my best interest to _____

I praise Your name for helping me to _____

YT "RESPECT" ARETHA FRANKLIN

I JUST NEED TO HEAR YOUR VOICE.
Solomon 2: 8, 10, The voice of my beloved! Behold... My beloved spake, and said unto me, Rise up, my love, my fair one, and come away. **Matthew 21:21,** "Jesus answered and said unto them, Verily I say unto you, If ye have faith, and doubt not...also if ye shall say unto this mountain, Be thou removed, and be thou cast into the sea; it shall be done."

Psalm 29:3-4, "...The voice of the LORD is over the waters; the God of glory thunders, the LORD thunders over the mighty waters. The voice of the LORD is powerful; the voice of the LORD is majestic." **Proverbs 10:31,** "The mouth of the godly person gives wise advice." Proverbs 12:18, "... but the tongue of the wise brings healing." Proverbs 15:2-4, "The tongue of the wise commends knowledge... A gentle tongue is a tree of life..." Proverbs 16:24, "Gracious words are a honeycomb, sweet to the soul and healing to the bones." John 10:27, "My sheep hear my voice, and I know them, and they follow me." Hebrews 4:12, "For the word of God is quick, and powerful, and sharper than any two-edged sword, piercing even to the dividing asunder of soul and spirit, and of the joints and marrow, and is a discerner of the thoughts and intents of the heart."

The power of life and death are in the tongue. Do you understand how much power God has given you when I hear your voice speaking to me? I feel such comfort, peace, and joy when I hear that voice that I recognize as yours. God speaks and things happen. Mountains are moved. Rivers stay in their boundaries. My heart beats. I breathe. He speaks words of life when He tells me how to live healthfully. The dead rise. The lame walk. The blind see. The deaf hear. God has given power to your voice just as He has power in His.

Your voice connects me to your heart's energy, and it makes me comfortable and safe. I feel free to risk my vulnerability when I hear you call my name. The safety I feel when I hear your voice frees me, so that I feel okay to share my deepest, innermost thoughts and feelings with You. The calmness and evenness of your voice inspires me to reflect on where I am in my life and gives me the desire to move forward. I value your opinion. I value your purpose. I hear your mission projected in your voice. I am empowered by the wisdom that comes via your voice. Your gentle tongue has restored me in times when I wanted to give up. Your kind tongue has given me hope when things seemed pretty hopeless. I hear you speak to me in the midnight hour, at noonday, in the evening when the sun goes down.

Christ in you, the hope of glory, speaking to me through you. I love to hear your voice for I recognize that it is Christ speaking to me through you. I need to hear your voice. Please keep Christ in your heart and keep speaking words of life into me.

Love looks like _____

My strength in this area _____

My weakness in this area _____

Dear God, You have promised_____

You have told me that it is in my best interest to_____

I praise Your name for helping me to_____

YT "Comforter" CeCe Winans
YT "My help" Donnie McClurkin

I WANT YOU TO THINK ABOUT ME.
Phillipians 1:3-11, "³ I thank my God upon every remembrance of you. Always in every prayer of mine for you all making request with joy. For your fellowship in the gospel from the first day until now… Even as it is meet for me to think this of you all, because I have you in my heart…ye all are partakers of my grace. For God is my record, how greatly I long after you all in the bowels of Jesus Christ."

Do you think about me? Will you remember me? Do you miss me when you don't see me? Why are you silent? Why haven't I heard from you? Is our relationship worth it, or has it just been a convenience for you? Do you still love me? Have you ever really loved me? Have I treated you dishonorably or disrespectfully? Have I been unkind to you? Have I put you down? Have I been for real with you? Have I taken from you more than I have given to you? Don't you believe I love you? These same questions that I ask you, Jesus asks me. He wants me to think about Him just like I want you to think about me. We are created in His image. The same desire He has for me to think about Him, He has placed within me, and I want you to think about me.

I need you to think about me. I need you to think about the things I have shared with you. I need you to think about the good time we had together. I want you to think about what you want to share with me the next time we are together. I want you to re-read that card I sent you and tell me what it means to you. I want you to think about what you want to share with me about what's going on in your life. I have my own life, but you thinking about me makes it so much better. When Jesus thinks about me, He thinks about these things and so much more. 1 Thessalonians 3:6, "…that you always think kindly of us, longing to see us just as we also long to see you."

Joseph asked that his friend think about him when he was unfairly put in jail. Genesis 40:14, "But think on me when it shall be well with thee, and shew kindness, I pray thee, unto me, and make mention of me unto Pharaoh, and bring me out of this house." Abigail asked David to remember her after she kept him from needlessly killing or hurting someone. 1 Samuel 25:31, "…this will not cause grief or a troubled heart to my lord, both by having shed blood without cause and by my lord having avenged himself. When the Lord deals well with my lord, then remember your maidservant." The thief on the cross wanted Jesus to think about him. Luke 23:42, "And he was saying, "Jesus, remember me when You come in Your kingdom!" And Jesus responded to His request in Luke 23:43, "And Jesus said unto him, Verily I say unto thee today, shalt thou be with me in paradise." 2 Timothy 1:3, "I thank God, whom I serve with a clear conscience... as I constantly remember you in my prayers night and day.

Love looks like _____

My strength in this area _____

My weakness in this area _____

Dear God, You have promised _____

You have told me that it is in my best interest to _____

I praise Your name for helping me to _____

YT "Remember me" Whitley Phipps
YT "King of my heart" Demetria Stallings

I want you to be loyal to me.
Proverbs 21:21, "He who pursues righteousness and loyalty finds life, righteousness and honor."

Loyalty. A lifestyle that includes being true to myself as a key component for loyalty to you. Loyalty, emotional fidelity from you, sharing your thoughts and feelings with me, never lying or deceiving me. You consider my feelings when you make decisions concerning me. You empathize with me. You don't feel sorry for me but rather you put yourself in my shoes and walk that mile with me, so that you know how I feel. You give my needs and wants a priority place. You keep all the promises you make to me. Please forgive me, but there is a time requirement for me to test and prove your loyalty. Jesus allows me a time period to prove Himself loyal to me as well. That's why He gave me the word "testimony."

Ruth left her home of comfort and what she was used to, to go a place she didn't know just to be with her mother-in-law, Naomi. Peter, though later failing his initial test, told Jesus that he would die for Him. He ended up dying on a cross turned upside down for Jesus. When Ittai, leader of soldiers from Gath, joined David when he had hidden from Saul and David tried to send him home, Ittai was loyal to David. But Ittai replied to the king, "As surely as the LORD lives, and as my lord the king lives, wherever my lord the king may be, whether it means life or death, there will your servant be." 2 Samuel 15:21, When Sarah was asked by her coward of a husband to put herself in a compromising position so that he wouldn't be killed, she agreed to do so. Genesis 20:13. "Divided loyalty is unacceptable. 2 Kings 17:33, "They worshiped the LORD, but they also served their own gods in accordance with the customs of the nations from which they had been brought." Matthew 6:24, "No one can serve two masters. Either you will hate the one and love the other, or you will be devoted to the one and despise the other. You cannot serve both God and money." James 1:8, "Such a person is double-minded and unstable in all they do." God has proven His loyalty to me. He is always by my side. He doesn't forsake me, even when I am unfaithful to Him. He has never lied to me nor deceived me. He shares His thoughts and feelings with me. He gives me hope for a future. He is determined to redeem me, so that I can spend eternity with Him.

Recognize my ability to be loyal to you by noting these patterns in my life. I am optimistic about life. I am committed and determined. I am very predictable. I don't hold grudges. I am reliable and dependable. I keep my promises. I am by your side in good and bad times.

Love looks like _____

My strength in this area _____

My weakness in this area _____

Dear God, You have promised _____

You have told me that it is in my best interest to _____

I praise Your name for helping me to _____

YT "He's been faithful to me" Brooklyn Tabernacle Choir
YT If you don't know me by now" Harold Melvin/Blue Notes

I WANT YOU TO KISS ME, TOUCH ME, HUG ME.
Song of Solomon 1:2, "Let him kiss me with the kisses of his mouth— for your love is more delightful than wine. **Song of Solomon 4:11,** "Thy lips, O my spouse, drop as the honeycomb: honey and milk are under thy tongue; and the smell of thy garments is like the smell of Lebanon."

Whereas a little wine might be good for the belly's sake, overuse doesn't accomplish much good at all. Turns out Betty Everett was right! It really is "in his kiss." Now that's something I won't overuse and has long term benefits! Honey and milk are known to strengthen my immune response.

Kiss me. Release my oxytocin, dopamine, and serotonin, which make me feel euphoric, affectionate, and helps me bond with you. Reduce my cortisol (stress hormone) levels. I want that oxytocin released, so that I can feel attached to you and feel satisfaction in our relationship, so that we can have a trusting, enduring relationship. I want that oxytocin to help keep me calm and decrease my anxiety. Touch me. I want my stress levels to decrease, thereby decreasing my cortisol levels, which helps keep my blood glucose (sugar) levels under control. Hug me, so that my blood vessels will dilate and decrease my blood pressure. Touch me. Those dilated blood vessels takes care of my headache. Kiss me. Increase my salivation, so that I won't have as many cavities. Hug me so my cholesterol levels can be reduced and protect my heart. "Thy gentleness hath made me great," 2 Samuel 22:36 Your gentle touch, your thoughtful kiss, your encircling hug make me feel good physically, spiritually, and emotionally. Thank you for allowing God to work through you to meet my needs.

A caveat though! Due to many negative experiences in life, not everyone is as comfortable with hugging, touching, and kissing as I am. Make sure you get permission to kiss, hug, and touch. It's okay to ask. Pay attention to body language before kissing, touching, or hugging. I reserve kissing on my lips and neck for my husband. Kiss me on my forehead. Kiss me on my cheek. You can kiss my hand any time.

Remember Judas kissed Jesus to betray Him, but we are told multiple times in the Bible to greet each other with a holy kiss not as a betrayal but a sign of love. "Greet one another with a holy kiss," 2 Corinthians 13:12. The kiss is holy and helps to establish unity in brotherhood. A holy kiss expresses brotherly love and unity. It communicates acceptance and fellowship. Kiss, touch, and hug me often. I need it, so do you.

Love looks like _____

My strength in this area _____

My weakness in this area _____

Dear God, You have promised _____

You have told me that it is in my best interest to _____

I praise Your name for helping me to _____

YT "It's in his kiss" Betty Everett

I WANT YOU TO FOCUS ON MY STRENGTHS AND SUCCESSES AND TALK TO ME GENTLY ABOUT MY FAILURES AND WEAKNESSES. Proverbs 3:1-4, "My son, do not forget my teaching, but let your heart keep my commandments …So you will find favor and good success in the sight of God and man." **Proverbs 16:3,** "Commit to the Lord whatever you do, and your plans will succeed. **Psalm 21:**1 The king shall joy in thy strength, O Lord; and in thy salvation how greatly shall he rejoice!"

1 Samuel 18:6-7, "And it came to pass as they came, when David was returned from the slaughter of the Philistine, that the women came out of all cities of Israel, singing and dancing, to meet king Saul, with tabrets, with joy, and with instruments of musick. And the women answered one another as they played, and said, Saul hath slain his thousands, and David his ten thousands." David, with the confidence of having been protected by God from lions and wolves, in God's strength, slew Goliath with a sling shot and stones. After his success, the women sang and danced to celebrate his success.

When the wine ran out at a wedding and Jesus' mother, knowing her Son's strengths, told Him there was no wine and then she asked the servants to do whatever He told them to do. Jesus turned water into wine. The governor of the feast proclaimed this to be the best wine at the feast. John 2.

1 Kings 10:1-10, "And when the queen of Sheba heard of the fame of Solomon concerning the name of the Lord, she came to prove him with hard questions…she communed with him of all that was in her heart… And when the queen of Sheba had seen all Solomon's wisdom, and the house that he had built…she said to the king, It was a true report that I heard…of thy acts and of thy wisdom…behold, the half was not told me: thy wisdom and prosperity exceedeth the fame which I heard. Happy are thy men, happy are these thy servants, which stand continually before thee, and that hear thy wisdom. Blessed be the Lord thy God, which delighted in thee, to set thee on the throne of Israel: because the Lord loved Israel forever, therefore made he thee king, to do judgment and justice. And she gave the king an hundred and twenty talents of gold, and of spices very great store, and precious stones: there came no more such abundance of spices as these which the queen of Sheba gave to king Solomon."

I feel good when you recognize the strengths and successes that God has given me. I also need you to tell me about my weaknesses in a kind, gentle way, so that I can continue to grow.

Love looks like _____

My strength in this area _____

My weakness in this area _____

Dear God, You have promised _____

You have told me that it is in my best interest to _____

I praise Your name for helping me to _____

YT "Buy me a rose" Luther Vandross

I WANT YOU TO TREAT ME KINDLY.
Proverbs 19:11, "The discretion of a man deferreth his anger; and it is his glory to pass over a transgression." **Ruth 4:11,** "And all the people that were in the gate, and the elders, said, We are witnesses. The LORD make the woman that is come into thine house like Rachel and like Leah, which two did build the house of Israel: and do thou worthily in Ephratah, and be famous in Bethlehem."

When Boaz bought the property of Elimelech and took Ruth as his wife to keep the property in the family, the men who were called to be witnesses recognized the kindness of Rachel and Leah and wanted Ruth to be like them. They noted their kindness as having built the house of Israel, they bore the sons of Jacob. When men brought Mary to Jesus intending to stone her to death because of her adultery, Jesus wrote their part in contributing to her misdeeds on the ground. To whom was He showing kindness, Mary or the men who accused her?

What is kindness? Is it bearing sons to build up the house of Israel? Is it deferring your anger and passing over my flaws? Affection? Generosity? Warmth? Concern? Care? Is it being happy for me when I succeed? Is it telling me the truth when I need to hear it? Is it "doing" kind deeds or is it "being" kind? Is it limited to actions or are words involved? Or is it a blend of both, doing and being? Is being kind a sign of weakness? Research suggests that kindness is a blend of being and doing. Its presence is a predictor of satisfaction and stability in long-term relationships. Research demonstrates that being kind to others brings feelings of well-being to the giver of kindness as well as to the recipient, reciprocity.

I need your kindness. I need you to open your eyes, see my suffering, and kindly help relieve my suffering. I need you to smile at me when you open the door for me. I need you to celebrate me with honest compliments. I need you to tell me how special I am to you. I am elderly, so come by and visit me every now and then. I need help cleaning my house. Would you extend some kindness and help me? I need a reminder of you, can you send me a picture? I could sure use some of those clothes in your closet that don't fit you anymore. Mary washed Jesus' feet with her tears and dried them with her hair to express her gratitude because of the kindness He had shown to her. My hair isn't long enough to dry your feet, and I probably won't shed enough tears to get them clean, but I will be forever grateful for your kindness. Kindness to me shows your values, as well as your courage. Thank you for treating me kindly.

Love looks like _____

My strength in this area _____

My weakness in this area _____

Dear God, You have promised _____

You have told me that it is in my best interest to _____

I praise Your name for helping me to _____

YT "Alabaster box" CeCe Winans

I want you to tell me I am beautiful inside and out. Solomon 6:4, "Thou art beautiful, O my love…comely as Jerusalem…" **Isaiah 62:3,** "Thou shalt also be a crown of beauty in the hand of Jehovah…"

What was Solomon talking about when he told his wife she was beautiful? Was he focused just on her outward appearance? Was she tall, short, skinny, fat? What makes me beautiful to you on the outside? Is it my eyes? If you say they are beautiful, the song says, "It's because I'm looking at you and my eyes are just a window for my love to shine through." Is it because you are proud of me?

What do you see when you see beauty on my inside? What do you see inside of me that makes you think I am beautiful? You told me that you think I am astute, focused, caring, and trusting. You said I am loyal, dependable, loving, committed, and truthful. You said I am interested and introspective. You said I am a deep-thinker, unique, special. Thank you for telling me that I am beautiful. I need to hear it. It helps me in my life's journey to know that you recognize and acknowledge the Holy Spirit working in me to help me reflect God's image.

Here's what I see when I see your beauty. I see you. I see the smile on your face when you are in my presence. I see your eyes light up when you see me. I hear the tenderness in your voice when you answer the phone knowing that it's me calling. I see your inner beauty. I see your humility. I see the kind way you treat others. I hear you expressing concern for others. I hear you when you feel powerless to reach out and help others that you care about. I see your confidence, your self-control, your patience, your honesty, your loyalty. I see your optimism, your positivity, your passion, your intelligence. I see Christ in you, the hope of glory.

Isaiah 53:2, "For he shall grow up before him as a tender plant, and as a root out of a dry ground: he hath no form nor comeliness; and when we shall see him, *there is* no beauty that we should desire him." Wow! Jesus was not good to look at! So where do I get this need to be told that I am beautiful? Had Jesus been good-looking and rich, it would have made it harder for Him to carry out His purpose, so He chose to come as someone who would not draw attention to His outward appearance. He was more concerned with what the heart looks like. Beauty is created and sustained by Him and per **Isaiah 62:3,** "Thou shalt also be a crown of beauty in the hand of Jehovah, and a royal diadem in the hand of thy God." My beauty is and will continue to be restored. I look forward to looking like Him when He returns.

Love looks like _____

My strength in this area _____

My weakness in this area _____

Dear God, You have promised _____

You have told me that it is in my best interest to _____

I praise Your name for helping me to _____

YT "Worthy" Brandon Feat
YT "If you say my eyes are beautiful" Whitney Houston

I want to experience joy, peace, and happiness with you. John 16:22, 33, "And ye now therefore have sorrow: but I will see you again, and your heart shall rejoice, and your joy no man taketh from you. These things I have spoken unto you, that in me ye might have peace…"

"It (joy) is the result of the consciousness of the presence of Christ." *Ye shall receive power* E.G. White, 2012 p 83. In your presence, I want to feel joy. I want to respond to any external situation with inner contentment and satisfaction. I want to laugh. I want to feel good. In our shared consciousness of the presence of Christ when we are together, the endorphins will be released to help us both to feel joy. Joy is a choice, my choice. When I am with you, I want my spirit to feel exalted, lifted up. At the same time, I want to feel humble and grateful just for the opportunity to be in your presence. I will sparkle and be grateful for your support to dream my dreams and move toward fulfilling them.

Psalm 119:165, "Great peace have they which love thy law: and nothing shall offend them." Peace, not the absence of strife but the presence of Jesus with us both in our shared experience with each other. His law of love brings peace, a calm, inviting environment, even when the storm is raging outside. When the winds are blowing and the ship seems like it is going to sink, I want to feel safe and warm and loved when I am with you.

John 13:14-17, "If I then, your Lord and Master, have washed your feet; ye also ought to wash one another's feet. For I have given you an example, that ye should do as I have done to you. Verily, verily, I say unto you, The servant is not greater than his lord; neither he that is sent greater than he that sent him. If ye know these things, happy are ye if ye do them." Happiness is a byproduct of obeying Jesus. I want to feel happy in your presence. When in our shared experience, we are obedient to His commands, we will both feel happy. I won't wait to feel happy, I will feel it each time I am with you. I will not waste our time worrying about things that we cannot change. We will be positive to support an environment of happiness.

I want to experience joy, peace, and happiness with you.

Love looks like _____

My strength in this area _____

My weakness in this area _____

Dear God, You have promised

You have told me that it is in my best interest to_____

I praise Your name for helping me to_____

YT "Comforter" CeCe Winan
YT "My life is in Your hands" Kirk Franklin

I WANT TO FEEL LIKE I AM YOURS AND YOU ARE MINE.
Song of Solomon 2:16, "My beloved is mine, and I am his..." **Ecclesiastes 7:10,** "Say not thou, what is the cause that the former days were better than these? for thou dost not enquire wisely concerning this."

"But now thus says the Lord...I have called you by name, you are mine," (Isaiah 43:1). I belong to the God of the universe! I am His, He is mine! What a joy the feeling of belonging brings! This same feeling comes when we engage with each other. It happens in intimate relationships with each other, especially between a husband and wife.

What does it mean "I am yours, you are mine?" It means I enjoy your benefits and you enjoy mine. I invest myself in you and you in me. You have something that you are willing to give to me that I benefit from you. I have something that benefits you and I willingly share it with you. That is exactly what Jesus did and continues to do for me. He gave Himself away on that cross. He left heaven, took on the form of man forever! I give myself to Him in return. "I give myself away, so you can use me. My life is not my own, I give myself to you, to you I belong." The words of a beautiful song. In my relationship with you, we do the same with each other.

What happens between you and me, as well as in our relationship with Jesus, is that after a while, because we live in a sinful world, the relationship gets old. However, what is old can be made new again. Proverbs 5:16, "Why should your springs flow in the streets, your streams of water in the public squares?" When relationships are new, we indulge in the delight of getting to know one another. As time goes on, the new feeling of relationship begins to wane and a sense of normalcy sets in. Regular routines can become mundane, and one can long for the excitement that was prevalent in the beginning. Many times people look for the new feeling that comes from forging new relationships while forgetting that they have can have that same feeling in an existing relationship. Proverbs 15:17, "Let them be yours alone, never to be shared with strangers." The grass is not always greener on the other side. Have I watered my own grass to make it green again? What do I need to do to water that grass and restore those joyful feelings of belonging both to you and to Jesus?

Proverbs 5:18, "Let your wife be a fountain of blessing for you. Rejoice in the wife of your youth."

"Remember now thy creator..." Ecclesiastes 12:1 We often look back to our past and long for things that we cannot return to. The bond between two people is a relationship that can be tested by the trials of time. All we have is the present, the past is but a learning tool or glimmer in time that can never be returned. I am in a relationship with you, forever, I am yours and you are mine.

Love looks like _____

My strength in this area _____

My weakness in this area _____

Dear God, You have promised_____

You have told me that it is in my best interest to_____

I praise Your name for helping me to_____

YT I give myself away" William McDowell

I WANT TO FEEL POWERFUL WHEN I AM WITH YOU.
2 Timothy 1:7 "For God hath not given us the spirit of fear; but of power, and of love, and of a sound mind." **Acts 1:8** "But ye shall receive power, after that the Holy Ghost is come upon you: and ye shall be witnesses unto me… unto the uttermost part of the earth". **Philippians 4:13** "I can do all things through Christ which strengtheneth me. **Luke 10:19** "Behold, I give unto you power to tread on serpents and scorpions, and over all the power of the enemy: and nothing shall by any means hurt you." **1 Corinthians 4:20** "For the kingdom of God [is] not in word, but in power." **1 Corinthians 6:14** "And God hath both raised up the Lord, and will also raise us up by his own power." **Ephesians 6:10** "Finally, my brethren, be strong in the Lord, and in the power of his might."

Power, the ability to transfer energy to move something. Power in physics measures the rate at which work is done or energy is transferred. In other words, something changes when power is exhibited. Where does power come from, inside of you or do others have power over you? How is power related to influence? What does God mean when He tells me He has given me the spirit of power? What power from the Holy Ghost enables me to be a witness to the uttermost part of the earth? I was born in sin and shaped in iniquity. The Holy Spirit in me that Jesus' death provided for me to have to transform my character is the power that works within me to will and do of His good pleasure. Nehemiah 8:10, "…for the joy of the LORD is your strength." Joy, the conscious presence of Jesus in me, is my strength, my power.

God's power shared with me enables me to have influence with you and others that increases as I support you in serving you. Serving you provides sustainable growth for me. Help me feel powerful by allowing me to serve you and lift you up. Help me feel powerful by allowing me to help create an environment for you in which you are self-disciplined and have the opportunity to serve others, so that you also have an opportunity to use and grow your power. Help me to feel powerful by allowing me to share the energy God has given me with you, so that your power also grows. Real power is the impact that I have to change my environment. Help me be powerful by allowing me to impact your life in such a way that changes you for the better. Help me to be powerfully confident by living my God given assignment of reflecting His character as a witness of His love for both of us to you. Pray for me that my power will be reflected in positivity that helps to solve problems, create cooperation, and inform good decision making. I want to feel God's powerfulness extended through me in your presence. I really can do ALL things through Jesus Christ who empowers me. God has given me the spirit of power.

Love looks like _____

My strength in this area _____

My weakness in this area _____

Dear God, You have promised _____

You have told me that it is in my best interest to _____

I praise Your name for helping me to _____

YT "Nobody Greater" Vashawn Mitchell
YT "No one in the world loves me like you do" Anita Baker

I want to feel your warmth.
Ecclesiastes 4:11, "Again, if two lie together, then they have heat: but how can one be warm alone?"

"I want to feel the heat from somebody that loves me" are words in a popular song sung by Whitney Houston. The second law of thermodynamics states that heat moves from a place of higher concentration to a place where there is less heat. Ice cubes melt based on this law. A warm room with an open door gets colder because the heat moves from inside the room to the outside cold based on this law. Heat produced from the movement of muscles and other body processes moves from your body to a cooler environment.

Feelings of warmth elevate my mood and make me feel good. Research indicates that warm skin impacts areas of the brain that stimulate feelings of emotional warmth. People that feel lonely tend to identify the room as being cold and to take warm showers or baths more often than those that are not lonely. Heat is being used to treat depression. We know that warmth works throughout life. Physical and emotional warmth, love, generosity, and morality are needed for survival. These are integrated to assist in needed transformative processes that help us change, grow, and adapt in life just as heat is used to change flour, yeast, and water into bread.

When David was old, ill, and cold, a virgin was chosen to lie next to him to keep him warm. 1 Kings 1:1-2, "Now king David was old *and* stricken in years; and they covered him with clothes, but he gat no heat. Therefore his servants said to him. Let a young woman, a virgin, be sought for our lord the king, and let her stand before the king, and let her care for him; and let her lie in your bosom, that our lord the king may be warm." Newborns are placed next to their mothers for skin-to-skin contact that keeps them warm and increases bonding. When you hug me, your physical warmth is shared with me. When I drink the warm drink you shared with me, the heat is distributed to my body. Just being in the room with you means that we exchange and share heat with each other. When I lie in bed under the cover, the warmth that my body gives off is recirculated to keep me warm, but when my husband is in bed with me, we share each other's heat. Please share your heat with me. I need it for survival, and it makes me feel good.

Love looks like _____

My strength in this area _____

My weakness in this area _____

Dear God, You have promised _____

You have told me that it is in my best interest to _____

I praise Your name for helping me to _____

YT "I want to feel the heat" Whitney Houston
YT "One Summer night" - The Danleers

I WANT TO WAKE UP LYING NEXT TO YOU.
Solomon 5:2, "I sleep, but my heart waketh: it is the voice of my beloved that knocketh, saying, Open to me, my sister, my love, my dove, my undefiled: for my head is filled with dew, and my locks with the drops of the night."

In the night time, when I wake up, it is dark. I want to wake up knowing that God is there with me, to ensure that I am safe, that He still loves me, that He still cares about me. I want to feel His warmth and love. He assures me. "I will both lay me down in peace, and sleep: for thou, LORD, only makest me dwell in safety," Psalm 4:8

God knows the wants and desires of my heart. I yearn for that connection felt with another human being. I want to share in the love that has been bestowed upon me and in my heart with another. God said in the very beginning, "It is not good that man should be alone." He made Eve to stand at Adam's side. God did not intend for me to be alone. John 15:7, "If ye abide in me, and my words abide in you, ye shall ask what ye will, and it shall be done unto you." When you find that person that reflects God's love, you never want to be without that love. God who made me knows that when I consistently sleep with the one He has appointed in my life, I develop synchrony over time; our body habits and other habits become similar. I get better sleep that helps restore me. My blood pressure is lowered (oxytocin increased), there is less inflammation (cortisol levels are reduced), and my immune system is enhanced. Dopamine and serotonin are released, making me feel happier. I fall asleep faster. I feel safer. The warmth that you give off helps me have a deeper sleep, so that my REM sleep works to help me be healthy. When I wake up after lying next to you, I am energized to face the next day.

Ecclesiastes 4:9-11, "Two are better than one, because they have a good return for their labor. For if one falls, his companion can lift him up; but pity the one who falls without another to help him up. Again, if two lie together, then they have heat: but how can one be warm alone?" No one should be alone. Our purpose is to join and build each other up in love. Wanting the companionship that comes from love, spending one's life with another and starting each day together is a special bond desired for me by God. What does it mean to you to wake up lying next to the one you love? If you are alone and have that desire, ask Him. He knows your needs and has promised to give you the desires of your heart.

Love looks like _____

My strength in this area _____

My weakness in this area _____

Dear God, You have promised_____

You have told me that it is in my best interest to_____

I praise Your name for helping me to_____

YT "My song in the night" Mormon Tabernacle Choir

I WANT TO BE IN YOUR PERSONAL SPACE.
Revelation 3:20, "Behold, I stand at the door, and knock: if any man hear my voice, and open the door, I will come in to him, and will sup with him, and he with me."

I want you to open the door of your heart and let me come in. I want to be in your personal space. Even animals have a personal space. If you step into the personal space of a lion, watch out! When someone enters my personal space without permission, I take it as a threat and respond in such as way as to protect myself. Four spaces of personal interaction between humans have been studied in research: intimate space, personal space, social space, and public space. Intimate space is usually reserved for romantic relationships or for caring for those unable to care for themselves. Personal space is where strong powerful friendships grow and exist.

Jesus asks me to open the door to my heart to let Him in to my intimate space. Opening the door to my heart allows His love to come in and dwell with me. When He comes in, His light is with Him, light that provides warmth and guidance for my pathway of life. Light that helps me know who I am and where I am going. Ezra 9:8, "But now for a brief moment grace has been shown from the LORD our God, to leave us an escaped remnant and to give us a peg in His holy place, that our God may enlighten our eyes and grant us a little reviving in our bondage." Love and light in has to go somewhere, out, to you.

It is important to focus on the power of my heart for out of it are the issues of life. The issues of life coming from my heart and thoughts of my mind are then controlled by Jesus who has come in to sup with me. Jesus entering my intimate space empowers me to know that I am His child and helps me move forward to cooperate with Him in His plan for my life. My selfishness loses its power to control me and my heart is moved to imitate the love of Christ. If I block the unconditional love that comes with Him, I block myself from entering your personal space to show unconditional love for you. Through my heart connections with Jesus, unconditional love flows like a river from me to you. The more I open up and let Him in, the more my unconditional love grows. The more time I allow Him to spend in my intimate space, the more love grows. The more I hear His word, keep it in my heart, and talk to Him, the deeper my love and trust grows. Think about a tree planted by a river, how it grows! When my heart is open and I let Him come in, He brings a sense of peace, joy, and fulfillment that I feel strongly. When you let me into your personal space, you allow the Jesus in me to love the Jesus in you. We both benefit.

Helen Keller said, "The best and most beautiful things in the world cannot be seen or even touched. They must be felt with the heart" (Helen Keller, <u>*The story of my life*</u> p 203 1905). Please let me into your personal space.

Love looks like _____

My strength in this area _____

My weakness in this area _____

Dear God, You have promised_____

You have told me that it is in my best interest to_____

I praise Your name for helping me to_____

YT "Open the door to your heart" Darrell Banks
YT "My Jesus I love Thee" YT "It's growing" Temptations

I want to know where I stand with you.
Amos 3:3, "Can two walk together, except they be agreed?"

I need to know where we are in this relationship. Just where do I stand with you? Are we friends? Are we lovers? Are we acquaintances? What do you expect from me?

Psalms 51:5, Behold, I was shapen in iniquity; and in sin did my mother conceive me." This was my beginning status, but thank God for His grace, love, and mercy! Jesus got up on that cross and died for me! Making justification and sanctification through His Spirit possible! Now I can stand before the Creator of the universe as if I had never sinned! I am sanctified by giving His Spirit permission to dwell in me, controlling my thoughts, feelings, and behaviors. Romans 5:19, "For as by one man's disobedience many were made sinners, so by the obedience of one shall many be made righteous." I am covered by His righteousness. Habakkuk 2:4, "Behold, as for the proud one, His soul is not right within him; But the righteous will live by his faith" I live by faith in Him. 1 John 5:13-14, "These things have I written unto you that believe on the name of the Son of God; that ye may know that ye have eternal life, and that ye may believe on the name of the Son of God. And this is the confidence that we have in him, that, if we ask any thing according to his will, he heareth us. And if we know that he hear us, whatsoever we ask, we know that we have the petitions that we desired of him." I believe on Jesus name; I have eternal life. Whatsoever I ask of God, I know that my request will be granted in accordance with His will and knowledge of what is best for me. Behold, all things are made new. We are friends, we are lovers, we know each other. When He comes, I am going to be like Him and I am going to live forever with Him.

But where am I with you? I want to know where I stand with you. Will you share with me what you think about us? What do I need to do to gain your trust and confidence? What needs do you have that I can help meet? I know you want honesty, respect, kindness from me, but I need you to tell me what that looks like for you, so that I can share what that looks like for me with you, so we can be on the same page. Did you think about me today? Have you talked to me today? Did you pray for me today? When can we get together just to spend some time with each other? Where am I on your priority list? Where do I stand with you?

Love looks like _____

My strength in this area _____

My weakness in this area _____

Dear God, You have promised _____

You have told me that it is in my best interest to _____

I praise Your name for helping me to _____

YT "I will run to you" Alvin Slaughter
YT "You know my name" Brooklyn Tabernacle Choir
YT "For the love of you" Isley Brothers
YT "Tru" Lloyd

I don't want you to just hear me, I want you to listen to me.
Proverbs 20:12, "The hearing ear, and the seeing eye, the Lord hath made even both of them" **James 1: 10**, "Wherefore, my beloved brethren, let every man be swift to hear…" **Psalms 46:10**, "Be still, and know that I [am] God…"

I want you to listen to me, so that you can know me. When I know that you are listening, it makes me feel secure, warm, and loved. Hearing is passive and involuntary. Listening to me tells me you have made a decision to voluntarily actively engage with me. My preference is that you are physically present with me, although sometimes you will talk to me on the phone or by texting.

You are curious about me, who I am, what I like, what I am feeling, what bothers me, what makes me happy, so you listen to me. You ask me open ended questions, so that I control the conversation. You say things like, "Tell me all about that," so that I can guide the conversation into what is going on inside of me. Pay attention to the tone of my voice and the expression on my face. Those will tell you more about what's going on than my words most of the time because often I don't know how to say what I am feeling, but it registers on my face, in my voice, and in my body language. This will tell you whether I am happy, sad, relaxed, calm, angry. But don't assume that your interpretation is correct, ask me, "How does that make you feel?"

Face me, lean forward, keep your arms uncrossed, and look into my eyes. Honesty and truth are enhanced when you do this. Don't play with your keys or text on your phone. That makes me think you aren't really interested in listening to me. Sit at the same level that I am sitting, so that I will feel that we are equal. I want you to give me a kind, gentle critical analysis of my situation but timing is important, wait until you know for sure what is going on with me. Ask questions to clarify first. **Proverbs 18:13**, "He that answereth a matter before he heareth it [is] folly and shame unto him." Then please don't judge me. Judgment for me is "good or bad, right or wrong." A critical analysis helps me focus on the pros and cons and leaves the decision for outcomes in my hands, especially since I am the one that will take the responsibility for my decisions. Silence is ok. It gives me time to reflect on what I have said, and it gives you time to do the same thing.

Please listen to me, it makes me feel so good when you do.

Love looks like _____

My strength in this area _____

My weakness in this area _____

Dear God, You have promised_____

You have told me that it is in my best interest to_____

I praise Your name for helping me to_____

YT "BE SILENT, BE SILENT"
YT "STOP TO LOVE" LUTHER VANDROSS

I don't want you to ever forget me.
Psalm 103:2-6, "Bless the LORD, O my soul, and forget not all his benefits: Who forgiveth all thine iniquities; who healeth all thy diseases; Who redeemeth thy life from destruction; who crowneth thee with lovingkindness and tender mercies; Who satisfieth thy mouth with good things; so that thy youth is renewed like the eagle's."

God does not want me to forget Him. I would be very unwise, even foolish, to forget about Him after all the things He has done for me. I love Him because He first loved me. The benefits from Him loving me are characteristic of who He is. Yet it is not just because of what He has done for me that He doesn't want me to forget Him. The very nature of God is love and love seeks to be known, to be remembered.

Exodus 20:8, "Remember the Sabbath day to keep it holy." God doesn't want me to forget to spend time with Him who loves me far more than I can ever love myself. This is the time He Himself has set aside to reveal Himself to me that I may know Him noting in John 17:3 that my eternal life depends on knowing God and Jesus who He sent.

1 Chronicles 16:15, "Remember His covenant forever, The word which He commanded to a thousand generations."

Psalm 105:8, "He has remembered His covenant forever, The word which He commanded to a thousand generations." God wants me to remember the covenants He makes with me. He wants me to know that He remembers the agreements that He makes and He honors them. When He destroyed the world with a flood, He put a rainbow in the cloud as a reminder to Himself and to me of the promise He made to never destroy the world again with water.

Created in His image, I have the same desire. You will remember pleasure, discomfort, and fear from our relationship. When you met me, you took a chance on me. Although my desire is to always bring pleasure, in my selfishness, I may have created some memories for you that are painful. Forgive me for those memories. Those are not what I want you to remember. As time has passed, I hope that you are past fearing me and know that I love you and my intentions are for your best outcomes. Can you remember the good times? The songs we both liked that had so much meaning for us? The moments of quiet? The encouraging words? The birthday cards, the "just thinking about you" cards? How I supported your dreams? The promises that I made and kept? Look at my picture and remember my smile. Know that I truly do love you, please don't ever forget me.

Love looks like _____

My strength in this area _____

My weakness in this area _____

Dear God, You have promised_____

You have told me that it is in my best interest to_____

I praise Your name for helping me to_____

YT "Let me live life loving you" Barry White
YT "Let me love you" Mario YT "I'm so in love with you" Al Green

IF SOMETHING HAPPENS TO ME, I WANT YOU TO BE THERE WITH ME.

2 Kings 2:2, "And Elijah said unto Elisha, Tarry here, I pray thee; for the LORD hath sent me to Bethel. And Elisha said unto him, As the LORD liveth, and as thy soul liveth, I will not leave thee. So they went down to Bethel."

When God was ready to take Elijah to heaven, Elijah tried three times to get Elisha to stay behind, so that he would not witness the event. Although Elisha knew what was about to happen, he refused to leave his good friend. He wanted to be there with him through the entire event. They finally crossed over the Jordan River together on dry land. 2 Kings 2: 9-12, "And it came to pass, when they were gone over, that Elijah said unto Elisha, Ask what I shall do for thee, before I be taken away from thee. And Elisha said, I pray thee, let a double portion of thy spirit be upon me. And he said, Thou hast asked a hard thing: nevertheless, if thou see me when I am taken from thee, it shall be so unto thee; but if not, it shall not be so. And it came to pass, as they still went on, and talked, that, behold, there appeared a chariot of fire, and horses of fire, and parted them both asunder; and Elijah went up by a whirlwind into heaven. And Elisha saw it, and he cried, My father, my father, the chariot of Israel, and the horsemen thereof. And he saw him no more: and he took hold of his own clothes, and rent them in two pieces." Elisha was distraught because he would be with his friend no more, but he had held on to his promise to be there with him.

Jonathon was there with David when Saul tried to kill him. The angels were there in prison with Paul and Silas. Deborah was there with Barak when there was war. The Father was there watching when His Son died on the cross. Jesus was there with Mary when they ran out of wine at the wedding feast.

I need you to be there with me when something goes wrong. I need your comfort, your reassurance, your encouragement. I, like most people, am afraid of dying. I don't want to die alone. I need you to be at my bedside when I am dying. I need you to speak the words of Jesus that offer me the assurance that I will see Him when He comes. Don't be afraid to talk to me about death, it happens to all of us, and what I want to know most of all is where am I going to spend eternity. Hold my hand. Look at old pictures with me. Share memories with me. Will you be there with me if something happens?

Love looks like _____

My strength in this area _____

My weakness in this area _____

Dear God, You have promised _____

You have told me that it is in my best interest to _____

I praise Your name for helping me to _____

YT "The Anchor holds" Lawrence Chewning
YT "When you cry" Winans

I WANT YOU TO REMEMBER MY WORDS.
John 14:24, "Jesus answered and said unto him, If a man love me, he will keep my words: and my Father will love him, and we will come unto him, and make our abode with him." **Proverbs 7:1,** "My son, keep my words, and lay up my commandments with thee."

Keep my words. God tells me to remember what He said. When I hide them deep in my heart, I will not sin against Him. I recite them from time to time. I tell others what He has said. I ask them what they think about what He said. In the middle of the night, when I am alone and sad, I remember His words and it makes me feel better. When I am about to start on a new adventure, I remember that He told me to submit my plans to Him, and I will move forward and be successful. When I am afraid, I remember that He has told me to "fear not." When I am going through hard times, I remember that He has told me that the battle is His, not mine.

Read the words of love Boaz and Ruth spoke to or about each other in Ruth 2. "Then said Boaz unto Ruth, Hearest thou not my daughter? Go not to glean in another field, neither go from hence, but abide here by my maidens…And Ruth the Moabitess said (to Naomi) He said unto me also, Thou shalt keep fast by my young men, until they have ended all my harvest. Let thine eyes be on the field that they do reap, and go thou after them: have I not charged the young men that they shall not touch thee? And when thou art athirst, go unto the vessels, and drink of that which the young men have drawn." Ruth kept Boaz's words in her heart and shared them with Naomi. She ended up marrying Boaz.

When you remind me of what I have said, I know that you have remembered my words and that they have impacted you in some kind of way. It makes me feel good to know that you remember what I say for I know from Proverbs 18:21, "Death and life are in the power of the tongue: and they that love it shall eat the fruit thereof." I hope those words that I have spoken to you are words of life.

Your words of love. "I love you. I want you. I want to be with you. I don't want you to ever forget me. You are beautiful, inside and out. You are special. You are different. I want to tell everybody that you are mine." I am reminded that you love me when I remember your words. When you remember what I said, it reinforces for me that you know that I love you and you love me. Your words have powerfully impacted my life. I will keep your words in my heart.

Love looks like _____

My strength in this area _____

My weakness in this area _____

Dear God, You have promised _____

You have told me that it is in my best interest to _____

I praise Your name for helping me to _____

YT "My words have power" Karen Clark-Shearad
YT "It wasn't the nails" Mississppi Mass Choir

Chapter 4
Love God supreme? What is that all about?

I BELIEVE THAT YOU ARE WHO YOU SAY YOU ARE.
Hebrews 11:6, "But without faith it is impossible to please him: for he that cometh to God must believe that he is, and that he is a rewarder of them that diligently seek him."

God is truth. I believe that He is and He rewards me as I diligently seek Him.

God told Noah there was going to be a flood. People laughed at him because it had never rained before. Why would Noah believe something so seemingly impossible? Noah built an ark. God rewarded him by saving his whole family and he became an heir of righteousness that comes by faith. Hebrews 11:7

Abraham believed God, left his home, and went to a place that he knew nothing about. He looked for a city whose builder and maker is God. God told him that he was going to have a son and he was ninety-nine-years-old. Sex, a baby at 100! Come on! Isaac was born when Abraham was 100-years-old. God rewarded him by counting his belief as righteousness. Hebrews 11:8-10

Exodus 3:14, "And God said unto Moses, I AM THAT I AM: and he said, Thus shalt thou say unto the children of Israel, I AM hath sent me unto you." I AM – state of being. Always, forever, eternal. Moses' parents hid their three-month-old son in a basket in the Nile River! Child abuse by current standards. They believed God would take care of their son. He did and rewarded their faith by allowing their son to lead the Israelites from Egypt to the borders of the promised land. Moses chose to believe God and suffer with the people of God rather than enjoy the pleasures of sin for a short time. He was one of the three men seen by the apostles on the Mount of Transfiguration.

He told me He loves me, that He will never leave me. He told me He created all things. He told me that He is Alpha and Omega, first and last. He told me that He is all powerful, all knowing, and everywhere present. He told me that all the silver and gold and the cattle on a thousand hills is His. He told me that He will judge me based on His law. He told me that He is standing in the Most Holy Place looking at my record to verify for Himself that I really do love Him. He told me that when He is finished reviewing, He will come back to get me. He said to Moses, "…The LORD, The LORD God, merciful and gracious, longsuffering, and abundant in goodness and truth, keeping mercy for thousands, forgiving iniquity and transgression and sin, and that will by no means clear the guilty; visiting the iniquity of the fathers upon the children, and upon the children's children, unto the third and to the fourth generation." (Exodus 34:6-7). My merciful, gracious, longsuffering God, abundant in goodness and truth, forgiving my sins and transgressions! I know Satan tries hard to convince me not to believe You. Help Thou my unbelief.

Love looks like _____

My strength in this area _____

My weakness in this area _____

Dear God, You have promised_____

You have told me that it is in my best interest to_____

I praise Your name for helping me to_____

YT "GOD IS" JAMES CLEVELAND
YT" STOP, LOOK, LISTEN TO YOUR HEART" STYLISTICS

I have faith in You.

Hebrews 11:1, "Now faith is the substance of things hoped for, the evidence of things not seen."

My beliefs do not determine truth, but they do determine my outcomes. Belief and faith are not the same. My actions are based on my beliefs. Belief comes before faith. Faith has an evidence factor. I must believe that God exists before I will have faith in Him. Faith, testing, and proving God grows imperceptibly over time through exercise. Faith is a gift of God, a fruit of the Spirit, that comes by hearing the Word of God, spoken, written, or direct. Romans 10:17, "…these have been written so that you may believe" (John 20:3). Jesus pronounces a blessing on those who believe without first seeing, John 20:29.

Faith exercised requires that I recognize that He has chosen me before the foundation of the world that I should be holy and without blame before him in love. Ephesians 1:4. God's love draws me to Christ to be received and presented to Him. Faith exercised requires that I keep His commandments and claim His promise to abide in His love. I exercise my free will and choose to allow the Holy Spirit to dwell in my heart that I may have Christ's divine nature of love implanted in me. Exercised faith allows the Holy Spirit to transform my character. I come to Christ daily to behold Him, see Him, get to know Him, sup with Him at His table eating the Bread of Life and drinking from His everlasting water by reading His word and keeping it in my heart. I keep looking up towards heaven. I see what Jesus sees, and as a result, do what He tells me to do. I see myself as the son of God, created in His image, joint heir to His throne, priest in His kingdom. Exercised faith then empowers me to carry out the functions of those roles starting right here living on earth. I can't see the air, but I know that I need it to live. I can't see the wind, but I see the results of the wind's movement. I am not yet what He sees in me, His perfect love, but He tells me that when He comes, I will be like Him. My faith in Him guarantees that outcome as He promised to reward those that diligently seek Him. He tells me that if I believe in Him, I will be saved. My faith guarantees that outcome as stated in 1 John 5:13, "These things have I written unto you that believe on the name of the Son of God; that ye may know that ye have eternal life, and that ye may believe on the name of the Son of God."

He has given me everything I need for life and godliness. I have been purged from my old sins. His divine nature implanted in me helps make my calling and election sure by adding to my faith, goodness, and to goodness, knowledge, and to knowledge, self-control, and to self-control, perseverance, and to perseverance godliness, and to godliness, brotherly kindness, and to brotherly kindness, love. 2 Peter 1: 5-7.

Love looks like _____

My strength in this area _____

My weakness in this area _____

Dear God, You have promised_____

You have told me that it is in my best interest to_____

I praise Your name for helping me to_____

YT "Just have faith when you pray" Tremaine Hawkins
YT " Prayer is the key but Faith unlocks the door" Andrae Crouch

I WANT TO KNOW YOU.
John 17:3, "And this is life eternal, that they might know thee the only true God, and Jesus Christ, whom thou hast sent." **Psalm 139:1-3,** "O lord, thou hast searched me, and known me. Thou knowest my downsitting and mine uprising, thou understandest my thought afar off. Thou compassest my path and my lying down, and art acquainted with all my ways."

God, You have searched me and You know me. I know about You, Lord, but that is NOT enough. I have to know You, God, and Jesus whom You sent. My eternal life hinges on it, Father. You have told me how to know You. "And I will give them an heart to know me, that I am the LORD: and they shall be my people, and I will be their God: for they shall return unto me with their whole heart", (Jeremiah 24:7). "And ye shall seek me, and find me, when ye shall search for me with all your heart," (Jeremiah 29:13). You have given me a heart to know You and have promised that when I search for You with that whole heart, I will find You. Just like I discovered how to distinguish an acid from a base by experimenting with litmus paper in the lab, I will test and discover you as You have instructed me to. "…prove me now herewith, saith the LORD of hosts…" (Malachi 3:10).

Esther, who knew that her life and the lives of her people were on the chopping block, proved You when she went to stand before King Xeres and the whole nation of Israel was saved. Sarah, after first laughing at You in disbelief when You told her she was going to get pregnant and have a son at ninety years of age, proved You right, when she gave birth to Isaac. Peter proved You. "Then Peter said, Silver and gold have I none; but such as I have give I thee: In the name of Jesus Christ of Nazareth rise up and walk," (Acts 3:6). Jews are known today as people with money because You told Abraham You would bless his descendants and asked them to show that they believed You by returning tithe and offering.

My heart is searching for You, God. I am reading Your word daily. I am looking for You when I meet with two or three because You are there in the midst of us. I know it made You unhappy when I misrepresented Your kingdom of grace. I'm sorry. I know it made You feel good when I cried out to You for help when I almost hit that car, when I praised Your name for helping me get three boxes of cereal for six dollars at Dollar General. I know You keep my car keep running and every good and perfect gift that I have came from You. I know that You sent angels to watch over me as I traveled to Michigan last week. I know that You want me to be where You are. I know that You want me to model Your love for others. I know that I will spend eternity just getting to know You. Thank You for letting me test and know You.

Love looks like _____

My strength in this area _____

My weakness in this area _____

Dear God, You have promised _____

You have told me that it is in my best interest to _____

I praise Your name for helping me to _____

YT "Center of my joy" Richard Smallwood
YT "Holy, holy, holy" Brooklyn Tabernacle Choir

Let me show You some affection.
Psalm 86:12, "I will praise thee, O Lord my God, with all my heart: and I will glorify thy name for evermore."

Affection, a feeling associated with love. Fondness. "Can a woman forget her sucking child, that she should not have compassion on the son of her womb? yea, they may forget, yet will I not forget thee. Behold, I have graven thee upon the palms of my hands…" (Isaiah 49: 15-16). I remember those feelings of warmth with that first born child. That tenderness, that protective feeling. The fear I might roll over on her during the night. I remember stroking her cheeks, looking in her eyes. Feelings of warmth. Wrapping her tightly in a blanket to keep her warm, even though it was summertime. Taking her with me everywhere I went. Not letting her out of my sight.

You, God, have those same feelings of affection for me. You have graven me on the palms of Your hands. I may forget that child You gave me, but You will never forget me. Words from that song I learned in high school, "There's a longing in my heart for Jesus, there's a longing in my heart to see His face," still ring true for me.

Let me be with You, Lord. Let me go where You go. Let me touch You. Let me embrace You. Let me feel Your warmth. Let me know the real You. Let me whisper how much I love You. Tell me about Your broken heart and let me show You compassion. Listen to this song with me Lord and hear the gentle, tender melody. Let me laugh with You. Let me into Your heart. Let me put You on that pedestal and keep You as a priceless treasure. Let me make You comfortable. Let me make You feel good. Let me tell You how good You are, how joyful and satisfied I am to be in Your presence.

God responded to me. "And it shall come to pass, that before they call, I will answer; and while they are yet speaking, I will hear," (Isaiah 65:25). I want your affection. I want your warmth. I want your tenderness. I want your kindness. I want you to whisper, "I love you." I want your love. I want to let you into My heart. "…I say unto you, Inasmuch as ye have done it unto one of the least of these my brethren, ye have done it unto me" (Matthew 25:40). Give Me your affection, I desperately want it.

Love looks like _____

My strength in this area _____

My weakness in this area _____

Dear God, You have promised _____

You have told me that it is in my best interest to _____

I praise Your name for helping me to _____

YT "I give You my heart" Hillsong
YT "Jesus, You are beautiful to me" CeCe Winans
YT "A heart like yours" CeCe Winans

GOD, YOU ARE MY EVERYTHING.
Philippians 4:18, 19, "But I have all, and abound: I am full.... But my God shall supply all your need according to his riches in glory by Christ Jesus."

You are my everything, God. You are my Bread of Life. You are my Living Water. This concept you reinforce by reminding me that my body is some sixty percent water and the remaining part of my body is made of what I eat. How wonderful You are to help me understand even at this level what it means to eat Your flesh and drink from the everlasting fountain.

In John 4:24, You are Spirit. You are Truth. Your Word is truth. I come to You through Your Son for there is no other name given among men whereby I can come to You. Your created angels cover their faces in Your presence and bow before You to worship you. I bow down and worship You in spirit and in truth. Your angels come and go at Your command to minister to me, an heir of salvation. I hide Your Word in my heart, so that I won't resist Your authority, disobey You, and sin against You. I say in answer to Your question, "Who shall I send and who will go for Me?" Here am I, Lord, send me.

"Because it is written, Be ye holy; for I am holy," (I Peter 1:16). "...ye also trusted, after that ye heard the word of truth...in whom also after that ye believed, ye were sealed with that holy Spirit of promise, which is the earnest of our inheritance until redemption of the purchased possession..." (Ephesians 1: 13-14.) You are holy. You are righteous. You make me holy through the indwelling of Your Spirit, so that I can stand in Your presence. You see Your Son's righteousness covering me and count it as my righteousness. You sent Your Son to die for me and justify me, so that I can stand in Your presence as if I have never sinned. Your Son's death makes it possible for Your Spirit to dwell in me, the same Spirit that dwelt within Adam before he sinned, the Spirit that implants your Divine nature in me, that sanctifies me by working within me to do Your will and accomplish Your good pleasure. Your indwelling Spirit is restoring in me Your perfect image of love, trust, and obedience, so that when You come, I will be like You. I am Your Son, heir to Your kingdom with the privileges and responsibilities of an heir. You have made me a priest in Your dwelling place and allowed me the privilege of ministering as a priest for You.

You are my Creator. You are my Redeemer. You are my King. You are my Lord. Every good and perfect gift, comes from You. You are my Protector. You are my Healer. You are my Bread. You are my Water. You are mine and I am Yours. I have need of nothing or no one. Hallelujah! You are my everything!

Love looks like _____

My strength in this area _____

My weakness in this area _____

Dear God, You have promised _____

You have told me that it is in my best interest to _____

I praise Your name for helping me to _____

YT "He's everything to me" Kim McFarland
YT "You're my everything" Temptations
YT "You're the best thing that ever happened to me" James Cleveland

I love to hear Your voice.
Psalm 68:33, "To Him who rides upon the highest heavens, which are from ancient times; Behold, He speaks forth with His voice, a mighty voice." **Isaiah 28:23,** "Give ye ear, and hear my voice; hearken, and hear my speech."

For He spoke and it was done. He commanded and it stood fast. Psalm 33:9, Life and death are in the power of the tongue. Proverbs 18:21, Speak to me Lord, I want to hear Your voice. Your voice is like the sound of many waters, powerful to change me in to what You want me to be through the power of Your word.

"The voice of the LORD is upon the waters; The God of glory thunders, The LORD is over many waters. The voice of the LORD is powerful, The voice of the LORD is majestic. The voice of the LORD breaks the cedars; Yes, the LORD breaks in pieces the cedars of Lebanon. He makes Lebanon skip like a calf, And Sirion like a young wild ox. The voice of the LORD hews out flames of fire. The voice of the LORD shakes the wilderness; The LORD shakes the wilderness of Kadesh. The voice of the LORD makes the deer to calve And strips the forests bare; And in His temple everything says, 'Glory!'" (Psalm 29:3-9).

Elijah experienced the earthquake and a fire, but You spoke to him in a still, quiet voice. In the quiet of the night, I hear Your voice as I lay me down to sleep, telling me how much You love me, how much You want me to be with You, reminding me that You are coming soon to take me back to be forever with You in glory. I hear You tell me in Luke 22: 29, 30 that "I appoint unto you a kingdom, as my Father hath appointed unto me: that ye may eat and drink at my table in my kingdom, and sit on thrones judging the twelve tribes of Israel." I hear You, Lord. Speak to me through Your Spirit in Your word to empower me to be able to sit at that table with You. Give me the wisdom that I need to be able to judge the twelve tribes of Israel.

Every time I see a leaf falling from a tree, I hear Your voice reminding me that when I am disconnected from the Source of Life, I will die. When I hear the thunder and see the lightning, I hear Your voice telling me that just as you take care of the horses and deer outside in the storm, that You take care of me when the storms of life are raging. I hear Your voice in the child crying from hunger. I hear Your voice in the blowing wind telling me that God is in charge. He has it all under control.

1 Samuel 3:10, "And the Lord came, and stood, and called as at other times, Samuel, Samuel. Then Samuel answered, Speak; for thy servant heareth." I say like that little child Samuel, speak, Lord, Thy servant heareth. Speak to me in the morning, speak to me at noon, speak to me at night. Speak to me all day long.

Love looks like _____

My strength in this area _____

My weakness in this area _____

Dear God, You have promised _____

You have told me that it is in my best interest to _____

I praise Your name for helping me to _____

YT "He's preparing me" Malaco
YT "God is trying to tell you something " Color Purple

God, I just love to talk to You!
1 Thessalonians 5:17, "Pray without ceasing."

The voice impacts the senses. It is my primary mode of self expression. It tells a lot about who I am and where I come from. I can change the meaning of what I say simply by changing my tone of voice. My voice has the ability to make one feel comfortable, scared, motivated, attracted, or repelled by what and how I speak.

Every evening before sin, God came down into the Garden of Eden to talk with Adam and Eve. God wants me to talk to Him as well. He wants to be in constant, ongoing dialogue with me. He wants to hear me say thank you. He expects me to talk to Him about what He commands me to do in His word, so that I understand His plan and purpose for my life. He rejoices to hear me say I love You, I am Yours, I want You to be in my life. He is so glad when I say to him the door of my heart is open, come in. I talk to Him about every verse that I read in His word. When I don't understand everything He tells me initially, He is ready to answer my how and why questions.

God commended Cornelius, whose heart had been renewed by grace and who was filled with gratitude for that grace, for talking to Him. "Thy prayers and thine alms are come up for a memorial before God," Acts 10:4. He wants me to grow and perfect my skills in talking to Him. I will be sitting with Him in heaven at the dinner table soon. I am practicing now for the conversations at that table. I am developing my communication skills now that I will use to talk to Him, to talk to the angels, to talk to other beings that He has created. I need those skills to communicate when I am judging the twelve tribes of Israel. There are angels that stand in His presence, say hallelujah, and praise Him all the time. I am developing those praise skills now that I will use to talk to Him throughout eternity.

Talking to God has a reciprocal affect on me. 1 Thessalonians 5:18, "Give thanks in every circumstance, for this is God's will for you in Christ Jesus." I find myself praying to Him when I am in need of a desired outcome. When He responds, I give thanks and praise to God for this is what He wants from me. Expressing gratitude to God increases my feeling of happiness and joy. It impacts my health and well being.

Romans 12:12, Rejoicing in hope; patient in tribulation; continuing instant in prayer. Rejoicing with laughter impacts my mood and enhances my immune system. God knows that talking to Him with rejoicing for the many blessings He has given to me not only makes Him happy to hear me but improves my outcomes as well, a wonderful reciprocal relationship. This rejoicing then becomes an outward reflection of what I am able to give to others to fulfill the command in John 13:34, "…that you also love one another." God loves me and He wants me to love Him back. Part of that reciprocal love relationship is talking to Him, everyday, all day, developing skills that I will use to talk to Him throughout eternity.

Love looks like _____

My strength in this area _____

My weakness in this area _____

Dear God, You have promised _____

You have told me that it is in my best interest to _____

I praise Your name for helping me to _____

YT "I COME TO THE GARDEN ALONE " MAHALIA JACKSON
YT "TALK TO ME" LITTLE WILLIE

LET ME KISS YOUR SON.
Psalm 2:12, "Kiss the Son, lest he be angry, and ye perish from the way, when his wrath is kindled but a little. Blessed are all they that put their trust in him."
Luke 7:45, "Thou gavest me no kiss: but this woman since the time I came in hath not ceased to kiss my feet."

God wants me to love His Son. He wants me to kiss His Son. A kiss is holy and increases the bonding that occurs between two people. When Jesus was having dinner at Simon's house, a woman, who had come specifically to see Jesus, washed His feet with her tears, kissed His feet, and dried them with her hair. Simon made no such offer. Jesus had walked through sand and dirt in the sandals worn during those times. His feet were dirty. Yet in her response of gratitude to Jesus' love for her, the woman had no problem kissing His dirty feet. She loved Him because He had first loved her.

How do I kiss a God that I cannot see? He tells me how in Matthew 25: 40, "And the King shall answer and say unto them, Verily I say unto you, Inasmuch as ye have done it unto one of the least of these my brethren, ye have done it unto me." I was hungry and you fed me. I was thirsty and you gave me drink. I was in jail and you visited me. I was a stranger and you took me in. I was naked and you clothed me. I was sick and you visited me. I needed a kiss and you kissed me. Kiss those that He loves. Kiss those that He died for. Kiss those that He is coming back to take to spend eternity with Him. The poor. The lonely. The broken-hearted. The hungry. The lame. The blind. The homeless. The immigrant. The white man. The black man. The Jew. Inasmuch as you have kissed the least of these His brethren, you have kissed Him. Don't be like Simon, avoid kissing Him, even though He is in your presence, having dinner with you. Isaac kissed Jacob, thinking he was kissing Esau. Jacob kissed Rachel, and it affected him so much that he wept. Laban was so happy to see his sister's son Jacob that he started running towards him when he saw him and kissed him. He also kissed his sons and daughters good-bye when they were leaving to go back with Jacob. Esau had missed Jacob so much during the time he was gone that they embraced and kissed each other, forgetting the strained feelings between them. Joseph had been separated from his father for a long time while in Egypt. When he saw him, he kissed him and wept. Moses kissed his father-in-law out of respect for him. Samuel kissed David after he anointed him to be king. Jonathan kissed David because he loved him so much. The prodigal son's father, so happy that his son came home, kissed him, and wept. I will kiss the Son, lest His Father be angry with me and I perish from the way.

Love looks like _____

My strength in this area _____

My weakness in this area _____

Dear God, You have promised _____

You have told me that it is in my best interest to _____

I praise Your name for helping me to _____

YT "I love the Lord" Whitney Houston

CAN I WASH YOUR FEET WITH MY TEARS AND DRY THEM WITH MY HAIR?

Luke 7:37-38, "And, behold, a woman in the city, which was a sinner, when she knew that Jesus sat at meat in the Pharisee's house, brought an alabaster box of ointment. And stood at his feet behind him weeping, and began to wash his feet with tears, and did wipe them with the hairs of her head, and kissed his feet, and anointed them with the ointment."

Picture the scene. A known woman of the streets, uninvited to dinner, standing behind Him, crying uncontrollably about what? What about Jesus' interaction with her would bring her to such dramatic display of emotions? She had to be crying an awful lot to be able to wash His feet with her tears. Then she wiped them with the hair on her head. Then she kissed them. She kissed His feet! Then she put the ointment from the box she had brought with her on His feet. His feet were dirty, and we know that because Jesus told Simon who was looking on with unhidden contempt that he (Simon) hadn't bothered to give Him any water to wash His feet. He also told Simon that her many sins were forgiven and she loved much because she had been forgiven much.

God is seated on the throne of grace in heaven. Jesus is in the role of High Priest there. God's throne is established in righteousness and judgment. His everlasting, unchanging law of love is the standard He uses to judge me. Satan is forever taunting me, you sinned; you are not good enough. You are not worthy, you are condemned to die. He is absolutely right! Sin is in my DNA, inherited from Adam. When I break the law, I am condemned to die. Jesus' intercession for me is based on His wounded hands, broken body, wounded feet, His spotless life, a substitute for my sin. He knows what I have been through, points to His wounds, and pleads with the Father for me. "My blood, Father, My blood for her sin."

Jesus is at my house to sup with me. He has forgiven me for many, many sins. I bow down with my tears. I am so sorry I opened up those wounds in Your hands, feet, and side. I am so sorry for reopening the wound on Your forehead. I was thoughtless, forgetful, inconsiderate, selfish. I was allowing the flesh of my nature to rule instead of giving Your Spirit control. I am so very sorry. Can I wipe the blood from Your wounded feet with my tears? Can I dry them with my hair? You forgave Mary much, will You please forgive me much? I am so very sorry. Please, I beg you, help me not to hurt You again. Thank You for Your forgiveness. Thank You for Your grace. Thank You for

Your mercy. Thank You for Your salvation. Thank You for allowing me to stand in Your presence as if I had never sinned. Thank You, thank You.

Love looks like _____

My strength in this area _____

My weakness in this area _____

Dear God, You have promised _____

You have told me that it is in my best interest to _____

I praise Your name for helping me to _____

YT "Alabaster Box" CeCe Winans
YT "Mercy said No" CeCe Winans

I Call You "Master."

John 13:13, "Ye call me Master and Lord: and ye say well; for so I am."

Jesus is King of kings, Lord of lords, appointed to this position by His father. Luke 22:29, "And I appoint unto you a kingdom, as my Father hath appointed unto me." He is Jehovah, My God. He is ELOHIM, Creator. He is Redeemer. I am twice owned by Him, first through creation and second through redemption. Psalm 97:1, The LORD reigneth; let the earth rejoice; let the multitude of isles be glad thereof."

Adonai Lord, Master. I accept His rule. I recognize His authority. I recognize that He alone is worthy to be praised. He is El Shaddai – Almighty God. He is El Elyon – The Most High God. I recognize His power. I recognize that He is all knowing. I acknowledge that He is everywhere present. He is holy. He is righteous. He is longsuffering and full of grace and mercy.

He is Abba, Father. Jehovah Jireh, My provider. Jehovah Rophe, My Healer. Jehovah Nissi – His banner over me is love. Jehovah Makadesh, My sancitifier.

I bow down and worship You, Almighty God. There is none other than You. I praise Your holy name. What is man that thou art mindful of him? For You have made me lower than the angels. Yet You loved me so much You sent Your very own Son, Your only Son, to die so that I could escape death, so I could be restored in your kingdom, so I could live with You forever, so I could rule in Your kingdom. You didn't want to do it, God, but You did it. The angels were sad when they heard He was going to die and offered to do it in His place, but He said no, I have to do it.

You rule in the heavens and your kingdom rules over all, Psalm 103:19. Yet You have appointed Your son to be Emmanuel, God with us. Why Lord? Why? Angels can't even understand. I can't understand why You would do such a thing. We spat in Your Son's face. We rejected Him. We called Him names. We mocked Him and laughed at Him. We drove those awful nails through His hands, that sword through His side. And all He would say is, "Father, forgive them, they don't know what they are doing." He told the thief, a thief, God, dying next to Him on the cross that he would be in heaven with Him. Have mercy, Lord. I don't understand it! But I am glad, so glad You did! You are Master! You are Lord! You are King! You only are worthy to be praised.

Love looks like _____

My strength in this area _____

My weakness in this area _____

Dear God, You have promised _____

You have told me that it is in my best interest to _____

I praise Your name for helping me to _____

YT "I GIVE MYSELF AWAY" WILLIAM MCDOWELL
YT "HOLY, HOLY, HOLY" DONNIE MCCLURKIN

I will try not to make You cry.
John 11:35, "Jesus wept."

Jesus' good friend Lazarus had died. When Jesus saw his sisters, Mary and Martha, in inconsolable grief, crying their hearts out, He lost it. He cried with them, so much so that those looking on said, "Wow, see how much He loved him! Look at how He is crying." John 11:33-43, "…He was deeply moved in spirit and troubled…came to the tomb… Take away the stone, he said…so they took away the stone. Then Jesus looked up and said Father…when He had said this, Jesus called in a loud voice, Lazarus, come forth. And the dead man came forth."

Jesus, moved in spirit? Troubled? At the death of His friend who He knew He was going to call back to life? Not so much so for Lazarus but more so for the people standing around crying with no faith, even when the Life-giver was present among them. Lack of faith seen in those He loved, lack of faith in His ability to give life brought Jesus to tears. Watching them crying and suffering needlessly brought tears to His own eyes. He had known that Lazarus was going to die. He had told his disciples he was dead. He didn't come to Lazarus before he died as a "test" of faith for those around Lazarus.

Trials are needed to develop my character. Jesus' heart is wounded when He sees me doubting His ability to do what He has told me He will do. It makes Him awfully sad. Jesus was on the boat sleeping when a storm came up that shook up the disciples so much, they feared for their lives. "Master, carest thou not that we perish. How canst thou lie asleep?"

Jesus got up and said "Peace, be still." The winds and waves obeyed Him. Peace was restored. How disappointed He was with the disciples who didn't even recognize who was in their midst and the abilities that He had although they had just witnessed His power in feeding 5,000 hungry people. Don't make Him cry by doubting Him. He is all powerful. He is in control of all things. "Be thou faithful unto death and I will give thee a crown of life," (Revelation 2:10).

Love looks like _____

My strength in this area _____

My weakness in this area _____

Dear God, You have promised_____

You have told me that it is in my best interest to_____

I praise Your name for helping me to_____

YT "Waymaker" Jesus Image Choir
YT "Break every chain" Tasha Cobbs

I want to tell everybody that You are mine and I love you. Psalm 96:3-4, "Declare his glory among the heathen, his wonders among all people. For the Lord is great, and greatly to be praised: he is to be feared above all gods." **Psalm 105:1,** "O give thanks unto the Lord; call upon his name: make known his deeds among the people."

God told Ezekiel to talk about Him. Ezekiel 20:45-47, " Moreover the word of the Lord came unto me, saying, Son of man, set thy face toward the south, and drop thy word toward the south, and prophesy... And say to the forest of the south, Hear the word of the Lord." He told the disciples to tell the gospel story to all nations, and when that was done, He would come back again to take them and me to heaven.

Jesus wants me to talk about Him. He wants me to tell people how beautiful He is. He wants me to talk about how He shows His love for me. He wants me to tell others that He adopted me as His Son, introduced me to His Father who gave Him permission to make me an heir to His kingdom. He wants me to tell others that His Father loves me because I belong to His Son. He wants me to tell others that He has never lied to me. He wants me to tell others that He held my hand when it needed to be held. He wants me to tell others that He held me in His arms when I was feeling so sad about the death of my child. He wants me to tell others that He has never mistreated or disrespected me. He wants me to tell others the words of love that He has shared with me. I want you, I want to be with you, I want to touch you, I want to hold you, I will never leave you nor forsake you, I will be your friend, forever. He wants me to share how safe, warm, and happy I feel in His presence. He wants me to tell others how kind He has been to me. He wants me to tell others how He made a way for me to go to school when it didn't seem to be possible. He wants me to tell others how He arranged to get my lights turned back on when the bill wasn't paid on time. He wants me to tell others how He helped me get to know Him by sharing His experiences while He lived here on this earth with me. He wants me to tell others how He is careful to explain things to me in a way that I can understand. He wants me to tell others that He only shares as much with me as I can handle at the time. He wants me to tell others that my experiences with Him in the past are what makes me trust His judgment more than I trust my own. He wants me to tell others that He is coming back soon to get me to take me to live with Him forever. He wants me to let others know that talking about Him is like a fire burning in my bones, I just can't keep it to myself. I talk about Him to anybody who will listen. Because I love Him so very much.

Love looks like _____

My strength in this area _____

My weakness in this area _____

Dear God, You have promised _____

You have told me that it is in my best interest to _____

I praise Your name for helping me to _____

YT "The Presence of the Lord" Byron Cage
YT "Psalm 34" Brooklyn Tabernacle Choir
YT "Get all excited, tell everybody" Clark Sisters

I WANT TO TOUCH YOU, HUG YOU, HOLD YOU CLOSE TO ME. Matthew 9:21-22, "And, behold, a woman, which was diseased with an issue of blood twelve years, came behind him, and touched the hem of his garment: For she said within herself, If I may but touch his garment, I shall be whole. But Jesus turned him about, and when he saw her, he said, Daughter, be of good comfort; thy faith hath made thee whole. And the woman was made whole from that hour."

Babies that are not physically touched on a regular basis will fail to gain weight and thrive. They may even die if not touched. The woman with the issue of blood recognized the importance of touch knowing if she touched Jesus, she would be healed. Jesus put spit on the eyes of a blind man, and the man was able to see. How important it is to touch Jesus! To hug Him. To hold Him in your arms. To feel His suffering. To know His pain.

"We must be partakers with Christ in His sufferings if we would sit down in triumph with Him on His throne… He suffers in the person of His saints, and whoever touches one of His chosen ones touches Him," (_God's Amazing Grace,_ White, Ellen G. p 90, 1973). See the eighty-three-year-old white man in the intensive care unit, emaciated, skin and bones, having to sell his body to get food just to live. Touch him, you are touching Christ. See that six-year-old abandoned by her mother who is addicted to drugs. Hug her. You are hugging Jesus. See that lonely, elderly black man walking down the road with a bag with his clothes on his back with nowhere to stay. Bring him into your house, feed him. You are feeding Jesus. See that fourteen-year-old foul mouthed teenage boy who you think is very disrespectful. Talk to him. He is in pain, torn between two divorced parents who are fighting over him, caught in the middle and doesn't know which way to go. You are talking to Jesus. See that drunk man trying to rub your arm and make a pass at you while you are waiting for your friend in the bar? He's hurting. He just found out his wife was cheating on him. Let him rub your arm, it's not going to make you a better or worse person; you will be the same when you leave. You are letting Jesus rub your arm to relieve His pain.

By the way, the God who made and loves me knows that when I touch others, it has a reciprocal impact on me. That's one of the reasons He told me to do it. When I touch, hug, and kiss you, it is releasing those wonderful hormones that increase my immunity, lower my blood pressure, improve the appearance of my skin, make me feel good, and a whole lot of other things to go along with it. Touch Jesus, hug Him, go on, make yourself feel good, see your eyes light up, that smile on your face, for "inasmuch as you have done it unto one of the least of these my brethren, you have done it unto me," (Matthew 25:40).

Love looks like _____

My strength in this area _____

My weakness in this area _____

Dear God, You have promised _____

You have told me that it is in my best interest to _____

I praise Your name for helping me to _____

YT "IF I CAN TOUCH THE HEM OF HIS GARMENT" SAM COOKE
YT "TOUCH ME IN THE MORNING" DIANA ROSS

YOU MAKE ME FEEL SO SAFE.
Psalm 91:1-2, "He that dwelleth in the secret place of the most High shall abide under the shadow of the Almighty. I will say of the LORD, He is my refuge and my fortress: my God; in him will I trust."

I feel so safe in Your presence. The winds and the waves obey Your will when You say "peace be still." Demons tremble at Your name. The sun stands in its place when You tell it to. The oceans stay in their boundaries at Your command. You make my enemies my footstool. You faithfully protect me from the evil one. You cover me with Your righteousness, so that I will never be shaken. You are my refuge in any time of trouble. You help me to see danger and tell me to take refuge in You. You will vindicate me, You will not abandon the work of Your hands. You will keep me in perfect peace because my mind is stayed on You and I trust You. Your name is a strong tower and I run to You, so I can be safe. I trust in You and do good, so that I can abide in safe pastures. When I see Your rainbow in the clouds, I know that it reminds You that You will never destroy the earth with a flood again.

"You are my hiding place; you will protect me from trouble and surround me with songs of deliverance," (Psalm 32:7). "In peace I will lie down and sleep, for you alone, Lord, make me dwell in safety," (Psalms 4:8). "Be strong and courageous. Do not be afraid or terrified because of them, for the LORD your God goes with you; he will never leave you nor forsake you," (Deuteronomy 31:6). " No weapon that is formed against thee shall prosper; and every tongue that shall rise against thee in judgment thou shalt condemn. This is the heritage of the servants of the LORD, and their righteousness is of me, saith the LORD," (Isaiah 54:17).

You kept Noah and his family safe on the ark. You delivered Lot and his daughters from burning Sodom. You brought Joseph out of the pit and made him ruler in Egypt. You delivered Jonah from the belly of a whale. You lead Abraham from Canaan to a land that he knew not. You saved Elijah from Jezebel. Yet God, John died in a pot of boiling oil. Peter was crucified upside down on a cross. Stephen was stoned to death. Your Son was crucified on a cross. I say like your servant Job, though You slay me, yet will I trust You. I say like the Hebrew boys, even if You choose not to deliver me this time, I will not bow down to idols. I say like Daniel, my God is able to deliver me from the lion's mouth. I trust You God. My life is in Your hands.

Love looks like _____

My strength in this area _____

My weakness in this area _____

Dear God, You have promised _____

You have told me that it is in my best interest to _____

I praise Your name for helping me to _____

YT "Master the tempest is raging" James Cleveland
YT "Thank you" Walter Hawkins

IT IS SO PEACEFUL AND JOYFUL WHEN I AM WITH YOU!
Romans 15:15, "Now the God of hope fill you with all joy and peace in believing, that ye may abound in hope, through the power of the Holy Ghost."

On a regular basis, I am surrounded by people that love You, and they are full of positivity waiting for You to come back to get us. I know You are there with us because You have said that where two or three are gathered in Your name, You are in the midst of them. Such joy, knowing that I will stand with them on the Sea of Glass and spend eternity with them and You!

"Thou wilt keep him in perfect peace whose mind is stayed on Thee because he trusteth thee," (Isaiah 26:3). When I lay down at night to sleep, I have no trouble getting to sleep and staying asleep because with You present, I have perfect peace. You increase my trust in You with every met need, with every day of care, with every prayer answered. You have kept my children safe. You have kept my grandchildren safe. You consistently follow through on every promise that You make. I trust you and my mind is stayed on You. Just being in Your presence reinforces for me that I want to be with You forever.

You have made it possible for me to pay tuition for several children to go church school or college. What hope that brings for their future outcomes knowing that You have said, "Train up a child in the way that he should go and when he is old he will not depart from it!" (Proverbs 22:6). You helped me with a nursing program for students that would not have been able to get into another program. Not only did You help me with that privilege of providing hope for their future, You empowered the majority of them to pass the nursing exam to become professional nurses when they finished on their first try! What wonderful feelings I have when I go on Facebook and see that those students are reaching out to help others because You worked with me and allowed me to share Your hope that gave them a future! How can I ever praise You enough? How can I say thanks?

You have given me the opportunity to bless and bring hope to so many others, and it has been such a privilege and joy to do so. You were with me every step of the way, bringing peace and joy and providing the wisdom and power to bless even when I thought that I was doing it on my own. You were the One that filled me with the joy and peace. You were the one that helped me to believe. You honored Your promise, so that I truly abounded in hope. You allowed me the privilege of seeing that hope passed on to others and experience the joy of their success as a result of that hope. Hope and joy and peace that came from You! It is true. You do honor Your promises. You do fill me with joy and peace, which brings a lot of hope not only to me but to others that You love and died for.

Love looks like _____

My strength in this area _____

My weakness in this area _____

Dear God, You have promised_____

You have told me that it is in my best interest to_____

I praise Your name for helping me to_____

YT "To God be the glory" Andre Crouch
YT "You give me joy" Anita Baker

THANK YOU FOR THE STRENGTH AND POWER THAT YOU GIVE ME BECAUSE YOU LOVE ME.

Luke 10: 19, "Behold, I give unto you power to tread on serpents and scorpions, and over all the power of the enemy: and nothing shall by any means hurt you." **Acts 1:8,** " But ye shall receive power, after that the Holy Ghost is come upon you: and ye shall be witnesses unto me both in Jerusalem, and in all Judaea, and in Samaria, and unto the uttermost part of the earth."

Strength is associated with resistance. When I move a book across a table, friction causes the book to resist the movement. Power is the ability to do something. Strength and power are increased by exercise. "The name of the Lord is a strong tower; the righteous run into it and are safe," (Proverbs 18:10). "Do not grieve, for the joy of the Lord is your strength," (Nehemiah 8:10). Your power, God, in me. Your joy, God, my strength.

You have given me power over the enemy and nothing shall hurt me. You told Zerubbael, "…Not by might, nor by power, but by my spirit, saith the LORD of hosts," (Zechariah 4:6). You told me that I would receive power after the Holy Ghost comes on me and that I am to use that power to witness unto You in all the earth. You give me strength to resist the power of Satan, my enemy. You give me power to do Your will, to do justly, to have mercy, to walk humbly with You. You give me power to, "Be ye therefore perfect, even as Your father which is in heaven is perfect," (Matthew 6:48). Because of the Holy Ghost power You give to dwell inside of me that places Your divinity within me, I am able to live a life that carries out Your purpose.

You give me faith and tell me to exercise it, so that my strength and power will increase. Faith in You. Trust in You to do everything You say You will do. I need to be sure that I grow my strength by spending time with others who love You that will encourage me. I need to spend time in the sun and in nature to be reassured by seeing how You take care of Your creation that You will do exactly the same for me. I need to reduce the distractions and be careful of those who give me a false picture of You or who lie about You to make me doubt Your word. I will step out in faith remembering that the Red Sea did not open until the people stepped into the water. I will through the strength and power that You give me serve others and witness for You as you have instructed. I will continue my habit of praying to You everyday, so that the strength and power You give me will increase. Thank You for strength and power.

Love looks like _____

My strength in this area _____

My weakness in this area _____

Dear God, You have promised _____

You have told me that it is in my best interest to _____

I praise Your name for helping me to _____

YT "Lord, help me to hold out" James Cleveland
YT "Not by might" Eden's Bridge

Tell me what You want!

Micah 6:8, "He hath shewed thee, O man, what is good; and what doth the Lord require of thee, but to do justly, and to love mercy, and to walk humbly with thy God?"

I know that You are all knowing, all powerful, and every where present. I know that Your kingdom lasts forever. You have told me to do justly. Justice demands a standard by which I am evaluated. Your law, love in practice, the foundation of Your throne based on righteousness and justice is the standard. Jesus came and died because Your law is everlasting, cannot be changed, and is in place to provide righteous government. Thus my justification is possible, so that I can stand in Your presence as if I have never sinned. You put Your law in my mind and on my heart as Your standard of righteousness. I need Your Spirit to explain it to me in terms that I can understand and empower me to put it into practice in my life. You told me not to kill, steal, commit adultery, lie, or envy what my neighbor has. You told me to honor my mother and father. Show me how and empower me to obey Your law that I may do justly.

You told me to love mercy. You mingled mercy with justice at the cross to confirm that Your law does not change. You show me mercy by not giving me the punishment that I deserve for the wrong things that I do. I deserve death for my sins, but You have extended mercy, so that I don't have to experience the punishment I deserve. Your expectation is that I extend the mercy that You give me to others.

You want me to walk humbly with You. Humility enables me to know the terms of my salvation, to understand Your word, to see Your light, to hear You speak to me, to receive the things of God, and become changed into Your image. This pride that I have. This independence. This self-sufficiency. This feeling that if I work hard enough, I can be good enough to go to heaven on my own. I have been taught that being independent and self-sufficient is a good thing and everyone should strive for it. Do I need to go around with my head hung down? Do you want me to be a weakling and let everybody walk all over me? Lucifer wanted to exalt himself above You, thought he knew more than You, and did not need rules to live by. He refused to submit to Your authority. You created all things, all power is in Your hands. I yield my will to Your authority. I trust Your judgment. I walk humbly remembering that You are King. You are Lord. You made the eternal laws that provide righteous judgment for the entire universe. I am your friend. "Ye are my friends if ye do whatsoever I command you," (John 15:14).

Love looks like _____

My strength in this area _____

My weakness in this area _____

Dear God, You have promised _____

You have told me that it is in my best interest to _____

I praise Your name for helping me to _____

YT "I surrender" Brooklyn Tabernacle Choir
YT "Lord Don't Move my mountain" Inez Andrews

I fear You and respect Your name.
Jeremiah 33:16, "In those days shall Judah be saved, and Jerusalem shall dwell safely: and this is the name wherewith she shall be called, The Lord our righteousness." **Matthew 6:9,** "…Hallowed be thy name." **Ecclesiastes 12:13,** "…Fear God, and keep his commandments: for this is the whole duty of man."

Seraphim are six-winged angels that stand in the presence of God. "Above it stood the seraphims: each one had six wings; with twain he covered his face, and with twain he covered his feet, and with twain he did fly. And one cried unto another, and said, Holy, holy, holy, is the Lord of hosts: the whole earth is full of his glory," (Isaiah 6:2-3). In covering my face in the presence of the Most Holy God, in humility bowing before Him in worship and praise, I recognize that You are God, have all power, and are worthy to be praised. Moses was told to take his shoes off. The ground that he was standing on was holy. "And he said, Draw not nigh hither: put off thy shoes from off thy feet, for the place whereon thou standest *is* holy ground," Exodus 3:5. Angels cover their feet; Moses took of his shoes in the presence of the Holy One. When Joshua approached a Man that he did not recognize and asked if the Man was on his side or on the enemy's side, the Man told him to take off his shoes for the ground that he was standing on was holy. Joshua fell on his face and worshipped the Man.

God's presence requires that I humbly acknowledge, respect, and honor Him. He tells me that the ground where He stands is holy. Fearing God means that I recognize who He is, Creator and Sustainer of all things, Lord of the Universe, King of all kings, the Life-giver. He made me, and I give Him the respect due Him. Angels stand in His presence and continually declare, "Holy, holy, holy." I recognize His holiness. Should I respect and honor Him any less than the angels? Moses? Joshua?

God's name is important to Him. "I Am" is what He told Moses when Moses asked who he should tell Pharaoh and the Israelites who sent him to deliver Israel from Egypt. I AM beginning, in the middle, always, forever. I honor and respect His name. I worship Him. "O come, let us worship and bow down: let us kneel before the Lord our maker. For he is our God…" (Psalm 95:6, 7). Lord, You are holy! You alone are worthy to be praised! I will bless the Lord at all times. His praise will be continually on my lips.

Love looks like

My strength in this area _____

My weakness in this area _____

Dear God, You have promised _____

You have told me that it is in my best interest to _____

I praise Your name for helping me to _____

YT "I BOWED ON MY KNEES AND CRIED HOLY" MICHAEL ENGLISH

I AM YOURS AND YOU ARE MINE. I AM COMPLETE IN YOU.
Colossians 2:10, "And ye are complete in him, which is the head of all principality and power." **John 17:23,** "I in them, and thou in me, that they may be made perfect in one; and that the world may know that thou hast sent me, and hast loved them, as thou hast loved me."

I feel so whole and complete in Your presence. I feel as if I have need of nothing but You. I feel totally at home. You make me feel so welcome, so accepted. I feel so calm and have so much peace. You help me to feel that I really can do all things as You have told me, "I can do all things through Christ which strengtheneth me," (Philippians 4:13). I know that You will not reject me. I know that when You correct me it is because You really do care about me. You know my weaknesses and You are working with me to change them into strengths. You listen to me so intently and enjoy it when I talk to You. I hear You speaking to me in my quiet times and in my not so quiet times. You walked in my shoes when You were on this earth, so You understand what I am going through. You want eternal life for me.

"That they all may be one; as thou, Father, art in me, and I in thee, that they also may be one in us: that the world may believe that thou hast sent me," (John 17:21). Just as You are one with Your Father, You know that my completeness is associated with unity with others. You want me to share those same feelings with others that You love and that love You. In Ephesians 4:13, You tell me, "Till we all come in the unity of the faith, and of the knowledge of the Son of God, unto a perfect man, unto the measure of the stature of the fulness of Christ." In Philippians 2:2, You say, "Fulfil ye my joy, that ye be likeminded, having the same love, being of one accord, of one mind." In Ephesians 4:3, You say, "Endeavouring to keep the unity of the Spirit in the bond of peace." Your Spirit is the Source of the unity that will bring unity of the faith, knowledge of You, the unity that love brings, and put me on one accord and of one mind with those that love and serve You. Your Spirit will empower me to obey Your command in Romans 12:10, "Be kindly affectioned one to another with brotherly love; in honour preferring one another." You want me to have the same affection for my brothers that You have for me. "Seeing ye have purified your souls in obeying the truth through the Spirit unto unfeigned love of the brethren, see that ye love one another with a pure heart fervently," (1Peter 1:22). Because You have reassured me that I can do all things through You, I promise to cooperate with Your Spirit to have the unity that enables the world to believe that He has sent You. Please help me keep my promise.

Love looks like _____

My strength in this area _____

My weakness in this area _____

Dear God, You have promised _____

You have told me that it is in my best interest to _____

I praise Your name for helping me to _____

YT "MAKE US ONE" PHILLIP BAILEY
YT "WE ARE ONE IN THE SPIRIT" WALT WHITMAN/SOUL CHILDREN OF CHICAGO

I will never forget or leave You.
Hebrews 13:5, "…for he hath said, I will never leave thee, nor forsake thee."

You have promised me that You will never leave or forsake me. I promise You the same. Knowing what I know about You, I would be very foolish to ever leave you. I also know my weakness in making promises that I sometimes do not keep. I know that I am going to need Your help to keep this promise, but it is a promise that I make to You from the bottom of my heart. You are always there for me. You do indeed walk right with me. You do protect me. You provide light to show me the way. You have a plan for my life. You have invested Yourself in me. You think about me all the time. You even know the number of hairs on my head. You know my every thought. My every deed. You know my ups and downs, my comings, and goings. You know me better than I could ever know myself.

You told me that for my good, You had to go away but that You would send me help. "Nevertheless I tell you the truth; It is expedient for you that I go away: for if I go not away, the Comforter will not come unto you; but if I depart, I will send him unto you," (John 17: 7). Empower me through Your Spirit to keep Your word in my heart. Empower me through Your Spirit to cry to You. Empower me through Your Spirit to get the victory over every sin, fully sanctified, so that I reflect Your image of love and to assure that I will look like You when You return. You have said that Your Spirit would convict me of sin, righteousness, and judgment. So be it unto me. In John 17: 15, You promise me "All things that the Father hath are mine: therefore said I, that he shall take of mine, and shall shew it unto you." Show me, Holy Spirit, give me what the Father has given You to give to me so I never forget You or leave You. Jesus, fill me with Your Spirit and cover me with Your righteousness like You said You would do if I ask.

What would my life be without You? I believe You call that "death." I would be insane to leave You. Yet I know that if Your Spirit does not work with me on a daily basis, I will easily fall into that trap. I do not want to die, Lord. I do not want to be separated from You. I want to be with You forever. Nobody loves me like You do. Nobody knows me like You do. Nobody treats me like You do. Nobody wants to be with me like You do.

Love looks like _____

My strength in this area _____

My weakness in this area _____

Dear God, You have promised _____

You have told me that it is in my best interest to _____

I praise Your name for helping me to _____

YT "He's that kind of Friend" Tremaine Hawkins

I will bear fruit for Your glory.
John 15:8, "Herein is my Father glorified, that ye bear much fruit; so shall ye be my disciples."

Grape vines produce grapes, which contain the seed to produce more grapes. The primary purposes of fruit are to feed others and produce seeds that produce more fruit. I am His disciple, thus Jesus tells me to bear much fruit. He tells me how to bear fruit. " I am the vine, ye are the branches: He that abideth in me, and I in him, the same bringeth forth much fruit: for without me ye can do nothing. If a man abide not in me, he is cast forth as a branch, and is withered; and men gather them, and cast them into the fire, and they are burned. If ye abide in me, and my words abide in you, ye shall ask what ye will, and it shall be done unto you," (John 15: 5-7).

I stay attached to the vine because through the vine comes the water and nourishment I need to grow to produce fruit. Note that the grape can only produce more fruit when the grape dies, and the seed inside the grape goes into the ground. I die daily as I allow Jesus to abide in me. I abide in Jesus when I eat His flesh and drink His everlasting water as I feed on His word daily. I abide in Jesus as I allow His Spirit to dwell within me bringing with Him His divinity, righteousness, and holiness that is placed in me. Thus the fruit of the Spirit will be produced and seen in my life as evidence of my abiding and His indwelling. "But the fruit of the Spirit is love, joy, peace, longsuffering, gentleness, goodness, faith, meekness, temperance: against such there is no law," (Galatians 5:22, 23).

When I die to self daily, that love feeds others and produces more love. Hallelujah! I am recognized as His disciple by the fruit I bear. "By this shall all men know that ye are my disciples, if ye have love one to another," (John 13:35). I die daily when I surrender my thoughts, my feelings, my behavior, my will to Jesus. I ask daily for His Holy Spirit to live in my heart, so that I may: continuously abide with Him, understand, keep, and apply His word to my life; receive His flesh, drink His everlasting water, and be empowered to cooperate with Him to bear fruit love. I am Your disciple Lord, help me to abide in You that I may bear not just a little bit of fruit, but much fruit, so that Your Father may be glorified.

Love looks like _____

My strength in this area _____

My weakness in this area _____

Dear God, You have promised _____

You have told me that it is in my best interest to _____

I praise Your name for helping me to _____

YT "He's preparing me" Wilmington/Chester Mass Choir

I KEEP YOUR WORDS IN MY MIND AND IN MY HEART.
Psalm 119: 11, "I have hidden your word in my heart that I might not sin against you." **Psalm 40:8,** "I delight to do Your will, O my God; Your law is within my heart."

Each step of my life I am faced with decisions. When I have His love letter written to me deep in my thoughts and feeling, those decisions help me stay on course and firmly anchored to His plan and purpose for my life. The path of right or wrong, the power that resides within my own ability to make conscious decisions, is rooted in the word of the Lord. The free will that He has given to me is a test of my endurance to fulfill His will and show Him that I really do love Him. His Spirit empowers me to keep His word in my heart by remembering what He says to me. He reminds me to think about those words often, to allow them to influence my life, and have control over my decisions. He reminds me that He told me He loves me, that He will take care of me, that He wants me to be where He is. I have those words hidden deep in my heart. He wants me to remind Him often of what He has said, not really as a reminder to Him because He has not forgotten but because He knows that it is my tendency to forget.

The bible, His love letter to me filled with truth, peace, and joy, was given so that I may understand the lessons and commandments that are written on my heart as I walk the path of life. "The law of his God is in his heart; none of his steps shall slide," (Psalms 37: 31). When I walk in the path lighted for me in His word, my decisions and steps are certain. Many times along this path outside influence can make it difficult to stay on the course meant for me. All kinds of worldly things, money, inappropriate relationships, power, may lead me from the path laid out for me but knowledge of His word in my mind and those words kept dear to my heart empowers me to say "no" to the temptations and stay anchored to the God who loves me. "If any man will do his will, he shall know of the doctrine, whether it be of God, or whether I speak of myself," (John 7:17). When the temptations of the world or the words of others make me question life, it is these times that God's words of love, fixed in my mind and heart, guide me. "There hath no temptation taken you but such as is common to man: but God is faithful, who will not suffer you to be tempted above that ye are able; but will with the temptation also make a way to escape, that ye may be able to bear it," (1 Corinthians 10:13).

"Give me understanding, and I shall keep thy law; yea, I shall observe it with my whole heart," (Psalm 119:34). The highlight of my faith each and every day comes with the comfort that I can say to God, who only speaks words of love to me, with resounding confidence, "Order my steps in Your word."

Love looks like _____

My strength in this area _____

My weakness in this area _____

Dear God, You have promised_____

You have told me that it is in my best interest to_____

I praise Your name for helping me to_____

YT "Order my steps" GMWA Women of Worship

THANK YOU FOR ALL THE THINGS YOU DO FOR ME!
Psalm 136:1, "O give thanks unto the LORD; for he is good: for his mercy endureth forever." **Psalm 97:12,** "Rejoice in the LORD, you who are righteous, and praise his holy name."

I was created to praise the Lord. When I give my testimony to others, I show others how God has seen me through a situation. Without Him, without His grace and mercy, I would be wandering without path or purpose. Psalm 30:40, "Sing to the LORD, O you His saints, and give thanks to His holy name." Psalm 32:11, "Be glad in the LORD and rejoice, O righteous; shout for joy, all you upright in heart." My testimony of the love given and received by God is my testament of thanks to His grace.

God told Abraham, let me bless you. Then go and tell everybody else how I blessed you. In this way, God's love was to be revealed to all nations, so that they would have the same opportunity that Abraham had of being blessed by God. When I say thank You to God and praise His name for all His goodness, it makes God happy to hear it, but it influences the lives of others that hear that testimony, as well as impacting me. It is an encouragement to them that the same God that loves me also loves them.

I have heard people say you have to have a test to have a testimony. Look at the "test"-imony of David in God's leading the children of Israel. Psalm 136:1-27, "O give thanks…for he is good: for his mercy endureth forever…to him who doeth great wonders…who made the heavens…that made great lights…the sun to rule by day…the moon and stars to rule by night…smote Egypt…brought Israel out…divided the Red Sea…and made Israel to pass through it…who remembered us in our low estate…and redeemed us from our enemies…who giveth food to all flesh…"

I love my family and friends. I love myself born out of gratitude that He first loved me. He is working with me to help me love my enemies. The love that He has given me is the first testimony of how I outwardly love others. "Take good heed therefore unto yourselves, that ye love the LORD your God," (Joshua 23:11). Telling Him thank you is just one of the ways that I say I love You. Loving you also says to Him, "I love You."

Love looks like _____

My strength in this area _____

My weakness in this area _____

Dear God, You have promised _____

You have told me that it is in my best interest to _____

I praise Your name for helping me to _____

YT "Thank You, Lord" Walter Hawkins
YT "Be grateful" Walter Hawkins

I AM LEAVING EVERYTHING TO FOLLOW YOU BUT, GOD, WHAT'S IN IT FOR ME?

Matthew 19:25-29, "Then answered Peter and said unto him, Behold, we have forsaken all, and followed thee; what shall we have therefore? And Jesus said unto them, 'Verily I say unto you, That ye which have followed me, in the regeneration when the Son of man shall sit in the throne of his glory, ye also shall sit upon twelve thrones, judging the twelve tribes of Israel. And every one that hath forsaken houses, or brethren, or sisters, or father, or mother, or wife, or children, or lands, for my name's sake, shall receive an hundredfold, and shall inherit everlasting life.'"

"We have forsaken all, and followed thee." Peter had a very forthright question for Jesus. "What shall we have therefore?" Jesus considered the question a reasonable question to ask and answered him without hesitating. "Ye shall also sit upon twelve thrones, judging the twelve tribes of Israel...shall receive an hundredfold, and shall inherit everlasting life." Peter didn't know all that Jesus meant when He said this to him, but over the course of his lifetime, he came to understand this text. "For all the promises of God in him are yea, and in him Amen, unto the glory of God by us," 2 Corinthians 1:20. God is consistent in what He says and keeps His word.

"By faith Abraham, when he was called to go out into a place which he should after receive for an inheritance, obeyed; and he went out, not knowing whither he went," Hebrews 11:8. Abraham left his home and his comfortable surroundings and didn't even know where he was going. Following God.

In Matthew 19:21, Jesus told the rich young ruler, "If you would be perfect, go, sell what you possess and give to the poor, and you will have treasure in heaven; and come, follow me." He chose his treasures.

"Give, and it shall be given unto you; good measure, pressed down, and shaken together, and running over, shall men give into your bosom. For with the same measure that ye mete withal it shall be measured to you again." The choice is mine. The promise along with requisite requirements are clear. Leave everything, follow Me. Father, mother, comfortable home, good paying job, drugs, alcohol, promiscuous lifestyle, worldly pleasures, good food, whatever He tells me to leave behind, so that God is glorified. I will sit upon a throne, judge the tribes of Israel, receive everything I give hundredfold, and have eternal life. I must deny myself, give up everything to follow Jesus. That's what He asks me to do if I truly love Him and want to be with Him. I choose You again, dear Lord, I choose You again. I am leaving all to follow You.

Love looks like _____

My strength in this area _____

My weakness in this area _____

Dear God, You have promised _____

You have told me that it is in my best interest to _____

I praise Your name for helping me to _____

YT "I choose you again, dear Lord" Wintley Phipps

I WANT TO BE WITH YOU FOREVER. I WANT TO SEE YOU FACE TO FACE – SOON!

John 14:1-3, "Let not your heart be troubled: ye believe in God, believe also in me. In my Father's house are many mansions: if it were not so, I would have told you. I go to prepare a place for you. And if I go and prepare a place for you, I will come again, and receive you unto myself; that where I am, there ye may be also."

You want me to be with You where You are! I am so excited! Just like You came every evening to be with Adam and Eve, You want to be with me! You want me to be where You are! O Lord, I cannot wait! Please make it soon! I want to see Your face. I want to kiss those nail-pierced hands. I want to put my finger in that scar on Your side like Thomas did. I want to bow at Your feet and wash them with my tears and dry them with my hair. I want to tell You thank You to Your face for dying for me and not rejecting me. I want You to put that crown on my head. I want to hear You say, "Well done." I want You to introduce me to that angel You sent to minister to me. I want to see Your throne of grace. I want to see the altar where You pleaded Your blood for me and interceded in my behalf. I cannot wait to sit at the welcome table and feast on the food of glory. I want to see what it feels like to walk next to You on the Sea of Glass. Is it really true that there are twelve gates to the city? I know the angels already are assigned the responsibility of standing by those gates, but could You let me do it just once? I want to see the mercy seat. Can I open the Ark of the Covenant and touch the Tables of Stone that God gave to Moses? Are You going to take me to introduce me to Your Father? I know You already told Him that I am Yours and He loves me because I belong to You, but can You take me to meet Him? I do not think I can handle being in His presence alone. He is just so awesome! And that mansion, Lord. What does it look like? You know I like orange. Is it orange? Where is that shelf where I get to put my crown? Even so come, Lord Jesus.

You told me to occupy until You come. So I will. I know You are preparing me for heaven. You are dwelling in me, so that I will be holy and righteous just like You. But I need Your help to put on the whole armor to continue to fight the fight of faith while I am waiting for You. Help me tighten the belt of truth securely. Cover my chest with the breastplate of Your invincible righteousness. Help me to hold that shield of faith, trusting in You to stop those darts that Satan is sending my way. Guide me in putting on that helmet of salvation and show me how to effectively handle the sword of the Spirit, Your word. Give me a new mind, a new heart. Change my behaviors. Let me hear Your voice. Let my prayers be a sweet song in Your ear. Help me, Lord, just to stand.

Love looks like _____

My strength in this area _____

My weakness in this area _____

Dear God, You have promised _____

You have told me that it is in my best interest to _____

I praise Your name for helping me to _____

YT "God will take care of you" Mississippi Mass Choir
YT "Stand" Donne McClurkin
YT "He's coming back" New Jersey Mass Choir
YT "Someday, we'll be together" Supremes

Chapter 5
I Love Myself So That I Know How to Love You

I ALLOW GOD'S GRACE TO TRANSFORM MY CHARACTER. (1) Luke 17:21, "Behold the kingdom of God is within you." **Matthew 13:31, 32,** The kingdom of heaven is like to a grain of mustard seed…when it is grown, it is the greatest among herbs, and becometh a tree…"

Psalm 51:6. I was born in sin and shapen in iniquity, loveless. There is no love for myself or others that exists in my natural tendencies. I need to be transformed from a loveless being to a being full of love for myself, so that I can love others like I love myself. The transformation needed can be compared to a seed that starts out small, continuously receiving nourishing soil and water, grows daily upward towards the light of heaven, and over time becomes a great tree. The tree is in the seed. Christ in me, His love, His divinity, His holiness, my hope of glory. God's grace that has been extended to me transforms my loveless character much like a mustard seed, planted in the ground in time to become a great tree. God's kingdom, composed of His kingdom of grace (fulfilled at the cross) and His kingdom of glory (started after the cross, fulfilled when He returns) is within me.

That transformation comes as a result of God's indwelling of me through the Holy Spirit. When I make the decision to accept Jesus as my Lord and Savior, this transformation begins. By this connection with Him, I receive "the hoarded love of eternity" that Christ came to earth to bring, and "this is the treasure" that I am "to receive, to reveal, and to impart," _God's Amazing Grace 1973 p 16_ White. I must receive His love for me in order to reveal it and impart it to others. My natural inclination is not to love. That transformation to loving myself and others occurs through the indwelling Christ in me, loving through me. An apple tree grows from an apple seed that produces more apples with apple seeds. The apple is a perfect apple at each stage of its development. The love seed, perfect at every stage in its growth, grows up into a tree that bears love fruit, that yields more seeds that are love seeds.

The transformation of my character grows from a very small beginning, like the mustard seed, to finally reflect fully and completely in me, the "hoarded love of eternity" manifested in Christ. I receive my nourishment and water by eating His flesh and drinking His everlasting water, His word. I grow continuously in the Light of Life all by the grace and power He gives me daily. I will be like Him when He comes, I will fully love myself and others, as He, loving me and knowing what is in my best interest, has told me to do. The song says, "Lord prepare me to be a sanctuary, pure and holy, tried and true. With thanksgiving, I'll be a living sanctuary…" God honors His promise to transform me. I want to reflect His image of love, pure and holy, tried and true. I want to love like He loves and be like Him when he comes. I want His divinity implanted in me to impart that holy love for myself, so that I may receive it, reveal it, and impart it to you. I want to be transformed by His grace. I want to be like Him.

Love looks like _____

My strength in this area _____

My weakness in this area _____

Dear God, You have promised _____

You have told me that it is in my best interest to _____

I praise Your name for helping me to _____

YT "LORD PREPARE ME TO BE A SANCTUARY" TD JAKES
YT "A HEART LIKE YOURS" CECE WINANS

I ALLOW GOD'S GRACE TO TRANSFORM MY CHARACTER (2)

Romans 12:2, "And be not conformed to this world: but be ye transformed by the renewing of your mind, that ye may prove what is that good, and acceptable, and perfect, will of God." **John 16:13,** "…when he, the Spirit of truth, is come, he will guide you into all truth…"

My character, thoughts, and feelings that motivate my behavior is transformed by the Holy Spirit in me. The seed of love that He implants will grow into a great tree of love. Like the branches on a tree, I must stay attached to the source, so that I can receive the "everlasting water" and the nourishment from the "Bread of life" so that I grow imperceptibly over time. I am empowered daily to receive the water and nourishment I need to grow and be transformed. I am empowered to spend time with Him, to feel His presence, to read His word and keep it in my heart. I talk to Him, listen to Him, and do what He tells me to do every day, and I am transformed.

God reveals to me how He will transform my character and what my love will look like when my character has been transformed. The Holy Spirit will "reprove the world of sin and of righteousness, and of judgment," John 16:8. As I hunger and thirst after Christ's righteousness, He will reveal His holy love to me and teach me all things that I need to know and do for my character to be transformed. Ephesians 1:3-5, "…God…hath blessed us with all spiritual blessings in heavenly places…he hath chosen us in him before the foundation of the world, that we should be holy and without blame before him in love." I hear from so many people that I cannot be holy, there is no one that can be perfect. Yet God tells me in Matthew 5:48, "Be ye therefore perfect, even as your Father which is in heaven is perfect." It is not my holiness but Christ who dwells in me, His holiness. It is not my righteousness but Christ's righteousness covering me, that enables me to stand holy and blameless before a holy and perfect Father. "I put away sinful thoughts. I renounce evil deeds. Love, humility, and peace replace anger, envy, and strife. Joy takes the place of sadness, and your (my) countenance reflects the light of heaven" (<u>Ye shall receive power</u> p 15 White, 2012). Cover me with Your righteousness. Fill me with Your Spirit, make me blameless and holy, not because of any good thing in me but because of Christ in me, the hope of glory. When He comes, I will be like Him, perfect in love, perfect in trust, perfect in obedience, because Christ who dwells in me, with my cooperation, daily transforms me.

Love looks like _____

My strength in this area _____

My weakness in this area _____

Dear God, You have promised_____

You have told me that it is in my best interest to_____

I praise Your name for helping me to_____

YT "The Potter's House" Tremaine Hawkins
YT "So you would know how much I love you" Brooklyn Tabernacle Choir

I forgive myself as God has forgiven me.
Ephesians 4:32, "And be ye kind one to another, tenderhearted, forgiving one another, even as God, for Christ's sake hath forgiven you." **John 3:3,** "…except a man be born again, he cannot see the kingdom of God."

Forgiveness is an intentional and voluntary process to which I have a change in feelings and attitude regarding a wrong that I have done or someone has done to me. I let go of negative emotions, such as anger, resentment, and a desire for revenge. Forgiveness elevates my mood, enhances my optimism, and decreases my blood pressure and the risk for heart disease. God's forgiveness establishes me to stand before the Creator of the universe as if I have never sinned and allows me to decide if I will remain in that justified position, so that I can have eternal life with Him. I show my love for myself when I forgive myself for things that I have done that have hurt me and others.

My heart is evil by birth; I cannot change it. When I am born again, as Jesus tells me I must be, I am born of the water and of the Spirit. John 3:5. The Holy Spirit tells me how and empowers me to forgive myself. Steps in that forgiveness process are similar to the new birth that Jesus told John that I must have if I am going to enter the kingdom of God (kingdom of grace and kingdom of glory). Those steps include: 1) acknowledgement of the specific wrong and the damage it has done 2) repenting of that wrong, "I am sorry" that I did that to myself while feeling compassion towards myself 3) allowing the Holy Spirit to provide the needed wisdom and power not do that to myself again while evaluating my growth related to the situation 4) Knowing that God does not lie, that He loves me, I accept that when He says "if you confess your sins, I am faithful and just to forgive your sins and cleanse you from ALL unrighteousness." I know based on what He has said, not on what I may feel, that I am forgiven and cleansed from my unrighteousness. I forgive myself, knowing that I stand before Him, justified as if I had never sinned. I let go of the negative doubts, the anger, the feelings of unworthiness, and accept that I am His child, heir to His throne, created in His image, empowered through His Spirit dwelling in me. I forgive myself just as God forgives me and I move forward in His strength, in His power because I love myself as He has commanded. I forgive myself and so I will not allow the enemy of mankind, Satan, to use my failures and my sins to hold me in his grasp.

Love looks like _____

My strength in this area _____

My weakness in this area _____

Dear God, You have promised_____

You have told me that it is in my best interest to_____

I praise Your name for helping me to_____

YT "Spirit fall down" Luther Barnes
YT "I did you wrong" Smokey Robinson/Miracles

I acknowledge that my body is the dwelling place of God and take care of it.

I Corinthians 6:19-20, "What? Know ye not that your body is the temple of the Holy Ghost which is in you, which ye have of God, and ye are not your own? For ye are bought with a price: therefore glorify God in your body, and in your spirit, which are God's."

My body, the temple of God, God's dwelling place, is holy. It is made holy by the presence of the indwelling Holy Ghost. God told Moses in Exodus 3:5, "…Draw not nigh hither, put off thy shoes from off thy feet, for the place whereon thou standest is holy ground." I am made holy by the indwelling Holy Ghost, not by any goodness in me. Jesus tells me in 1 Peter 1:16, "Be holy, because I am holy." He assures me that this is only possible through the Holy Ghost dwelling in me.

How do I "put off my shoes" related to God's presence in my body, His temple? 1 Corinthians 10:31, "…whatsoever you eat or drink or whatever you do, do it all for the glory of God." 3 John 1:2, "…prosper and be in health…" Loving myself means that I take care of God's dwelling place, His temple, my body. I take care of my physical body, my emotions, my intellect, and my spiritual components through the instructions He has given in His word. "…I have given you every herb bearing seed…and every tree, in which if the fruit of a tree yielding seed; to you it shall be for meat," (Genesis 1:29). "He that is slow to anger is better than the mighty; and he that ruleth his spirit than he that taketh a city," (Proverbs 16:32). "Get wisdom…" (Proverbs 4:5-9). "And be not drunk with wine…but be filled with the Spirit," (Ephesians 5:18). I love myself, knowing that my body is God's dwelling place, by taking care of it. I follow the laws of physical health. I follow the laws related to emotional health. I follow the laws related to my intellectual health. I am filled with His Spirit that enables me to follow all of those laws to demonstrate to God and myself that, through His grace and His power, I really do love myself.

Love looks like _____

My strength in this area _____

My weakness in this area _____

Dear God, You have promised _____

You have told me that it is in my best interest to _____

I praise Your name for helping me to _____

YT " THIS IS MY DESIRE/I GIVE YOU MY HEART" THE CHRISTIAN LIFE
YT "GOD IS HERE/THERE IS A SWEET ANOINTING IN THIS SANCTUARY" HEBER VEGA

I avoid things that are harmful to my body

Proverbs 20:1, "Wine is a mocker, strong drink is raging: and whosoever is deceived thereby is not wise."

Proverbs 23:20-35, "Be not among winebibbers; among riotous eaters of flesh. For the drunkard and the glutton shall come to poverty: and drowsiness shall clothe a man with rags… For a whore is a deep ditch; and a strange woman is a narrow pit. She also lieth in wait as for a prey, and increaseth the transgressors among men. Who hath woe? who hath sorrow? who hath contentions? who hath babbling? who hath wounds without cause? who hath redness of eyes? They that tarry long at the wine; they that go to seek mixed wine. Look not thou upon the wine when it is red, when it giveth his colour in the cup, when it moveth itself aright. At the last it biteth like a serpent, and stingeth like an adder. Thine eyes shall behold strange women, and thine heart shall utter perverse things. Yea, thou shalt be as he that lieth down in the midst of the sea, or as he that lieth upon the top of a mast. They have stricken me, shalt thou say, and I was not sick; they have beaten me, and I felt it not: when shall I awake? I will seek it yet again."

Solomon speaks a lot about the damage to the body from wine and by implication, drugs. He also talks a lot about the adverse effects of illicit sex. Much of what he said about both of these areas has been verified in the medical field. Cirrhosis of the liver is primarily caused by the use of alcohol over long periods of time. Because the liver controls so many body functions, damage to the liver causes wide spread damage to the body. Yellow eyes and yellow skin result from the deposition of bilirubin. Easy bleeding and bruising occurs because the blood does not clot like it should. Amber colored urine because the liver is unable to process bilirubin like it should. Enlarged veins in the throat that bleed because blood backs up into those veins when it is unable to flow through the liver like it should. Brain and nerve damage occurs due to destruction of brain cells and faulty processing of B vitamins.

Sexually transmitted diseases, gonorrhea, syphilis, Chlamydia, AIDs, are rampant in the world and produce damage to multiple organ systems in the body that lead to blindness, infertility, neurological damage, cancer, and death. Having multiple sexual partners is known to compromise the immune system, which decreases the body's ability to defend itself against disease.

"What? know ye not that your body is the temple of the Holy Ghost which is in you, which ye have of God, and ye are not your own? For ye are bought with a price: therefore glorify God in your body, and in your spirit, which are God's," (1 Corinthians 6:19-20). When I take alcohol, drugs, and other things into my body that interfere with its normal function, I am robbing myself of the opportunity to be able to cooperate with God in fulfilling my mission and purpose. My brain does not function like it should, so my thoughts are impaired. My feelings get twisted up and my behaviors that follow are not in my best interest. I love myself by avoiding those things that are harmful to my body.

Love looks like _____

My strength in this area _____

My weakness in this area _____

Dear God, You have promised _____

You have told me that it is in my best interest to _____

I praise Your name for helping me to _____

YT "I GIVE MYSELF AWAY" WILLIAM MCDOWELL

I get adequate sleep, rest, and fresh air.
Psalm 4:8, "I will both lay me down in peace, and sleep: for thou, Lord, only makest me dwell in safety." **Genesis 2:7,** "And the Lord God formed man of the dust of the ground, and breathed into his nostrils the breath of life; and man became a living soul." **Matthew 11:28,** "Come unto me, all ye that labour and are heavy laden, and I will give you rest."

The Creator God that made me knew even before sin that I would need rest, sleep, and fresh air. He made me a reciprocal interloper with other areas of His creation. The carbon dioxide that I breathe out is used by green plants and the sun through photosynthesis to make oxygen, which I breathe in.

Research documents that there are similar benefits from being outside in the fresh air and getting a sufficient amount of sleep. As I walk around outside in areas where there are trees and open nature, I get vitamin D from the sun and fresh air from nature. My blood pressure and heart benefit from this exposure due to decreased stress and cortisol. My mood is elevated, and I am able to relax. My energy increases and my mind is sharper. With the vitamin D, my bones are protected and I have decreased chance of osteoporosis, thus decreasing the chance of getting broken bones. I have decreased risk factors for getting cancer, depression, heart attack, and stroke because my immunity is enhanced. At least twenty minutes each day in the fresh air is good but more time is very beneficial. Keeping my windows cracked to allow fresh air to circulate in the house is also a good idea.

Sleep allows my body to shut down and repair itself during two stages REM (rapid eye movement) and non-REM sleep. Circadian rhythms and homeostasis regulate sleep. Adequate sleep is age-dependent, but I need at least eight hours of sleep with at least two of those before midnight. In addition to benefits similar to those from fresh air, getting adequate sleep aids in weight loss (more fat is lost) while allowing alertness and intellectual ability to increase. Memory is improved as the ability to store memorable episodes in the brain increases. Adequate sleep regulates blood sugar and decreases stress, which decreases risk of getting diabetes. For children especially, adequate sleep improves grades and functional ability in school. Watch for snoring and sleep apnea. These are health issues in which the airway is blocked and interferes with the exchange of carbon dioxide and oxygen.

Rest is considered a period of body inactivity where we do not perform a lot of physical activity. Rest was so important in God's creation plan that He provided one whole day at the end of the creation week that He designated "Sabbath" just for rest. "Remember the Sabbath day…six days shalt thou labor…but the seventh day is the Sabbath of the Lord Thy God. In it thou shalt do no work…(God) rested the seventh day…" Rest reduces stress and increases my mood, mental clarity, creativity, and motivation. The Sabbath, set aside for rest by God, allows me to spend time with God getting to know Him as He reveals Himself to me in line with "and this is life eternal, that you know God and Jesus…" (John 17:3) Come, Jesus says, and I will give you rest.

Love looks like _____

My strength in this area _____

My weakness in this area _____

Dear God, You have promised _____

You have told me that it is in my best interest to _____

I praise Your name for helping me to _____

YT "Forever yours" Whitley Phipps

MAY 10 I TAKE CARE OF MY SOCIAL LIFE.

Acts 2:46, "Day by day continuing with one mind in the temple, and breaking bread from house to house, they were taking their meals together with gladness and sincerity of heart."

Evaluating my social interactions and taking care of my social life helps me cooperate with the Holy Spirit by activating the hormones and processes that God has placed within me to contribute to my physical, emotional, intellectual, and spiritual health and growth. A number of benefits occur. I live longer. I boost my immune system decreasing the chance of getting colds, flu, and even some types of cancer. I boost my brain health, lowering the risk of dementia. I have feelings of well-being and decreased feelings of depression.

Not only eating the nourishing things that my body needs, but eating with someone else is important. "Breaking bread from house to house, taking meals together with gladness and sincerity of heart" is in my best interest and in the best interest of those that I am eating with. Walking through my neighborhood and saying hello benefits me as it benefits others. Babysitting my grandkids not only provides the opportunity to influence their long term outcomes, it provides joy for me that releases oxytocin and endorphins needed for bonding, trust, and obedience to God's commands.

Hebrews 10:25, "Not forsaking the assembling of ourselves together, as the manner of some is; but exhorting one another, and so much the more, as ye see the day approaching." Going to church is taking care of my social life. It benefits me in many ways. It also benefits those with whom I come in contact, empowering me to fulfill the commandment to love others as I love myself.

Knowing my impact on others is important in my social life. Taking a personality inventory helps me to know the tendencies that I have that impact my social interactions. OCEAN is a tool I can use to consider how I impact others. Do I have **openness**, do I like to learn new things and enjoy new experiences? Am I **conscientious,** am I reliable and prompt? Am I an **extravert**, do I get my energy from interacting with others? Am I **agreeable**, friendly, cooperative, compassionate? What is my level of **neuroticism**, emotional stability, negative emotions? I love myself through socializing with others.

Love looks like _____

My strength in this area _____

My weakness in this area _____

Dear God, You have promised_____

You have told me that it is in my best interest to_____

I praise Your name for helping me to_____

YT "We're gonna have a good time" Macedonia Mass Choir

I taste and see that the Lord is good.
Psalm 34:8-10, "O taste and see that the Lord is good: blessed is the man that trusteth in him. O fear the Lord, ye his saints: for there is no want to them that fear him. The young lions do lack, and suffer hunger: but they that seek the Lord shall not want any good thing."

I love myself by knowing that I have someone in my life that I can love and trust. Someone that I can believe in. Someone that has promised, and keeps that promise, to be with me forever. To be my friend forever. To be my protector. To be my light to guide my footsteps. To save me from myself.

"This poor man cried, and the Lord heard him, and saved him out of all his troubles. The angel of the Lord encampeth round about them that fear him, and delivereth them. O taste and see that the Lord is good: blessed is the man that trusteth in him. O fear the Lord, ye his saints: for there is no want to them that fear him," (Psalm 34:6-9).

I need someone that I can depend on to be merciful with my frequent misdoings like You were with David after he had Uriah killed. I need someone who loves me in spite of the mistakes I make as You loved Adam and Eve after they disobeyed and ate the fruit. I need someone in my life that can model kindness, love, gentleness, tenderness like You did when You raised the widow of Nain's dead son. I need someone in my life who will never lie to me similar to what You did when You told the woman at the well that the man she was with was not her husband.

I need someone to be there with me in the midnight hour when I am alone and afraid, like You were with Paul and Silas singing in jail. I need someone in my life who knows what I need and what I want and can provide it at the right time like You when You sent manna six days a week for the children of Israel in the wilderness. I need someone in my life who will speak words of encouragement to me when I am down and discouraged, like You spoke to Elijah when he ran from Jezebel. I need someone to walk with me when I am in trouble like the "Son of Man" walked in the fiery furnace with Shadrach, Meshach, and Abednego. Someone to be with me when I am in the lion's den like the angels You sent to be with Daniel that shut the lions mouths. I need someone that makes me feel accepted, wanted, needed, and inspires me to want to be in His presence forever like the woman felt who the men were about to stone because she had committed adultery. I need someone that tells me He loves me and wants to be with me like You did every evening when You came down into the

Garden to be with Adam and Eve. I need someone in my life that tells me when I am wrong but tells me in such a way as to help me focus on moving forward, not backward, like You did for Cain when he killed his brother. I need someone in my life, so that when my friends let me down, I have someone else I know for sure that I can turn to. I need someone in my life that will empower me to live my dreams like You did for Joseph. I need someone that can be my everything. I need You, Jesus. I have tasted and I see that You are good, very good!

YT "I surrender" Brooklyn Tabernacle Choir
YT "My Redeemer Lives" Nicholas Mullen
YT "I wanna be your everything" Manhattans

I CHOOSE LIFE OVER DEATH.
Deuteronomy 30:19-20, "… I have set before you life and death, blessing and cursing: therefore choose life, that both thou and thy seed may live. That thou mayest love the LORD thy God, *and* that thou mayest obey his voice, and that thou mayest cleave unto him: for he *is* thy life, and the length of thy days." **1 Corinthians 13:4-7,** "Love…always protects, always trusts, always hopes, always perseveres."

Death is not just the cessation of the heart beat and respirations. The second death is total, absolute, forever separation from the God that loves me. I show that I love myself when I choose life over death. John 17: 3, "And this is life eternal, that they might know thee the only true God, and Jesus Christ, whom thou hast sent." God intended from the very beginning of creation that I should live forever. While I am living in a world of sin, there will be many times that are hard and difficult to survive, but I love myself by choosing to trust, hope, and persevere when I have those down times.

Suicide is a major public health concern. Suicidal ideation refers to thinking about or planning to kill myself. In 2017, 47,000 people chose to end their lives. It was the second leading cause of death in the ages ten to thirty-four. It is the second leading cause of death in teenagers. The elderly, often feeling lonely and powerless, are also at great risk of suicide. Risk factors for suicide include: family history of suicide, previous suicide attempt, depression, feelings of hopelessness, history of alcohol and substance abuse, history of childhood sexual abuse, chronic illness, easy access to lethal methods, social isolation.

There are times in my life when I cry. There are times in my life when I don't feel like going on. Times when I don't want to deal with the pain any more. Times when I feel all alone. Times when no one knows what I am going through. There are times in my life when I feel like just giving up. Those are the times when I am at greatest risk of hurting or killing myself. I must remind myself during these times that I truly love myself. I am reminded that God has a plan for my life, and He wants me to live to carry it out. I remember that He is in charge of my life. I seek my support system. I get the help and support that I need to make it through the crisis time. I cry out, "Father, help me." I call my best friend just to talk. I remember and listen to the song "Peace be Still" by James Cleveland, a song learned in childhood, that helps me know I can get through my hard times. I recite poems that I learned in high school, "A psalm of life" or "Filling Daddy's place." I recall bible verses that remind me that God is right here with me to heal my broken heart and He has no problem with me calling the National Suicide Prevention lifeline if I need to have someone to talk to, 800-272-TALK. I love myself by not hurting or killing myself but by trusting, hoping, persevering, and getting the help I need when I have down times.

Love looks like _____

My strength in this area _____

My weakness in this area _____

Dear God, You have promised _____

You have told me that it is in my best interest to _____

I praise Your name for helping me to _____

YT "I ALMOST LET GO" KURT CARR
YT "LORD DO IT FOR ME" JAMES CLEVELAND YT "THERE'LL COME A TIME" BETTY EVERETT
YT "I FEEL LIKE GOING ON" 5 HEARTBEATS

I AVOID SEXUAL SIN.
Exodus 20:14, "Thou shalt not commit adultery." **Hosea 4:11,** "Whoredom and wine and new wine take away the heart." **1 Corinthians 6:13, 16, 18 ,** "…now the body is not for fornication, but for the Lord…know ye not that he which is joined to an harlot is one body? For two, said he, shall be one flesh…he that committeth fornication sinneth against his own body."

I love myself by not engaging in sex outside of the context in which God clearly defines it for me. Genesis 2:24, "Therefore shall a man leave his father and mother, and shall cleave unto his wife, and they shall be one flesh." The two become one flesh by the exchange of DNA, genetic material that determines who I am. This is mediated through sexual intercourse. When a man has sex and ejaculates, 40-200 million of his sperm cells with his DNA is placed within the vaginal tract of the woman. When these cells die inside the woman's body, the debris from the dead cells are recycled in the woman's cells, including the DNA. During that ejaculation, the penis acts like a vacuum, collecting material from the female, including her cells with her DNA, from the woman's vaginal tract. Research has found male DNA in the brain cells of females. Through this exchange of DNA during sexual intercourse, God's statement of the two becoming one flesh is mediated.

When a person gets a transplanted kidney or other organs, cells on that organ will die and other cells are generated from the transplanted organ with the donor's DNA. It has been demonstrated that an organ recipient may have tastes and characteristics that he or she did not have before the transplant and when investigated, found to be similar traits that the organ donor has.

When one has sexual intercourse with another, the two become one flesh. When God made Eve, he took a rib from Adam with cells containing Adam's DNA, the first stem cell transplant, to make her. Ephesians 5:29, "For no man ever yet hated his own body." Eve was literally his body. She had Adam's DNA. "…by one man, sin entered the world."

When a person is joined to a harlot, they become "one body." Literally he will never walk away from her. Neither will she ever be free of him. They have become "one." When having sex with multiple persons, the immune system, which normally adapts to recognize his cells as her cells and her cells as his in the singular marital sexual exchange, breaks down, which increases the risk of getting various diseases. God, who made me in His image and loves me more than I love myself, knows that it is in my best interest to engage in sex only as He has decreed. I love myself by engaging in sex only with my spouse.

Love looks like _____

My strength in this area _____

My weakness in this area _____

Dear God, You have promised _____

You have told me that it is in my best interest to _____

I praise Your name for helping me to _____

YT "Only you" Platters
YT "Unchained melody" Righteous Brothers

I HONOR MY PARENTS AND THE NAME THAT THEY HAVE SHARED WITH ME Exodus 20:12, "Honor thy father and thy mother that thy days may be long upon the land which the Lord thy God giveth thee." **Ephesians 6:1-3,** "Children obey you parents in the Lord, for this is right…"

Honor means "high" respect, great esteem. I love myself by honoring my parents. God's love promise to me for doing so is long life. That promise suggests that my health is protected by honoring and respecting my parents. The command, in my best interest, tells me to honor my parents, even if they do not honor me. My responsibility is to honor them regardless of how they may treat me. The end results, long life, relate only to my own actions. A woman carries a baby within her uterus for approximately nine months. During that time, the fetus acts much like we describe a parasite, it exists at the expense of its host. The goal of the baby is to preserve its own life, not the life of the mother. Her hold on fluid increases anywhere from four to five liters putting additional stress on her heart. Chemicals are released that makes her blood clot more easily, increasing the risk of stroke or a blood clot in the heart or lungs. The baby receives all of its nourishment and oxygen from the mother's blood. The mother is responsible for getting rid of the baby's waste that joins with her circulatory system. The baby is essentially a parasite, living at the expense of the mother.

I am reminded by my eyes on a regular basis that I have their DNA. I look like them. I have their blood in my veins. I am thankful for my parents. How helpless I was when I came into this world! I could not feed myself. I couldn't walk and had to be carried. I slept in the bed next to them and felt their warmth. I belonged to them. I am alive today because they took care of my needs.

I ask them for advice from their years of experience of handling problems. Proverbs 1:8-9, "Hear, my son, your father's instruction, and do not forsake your mother's teaching…" Not only does that benefit me, it makes them feel pretty special when I ask for their advice. I want them to live a long time so that my children can benefit from their expertise as I have. Hebrews 10:25 tells me to encourage others. My parents are on that list as they get older and need my help. In Mark 7:9-13, Jesus gets on me for not taking care of my parents as they get older. Paul says I am worse than an infidel when I abuse my parents. Old pictures remind me of living at the foot of that mountain in West Virginia where I walked a half mile to get water to do the laundry with my mother. I remember the garden that they planted to feed me. I remember the peach and cherry pies made from the trees not too far from our house. I remember the sacrifices they made for me. I remember my father taking me with him on his job and buying me potato chips and candy. I love myself by honoring my parents and protecting their name.

Love looks like _____

My strength in this area _____

My weakness in this area _____

Dear God, You have promised_____

You have told me that it is in my best interest to_____

I praise Your name for helping me to_____

YT "Sadie"

I am honest with myself.
Proverbs 17: 3, "Thou hast proved mine heart; thou has visited me in the night; thou has tried me, and shalt find nothing; I am purposed that my mouth shall not transgress." **Exodus 20:16,** "Thou shalt not bear false witness against thy neighbor."

I admit to myself how I truly feel, why I do what I do, because I truly love myself. When I am wrong or have made a mistake, I am willing to admit it. I reflect and share my true desires and motivations, my weaknesses. I will not wear a mask to hide myself from myself or from others. If I am going to be honest with you, I have to first be honest with myself. It is essential that I be honest with myself, so that I can honestly identify my needs and wants and be empowered to move forward toward my goals. I hear the negative opinions others may have of me, reflect on what I may be doing to impact those opinions, then consider the value of those opinions in deciding how to grow to love myself and others better. When I am honest with myself, I can be open, have inner joy, peace, and freedom. I have clarity about what I need from myself and from you. Being honest with myself is foundational to changing my life to move in positive directions. It takes away my need to judge and gossip about others.

I know that I am being honest with myself when I hear an inappropriate joke and I say with love and tenderness that it is inappropriate. I gently say no to your request when it is not in your or my best interest to say yes. I tell you kindly that I am not interested in doing what you want me to do rather than making an excuse. I don't hide the truth from you because I am afraid you will reject me or not like me. I am honest with myself about unhealthy addictions that are impacting my life.

Jacob spent many of his early years in life lying to himself and others. He reaped his reward when his father-in-law gave him Leah to wife instead of Rachel and when his father-in-law was deceptive after Joseph worked for him for years and was not given his just payment. But when returning home, God, who loved Jacob, allowed Jacob to wrestle with Him all night, then changed his name from Jacob (Supplanter) to Israel, "…for as a prince hast thou power with God and with men, and hast prevailed," Genesis 32:29. It is in my best interest to be honest with myself, so that I can also be honest with you.

Love looks like _____

My strength in this area _____

My weakness in this area _____

Dear God, You have promised _____

You have told me that it is in my best interest to _____

I praise Your name for helping me to _____

YT "Truth and Honesty" Aretha Franklin "What a wonderful world this would be" Otis Redding

I AM NOT JEALOUS OR COVETOUS OF WHAT BELONGS TO YOU.
Proverbs 14:30, "A sound heart is the life of the flesh: but envy the rottenness of the bones." **Exodus 20:17** "Thou shalt not covet thy neighbor's…" **Proverbs 15:27,** "He that is greedy of gain troubleth his own house…"

God knows that envy and covetousness are not in my best interest. Long term, the results of those emotions trigger the fight or flight hormones which impact my health. I feel anxious and have obsessive thoughts. My blood pressure and heart rate will be elevated from the epinephrine. I get sick to my stomach. I want the wrong things. I want the right things for the wrong reason. I want the right thing, but it is the wrong time or the wrong amount. How do I respond when I don't get what I want? Galatians 5:16-17. Do I walk by the Spirit and not carry out the desires of my flesh or do I give in and get what I want "by any means necessary?" How much time do I spend dwelling on the wrong thing that I want? The children of Israel kept looking back at the fish and onions that they had in Egypt, rejecting the manna God gave them, they asked for meat. God gave it to them and many of them died with the quail in their mouths. The Israelites rejected the sufficiency of God for their own desires. 1 Timothy 6:9, "…those who want to get rich fall into temptation and a snare and many foolish and harmful desires which plunge men into ruin and destruction."

When I am jealous of others or desire to have what belongs to someone else, it can blind me and alter my perception of reality. Jealousy characteristically stems from deep inside of me related to my inability to see my worth and appreciate all the things God has gifted me with. I am insecure and unsure of myself, and I think that you are better than I am and I relate that to the things you have or the talents you possess. If I have what you have, that will make me better, others will like me. Achan coveted a robe, silver, and gold, so he stole them and hid them. His whole family died as a result. Joshua 7:20-22. David coveted Uriah's wife, so he had him murdered to get her. Gehazi coveted the property of Namaan, lied to get it, and ended up with leprosy. I know that I am God's child, an heir to His throne, that He shall supply all my needs, that He loved me enough to die for me establishing my infinite worth to Him. I have no need to covet what He has given you or be jealous of you.

Love looks like _____

My strength in this area _____

My weakness in this area _____

Dear God, You have promised _____

You have told me that it is in my best interest to _____

I praise Your name for helping me to _____

YT "The Potter" Wintley Phipps
YT "No need to fear" Wintley Phipps
YT "My help" Brooklyn Tabernacle Choir

I LIVE A VICTORIOUS LIFE

I John 5:4, "For whatever is born of God overcomes the world. And this is the victory that overcometh the world, even our faith." **Proverbs 21:31,** "The horse is made ready for the day of battle, but victory rests with the Lord."

I love myself by living a consistently victorious life against a lot of different odds. I know what God's plan for my life is, and I have faith that the outcomes from that plan will be exactly as He has said in Jeremiah 29:11, "For I know the plans I have for you…plans to prosper you and not to harm you, plans to give you hope and a future." Faith in God's plan anchors me to His purpose. From this plan, my mission and purpose in life are identified. I establish my goals with outcome criteria identified in line with my mission and purpose. My plans include strategies for success in using the gifts God has given me to live that mission and accomplish those goals. When I am distracted and tend to move away from my victorious life, God reminds me of His plan, my mission, and my purpose to re-focus my attention. I am unafraid to move forward in cooperation with God to fulfill that purpose because He has reminded me of His command to be strong and of a good courage in Joshua 1:9. I recognize that fear is an inhibiting factor to living a victorious life. I seek advice from God and the presence of His Spirit on a daily basis, so I can consistently move forward to the goal.

After Joshua and the Israelites had taken Ai in battle, Adonizedec, king of Jerusalem, gathered the Amorites and other kings to move to take Gibeon, a great city, in response to Joshua's victory and fear that his kingdom would experience even greater losses. The king of Gibeon asked Joshua for help. God gave Joshua a message in Joshua 10:8, "And the Lord said unto Joshua, Fear them not, for I have delivered them into thine hand…" God made the sun stand still that day, and Joshua won the battle.

My victory is to overcome the world. I face life's challenges as a soldier in God's army, clad in the armor of God in Ephesians 6. I am girt with truth; I have on the breastplate of Jesus' righteousness, I use the shield of faith and the sword of God's word, and I am shod with the gospel of peace. God has promised me that my victory that will overcome the world is my faith and the victory rests with Him. Knowing that victory is mine, I am humbled, knowing that the battle is not mine, it's the Lord's. I have assurance for God's promises are yes and amen. I blossom with joy as I move forward toward the goal. I watch my heart with all diligence. I am focused. I get to know God and you, and because I love you, I share my victory with you, so that you can be encouraged to move forward with the plan God has for you.

Love looks like _____

My strength in this area _____

My weakness in this area _____

Dear God, You have promised _____

You have told me that it is in my best interest to _____

I praise Your name for helping me to _____

YT "The Battle is not yours" Yolanda Adams
YT "It wasn't easy" CeCe Winans YT "Celebration" Kool/Gang
YT "Miracle" Whitney Houston

I SPEAK WORDS OF LIFE TO MYSELF AS I WALK IN THE LIGHT.
Proverbs 16:24, "Pleasant words are as an honeycomb, sweet to the soul, and health to the bones." **1 John 1:7,** "But if we walk in the light, as he is in the light, we have fellowship one with another, and the blood of Jesus Christ his Son cleanseth us from all sin."

The Wernicke and Broca areas of the brain help to process language. The meaning of the words I say to myself and others is processed in the left hemisphere of my brain while the feeling associated with those words are processed on the right side of my brain. What I say to others, I hear myself. The words that I hear from others are processed in the same way. The words that I speak to myself are powerful for in the tongue is the power of life or death. Pleasant words promote learning in the brain, increase my motivation, and my resilience by stimulating the release of serotonin and dopamine.

I am reminded of the power of words when I remember that God spoke, and it was done. He commanded and it stood fast. Words cannot change reality, but they can change my perception of reality thus impacting my behavior. "…I have called thee by thy name; thou art mine," (Isaiah 43:1). God recognizes how important it is for me to hear my name called. He knows that calling my name impacts my perception of who I am. "And the LORD came, and stood, and called as at other times, Samuel, Samuel…" (I Samuel 3:10). I say to myself, I belong to the Creator of the universe. I speak words to myself that encourage high achievement. I speak words of truth in such a way as to build myself up, not break me down. I speak words of love, joy, peace, and comfort to help me cooperate with God's plan.

"Thy Word is a lamp unto my feet and a light unto my path," (Psalm 119:105) "The Word was made flesh and dwelt among us," (John 1:14). "Then spake Jesus again unto them, saying, I am the light of the world: he that followeth me…shall have the light of life," (John 8:12). There is no life without light. I was reminded of this on a walk through the woods when I saw a vine growing up from the ground that had wrapped itself around multiple trees, always reaching and moving upwards to where it could receive the most light. Even though the vine had all the water and nourishment it needed supplied from the ground, it could not grow without light. I hide His words in my heart that I may speak the words of God to myself, so that I will have the light needed to have life. I walk in the light of life, so that I will fellowship with you and the blood of Jesus cleanses both of us from all sin. Knowing that how I say the words impact my feelings, it is important that I read the word of God out loud, and I say those words with feeling, so that both areas of the brain are impacted in a way that increases my knowledge and love of God, myself, and you.

Love looks like _____

My strength in this area _____

My weakness in this area _____

Dear God, You have promised_____

You have told me that it is in my best interest to_____

I praise Your name for helping me to_____

YT "Walk in the light" Georgia Mass Choir
YT "I choose you again" Whitley Phipps

I DO NOT GIVE OTHERS CONTROL OVER MY THOUGHTS AND FEELINGS

Philippians 2:5, "Let this mind be in you which is also in Christ Jesus." **Matthew 5:8,** "Blessed are the pure in heart for they shall see God."

Thoughts and feelings are determinants of behavior. I love myself by maintaining control over my thoughts and my feelings. I refuse to accede this control over me to Satan or to you. Proverbs 4:23 tells me to guard my heart with diligence because the emotional attachments I make will determine the direction of my life. I will not accede this control to others because Luke 6:45 tells me that "a good man out of the goodness in his heart will do good things, while a bad person out of the evil in his heart will do bad things" and everything I do will come from the feelings I have inside. Jeremiah 17:9, "The heart is deceitful above all things and desperately wicked, who can know it?" As much as I may love you, I cannot give you that kind of power over me.

The senses are the way to my thoughts and feelings: sight, hearing, touch, smell, and taste. I receive information via my senses that I process. This impacts my outcome behaviors that will be good or evil.

I live in the country, and many times people will pass me on the road and comment later that they saw me and I didn't wave or see them. I remind them that I do as Solomon suggests in Proverbs 4:28, "Let your eyes look directly ahead. And let your gaze be fixed straight in front of you." This also reminds me to be careful of what I read, what I listen to, and what I watch on television or view on the internet. Peter reinforces this for me in I Peter 1:13, "Therefore prepare your minds for action, keep sober in spirit, fix your hope completely on the grace to be brought to you at the revelation of Jesus Christ." I am reminded that it may taste good, feel good, or smell good, but it may influence my thoughts and feelings to do evil, not good. Resource information to assist me in cooperating with God to guard my thoughts and feelings, so that I can cooperate with Him in His plan for my life is found throughout His word, the shield of faith needed to be able to quench all the fiery darts of the wicked. Ephesians 6:16.

Adam blamed Eve when God asked about eating the fruit. Eve blamed the snake. When I attempt to blame others for my misdoings, I am essentially saying that I have given them control over me. When I say, "You made me angry," when I say, "You made me do it," I am conceding that I have given you power and control over my thoughts and feelings. That kind of power and control, I am only willing to accede to God who loves me so much, He sent His Son to die for me. I want a heart like Jesus' heart. I want a mind like Jesus' mind.

Love looks like _____

My strength in this area _____

My weakness in this area _____

Dear God, You have promised _____

You have told me that it is in my best interest to _____

I praise Your name for helping me to _____

YT "My Redeemer lives" CeCe Winans
YT "A heart like yours" CeCe Winans

I live by mission and accomplish the goals, and plans for my life. I live my dreams.
Psalms 37:4-5, "Delight thyself also in the Lord: and he shall give thee the desires of thine heart. Commit thy way unto the Lord; trust also in him; and he shall bring it to pass." **Psalm 20:4,** "Grant thee according to thine own heart, and fulfil all thy counsel." May He give you the desire of your heart and make all your plans come true. **1 Chronicles 4:10,** "And Jabez called on the God of Israel, saying, Oh that thou wouldest bless me indeed, and enlarge my coast, and that thine hand might be with me, and that thou wouldest keep me from evil, that it may not grieve me! And God granted him that which he requested."

Eric Erickson, a well-known psychologist, describes eight stages of growth that a person goes through in life. The last stage of that growth is called "ego vs. integrity," and its core value is wisdom. During that stage, I will reflect on my life to answer the question, "Is it okay to have been me?" I will feel a sense of integrity if I look back over my life and determine that I have been successful. Achieving success requires that there have been goals that I have set and reached for myself. Research documents those that weather this stage most successfully have early in life identified a mission, with goals and a plan. This is very much in harmony with what God tells me when He reminds me that before I was conceived in my mother's womb, He had a plan for my life, plans to bring me to a good end. He promises me that with that plan for my life that He gives me everything I need to accomplish it.

In 1 Corinthians 12, He lists numerous gifts that He gives that brings balance to teams working in harmony to accomplish His goal of unity and the salvation of man. My job is to cooperate with Him in identifying the mission, goals, plans, and gifts that He has in place for my life. When I recognize that He that made me and loves me knows me best, His vision and plan for me becomes the center of my dreams. I delight myself in Him and He gives me the desires of my heart. I commit my plans to Him, trust Him, and He makes it happen. This is true in every area of my life, whether I am deciding on a career or looking for a life partner. Jesus knew when He was a child what His mission was. God began to tell me in childhood that I wanted to be in the medical field. He opened the doors and provided what I needed to move in that direction. He promised that He would make my plans come true just as He did for Jabez when he called on Him and asked that He enlarge his territory. God was with him, kept him from evil, and enlarged his territory as he asked. When I acknowledge His sovereignty, trust Him from the foundations of testing and proving Him as He has told me to do, then I know that I can believe in His goodness and trust Him to do what He says He will do. I then "step into the Red Sea," remembering that the waters did not open to allow Israel to pass through until the first step was taken. I know that because I have asked for His guidance and help, I will accomplish my goals.

Love looks like _____

My strength in this area _____

My weakness in this area _____

Dear God, You have promised_____

You have told me that it is in my best interest to_____

I praise Your name for helping me to_____

YT "Don't leave me by myself" Whitley Phipps
YT "I will run to thee" Alvin Slaughter

I RECOGNIZE, DEVELOP, AND USE MY GIFTS AND TALENTS FOR MY BEST OUTCOMES AND THE BEST OUTCOMES OF THOSE WHOM I LOVE

I Peter 4:10, "As every man hath received the gift, even so minister the same one to another, as good stewards of the manifold grace of God." **Exodus 31:1-5,** "See I have called by name Bezaleel… And I have filled him with the spirit of God, in wisdom, and in understanding, and in knowledge, and in all manner of workmanship, to devise cunning works…to work in all manner of workmanship."

I have gifts and talents that I recognize, develop, and use for my best outcomes and the best outcomes of those that I love as a measure of how much I know and love myself. I recognize that "Every good gift and every perfect gift is from above, and cometh down from the Father of lights," James 1:17

"Who taught the sun where to stand in the morn-ing? Who told the ocean you can only come this far? Who showed the moon where to hide 'til evening? Whose words alone can catch a falling star?" Words from the song, 'My Redeemer lives' - a strong reinforcement related to my gifts and talents. The same God to which creation testifies to as regulating the orbits of the universe, placed gifts and talents within me, to be recognized, developed, and used for the best outcomes of myself and others as a reminder of His love and the love He wants me to have for Him, myself, and others.

I can bake a loaf of bread. That's a gift I can use to feed myself and others. I know how to change the oil in my car. That's a talent He has blessed me with to help that older neighbor next door who still drives but doesn't have the same mobility that I have. I can teach a five-year-old how to add, so that her math scores are improved. I can listen to you. I am developing that skill, so that I can be more effective in loving you. I can sit next to you and hold your hand, so that you feel warmth and acceptance. He is still working with me to develop that skill, but He promises me in James 1:5, " If any of you lack wisdom, let him ask of God, that giveth to all men liberally, and upbraideth not; and it shall be given him."

I ask myself, what comes easier to me than anyone else? Does it set my heart on fire? What is important to me? What are the injustices that I see that really get on my nerves? I listen to what I complain about that I keep wanting others to fix. I ask family and friends what do they see as my strengths. I take the Strengths Finder assessment on the internet. I use my God-given gifts to glorify His name. I acknowledge God's role in giving me gifts and talents. "I praise you, for I am fearfully and wonderfully made. Wonderful are your works," Psalm 139:14

Love looks like _____

My strength in this area _____

My weakness in this area _____

Dear God, You have promised _____

You have told me that it is in my best interest to _____

I praise Your name for helping me to _____

YT "Use me Lord" James Cleveland
YT "I am a promise" Baby Reena YT "My Redeemer lives" Nicole Mullen

I know my strengths, weaknesses, and my resources.
Psalm 118:14, "The Lord is my strength and song, and is become my salvation. **Philippians 4:13,** "I can do all things through Jesus Christ who strengthens me. **Matt 6:33,** "But seek ye first the kingdom of God, and his righteousness; and all these things shall be added unto you.

Romans 15:4, "For whatsoever things were written aforetime were written for our learning, that we…might have hope." **Adam** took a look at that good looking woman, lost his mind, and let feelings rule his better judgment. He ate the fruit Eve offered him. **Jezebel** was unafraid to speak up and go after what she wanted, even though the long term outcomes were evil and were not in her best interest. **Ahab** was afraid to take a leadership role, had deep feelings for that good looking, powerful woman and chose behaviors that overruled his upbringing and training that led to poor outcomes. **Lot's** strength is displayed in his humility, hospitality, and using his resources to help others. He invited strangers into his house after bowing low to greet them, fed them, and protected them from homosexual men that tried to take them to their party. The "strangers" were actually angels that had come to warn Lot to leave Sodom. Genesis 19:1-38, **Job** would rise early in the morning and offer burnt offerings for each of his children "in case they had sinned and cursed God in their hearts." Job 1:1-22, **David** used his slingshot skills to protect himself, but he knew the real source of his power." I come to you in the name of the Lord." David also loved good-looking women inappropriately. He had sex with another man's wife and had him killed but showed his strength when he took ownership for his wrong doing, confessed his sin, married Bathsheba, and ask God to give him a clean heart (Psalm 51). **Martha** knew how to make a good meal and feed guests. **Mary**, her sister's strength, was knowing how to listen as she sat at the feet of Jesus. **Deborah** was unafraid to go forward and fight in battle. Having seen God's interventions in the past, she had confidence that He would give victory in the future. She was unafraid to stand up as a woman in a society ruled by men to lead and govern as God directed her. **Vashti** was unafraid to say no to a king that insisted she parade her good looks and body in front of his cronies. She was willing to lose her position as queen to stand up for what she knew was right. **Esther** was afraid that she would be rejected by the king if he knew she was Jewish, but she used her beauty to obtain a good position that later benefited her people. She turned a weakness into a strength by listening to her older cousin who had experience with the

Lord. **Peter** was afraid of what people would do to him if they knew he was associated with Jesus, so he denied Him three times.

Knowing my strengths, weaknesses, and resources is critical to my ability to love myself.

Love looks like _____

My strength in this area _____

My weakness in this area _____

Dear God, You have promised _____

You have told me that it is in my best interest to _____

I praise Your name for helping me to _____

YT "MUST JESUS BARE THE CROSS ALONE" SAM COOKE
YT "AIN'T NO NEED TO WORRY" ANITA BAKER/WINANS

I GET UP WHEN I FALL DOWN.
Proverbs 24: 16, "For though the righteous fall seven times, they rise again, but the wicked stumble when calamity strikes."

When about 3,000 Israelites soldiers went to fight at Ai and thirty-six of them were killed in the battle, the others fled. Achan had stolen items in a previous battle and caused the Israelites to be cursed, resulting in the loss of the thirty-six lives at Ai. When Joshua heard that the soldiers had fled from such a few men, he fell on his face and cried to God about how bad it looked for the soldiers to flee. God said to Joshua In Johsua 7:10, "…Get thee up; wherefore liest thou thus upon thy face?" He then told Joshua why the soldiers had died and what to do next. "Up, sanctify the people, and say, sanctify yourselves against tomorrow: for thus saith the LORD God of Israel, There is an accursed thing in the midst of thee, O Israel: thou canst not stand before thine enemies, until ye take away the accursed thing from among you." Joshua got up and took care of the problem with Achan.

When David's son, Absalom, was killed while trying to kill his father and steal his throne, David fell apart emotionally, as most parents would do when a child is killed. "But the king covered his face, and the king cried with a loud voice, O my son Absalom, O Absalom, my son, my son! And Joab came into the house to the king and said, Thou hast shamed this day the faces of all thy servants, which this day have saved thy life, and the lives of thy sons and of thy daughters, and the lives of thy wives, and the lives of thy concubines; in that thou lovest thine enemies, and hatest thy friends. For thou hast declared this day, that thou regardest neither princes nor servants: for this day, I perceive that if Absalom had lived, and all we had died this day, then it had pleased thee well. Now therefore arise, go forth and speak comfortably unto thy servants: for I swear by the LORD, if thou go not forth, there will not tarry one with thee this night: and that will be worse unto thee than all the evil that befell thee from thy youth until now" (2 Samuel 19:4-7). Joab confronted him with his behavior and the effect that it was having on the people who could have died had Absalom lived. David got up, did what he needed to do, and was restored to his rightful position as king.

When I fall down, I cry. I hurt. I am disappointed. I am ashamed. I am angry. I am frustrated. But the same Jesus that spoke to the disciples on the Mount of Transfiguration when they fell down and were afraid, assures me in Matthew 17:7, "…Jesus came and touched them, and said, Arise, and be not afraid." When I fall down, I get up and keep pressing forward to the mark of my high calling in Christ Jesus.

Love looks like _____

My strength in this area _____

My weakness in this area _____

Dear God, You have promised _____

You have told me that it is in my best interest to _____

I praise Your name for helping me to _____

YT "We fall down" Donnie McClurkin
YT "Keep on Pushin" Impression

I KNOW HOW TO HANDLE MY FINANCES.
Romans 13:8, "Owe no man anything, but to love one another: for he that loveth another hath fulfilled the law."

Proverbs 3:9, "Honour the Lord with thy substance, and with the first fruits of all thine increase." **Proverbs 11:15**, "He that is surety for a stranger shall smart for it: and he that hateth suretiship is sure."

God knows that "…where your treasure is, there will your heart be also" (Matthew 6: 21). He wants me to handle my finances in such a way that He will be able to say to me "…Well done, thou good and faithful servant: thou hast been faithful over a few things, I will make thee ruler over many things: enter thou into the joy of thy lord" (Matthew 25:21).

He gives wise instructions on how to handle my finances because He knows "a good name is rather to be chosen than great riches, and loving favour rather than silver and gold" (Proverbs 22:1). He tells me to start by recognizing that all that I have comes from Him and in acknowledging that fact return ten percent of whatever He gives me, tithe, to Him. "Bring ye all the tithes into the storehouse, that there may be meat in mine house, and prove me now herewith, saith the LORD of hosts, if I will not open you the windows of heaven, and pour you out a blessing, that there shall not be room enough to receive it" (Malachi 3:10). He promises when I do that He will reward me. The firstfruits of all my increase, honors Him.

He tells me not to owe anyone anything but love. I avoid credit cards and borrowing money. I have and manage a budget. I understand and prioritize my expenses. I know my income limitations, and I stay within my boundaries. I differentiate my needs and my wants and balance my wants, so that I spend money wisely. I create an emergency fund and save money for unexpected events, such as job loss, sickness, or other life events. He tells me that it is not wise to be surety for someone else, i.e. take responsibility for someone else's finances, co-signing for credit, loans. If I should find it necessary to borrow money, I pay it off as quickly as possible so that I can be free. I educate myself on saving, investing, and spending money wisely. I am honest in my financial dealings. I don't cheat. I do an honest day's work for an honest day's pay. I render to Caesar what belongs to him and to God that which belongs to Him. I share what He gives me with others in need. I am reminded that if I keep my hand closed, He cannot put anything in it, but as I am pouring from my cup, He is constantly refilling it.

Handling my finances effectively makes life smoother for me. It reduces my stress. It honors God to know that an heir to His throne handles wisely what He has given me and that I can be trusted with more that He wants to give me. I anticipate hearing Him say to me, "…Well done…thou has been faithful over a few things, I will make thee ruler over many things…"

Love looks like _____

My strength in this area _____

My weakness in this area _____

Dear God, You have promised_____

You have told me that it is in my best interest to_____

I praise Your name for helping me to_____

YT "TO GOD BE THE GLORY" ANDRE CROUCH
YT "I HAVE NOTHING WITHOUT YOU" WHITNEY HOUSTON

I USE MY INFLUENCE TO IMPACT OUTCOMES FOR GOOD.
Titus 2:7, "In all things shewing thyself a pattern of good works: in doctrine shewing uncorruptness, gravity, sincerity."

Proverbs 13:20, "He that walketh with wise men shall be wise: but a companion of fools shall be destroyed."

Matthew 5:16, "Let your light so shine before men, that they may see your good works, and glorify your Father which is in heaven."

Influence. The power to change a person in an indirect but important way. I will influence people in either one of two directions, for good or for evil. I choose to influence others for good.

Psychologists have identified several researched principles that impact my ability to influence others. Interestingly enough they each have a biblical foundation. **Reciprocit**y – Do unto others as you would have them do unto you. Matthew 7:12. **Consistency** – "Therefore, my beloved brethren, be ye stedfast, unmoveable, always abounding in the work of the Lord, forasmuch as ye know that your labour is not in vain in the Lord (1 Corinthians 15:58). **Social proof** –"I'll have what you are having" -"Be imitators of me, just as I also am of Christ" (1 Corinthians 11:1). **Authority** - "And they were astonished at his doctrine: for he taught them as one that had authority, and not as the scribes" (Mark 1:22). **Liking** - And Jonathan stripped himself of the robe that was upon him, and gave it to David, and his garments, even to his sword, and to his bow, and to his girdle. Then Jonathan and David made a covenant, because he loved him as his own soul (1 Samuel 18:3-4). **Scarcity** – "Some also there were that said we have mortgaged our lands, vineyards, and houses, that we might buy corn, because of the dearth" (Nehemiah 5:3). **Unity**- sense of belong "…keep the unity of the Spirit in the bond of peace" (Ephesians 4:3).

I will use my influence to move you to aim high. I will use the authoritative name of God to influence you to follow Him. I will tell you of your good qualities to influence you to use your strengths to reach out to change your environment. I will be quiet and listen to your dreams about your mission. I will ask what you want and use my influence to help you get it. I will use my influence to help you answer your question of what's in it for you just like Jesus did when Peter asked Him that question. I will use my influence to help you answer the question, why do I want this? I know that you trust my expertise and authority in certain areas, and I will use influence in those areas to put you in a better place. I will use my influence to help you feel like you belong. I will say yes when it is appropriate to say yes so that my influence can assist you in making wise choices. When you are unsure of which way to go, I will use my influence to lead you in a good path. I will follow through with my commitments, so that you can see that I am consistent and trustworthy. I will use my influence in such a way that you may see my good works and give the glory to my Father which is in heaven.

Love looks like _____

My strength in this area _____

My weakness in this area _____

Dear God, You have promised _____

You have told me that it is in my best interest to _____

I praise Your name for helping me to _____

YT "I will run to You" Alvin Slaughter
YT "Power of love" Luther Vandross
YT "Love buys love" Solomon Burke

I TAKE RESPONSIBILITY FOR MY THOUGHTS, FEELINGS, AND BEHAVIORS. Psalm 101:2-3, "I will behave myself wisely in a perfect way… I will walk within my house with a perfect heart. I will set no wicked thing before mine eyes: I hate the work of them that turn aside; it shall not cleave to me." **Psalm 116:9,** "I will walk before the LORD in the land of the living."

When God came to talk to Adam and Eve in the Garden of Eden after they had sinned, He asked Adam about eating the fruit from the tree, which he had been told not to eat. Adam put the responsibility on "the woman you gave me." Then God turned to Eve and she said, "The serpent You made tricked me." From that moment in time, man has always been tempted to put the blame for wrong doing on someone else. It is my mother's fault. It is my father's fault, he was not there when I needed him. It was my wife's fault that I cheated. If she had made herself look like she used to before we got married, I would not have been tempted to cheat. It's my teacher's fault, she did not teach me how to read. Always someone else's fault. Never mine.

God has given me the power of choice. He lets me know in His word what is in my best interest to choose, but He leaves the choice up to me. He tells me what the outcomes of my choices will be, life or death, but He allows me to make the choice. He even allows me to choose whether I will believe Him or not. I choose who I listen to. I choose what I read or see. I choose what I eat. I choose what I believe. I choose what I do. I choose life, or I choose death. I choose to do good, or I choose to do evil. I choose good thoughts, or I choose bad thoughts. I choose behaviors that are in my best interest, or I choose those behaviors that will destroy me. I choose feelings that put me in a good place, or I choose feelings that trigger behaviors that put me in a place that is not in my best interest. I choose to put the blame on someone else, or I choose to take responsibility for my own thoughts, feelings, and behaviors.

I choose either the pathway that Henley, poet and author, states in the poem *Invictus*, "It matters not how strait the gate. How charged with punishments the scroll, I am the master of my fate: I am the cap-tain of my soul." Or I choose the pathway of Dorothea Day, a poetess, wrote in *My Captain*, "I have no fear, though strait the gate, He cleared from punishment the scroll. Christ is the Master of my fate, Christ is the Captain of my soul."

I acknowledge the role that I play in my own life. I acknowledge that others and situations can influence that role, but ultimately I am the one that must make the choice. I am an heir to the throne of God. I choose thoughts, feelings, and behaviors in line with that role. I am the son of God. I choose thoughts, feelings, and behaviors consistent with that role. I recognize that "we must all appear before the judgment seat of Christ that everyone may receive the things done in his body, according to that he hath done, whether it be good or bad" (I Corinthians 5:10). I pray daily for the indwelling Holy Spirit to help me take responsibility for my thoughts, feelings, and behaviors, so that I may glorify God in all things.

Love looks like _____

My strength in this area _____

My weakness in this area _____

Dear God, You have promised _____

You have told me that it is in my best interest to _____

I praise Your name for helping me to _____

YT "Through it all" Andre Crouch
YT "I'm hanging up my heart for you" Solomon Burke

I TEST AND PROVE IF WHAT YOU HAVE SAID TO ME IS TRUE SO THAT I KNOW THAT I CAN TRUST YOU
2 Timothy 1:12, "…nevertheless I am not ashamed: for I know whom I have believed, and am persuaded that he is able to keep that which I have committed unto him against that day."

You told Abraham that You would make of him a great nation. The Jewish nation even now is proof of Your promise to Abraham. You told Daniel to tell King Nebuchadnezzar that his kingdom, Babylon, would be the first of four kingdoms to rule the earth. You identified that the three following in succession would be Media-Persia, Greece, and Rome. History books today verify that what You said would happen did happen. You told Mary that she would have a son and He was to be called Jesus. Mary had never had sexual intercourse with a man, yet it happened exactly as You told her it would.

You told me to come boldly to Your throne of grace that I might find mercy and grace to find help in my time of need. You told me to bring my tithes into Your storehouse and to prove that You would open the windows of heaven and pour me out a blessing so great that I would not be able to receive it. You told me, "…Verily I say unto you, There is no man that hath left house, or brethren, or sisters, or father, or mother, or wife, or children, or lands, for my sake, and the gospel's, but he shall receive an hundredfold now in this time, houses, and brethren, and sisters, and mothers, and children, and lands, with persecutions; and in the world to come eternal life" (Mark 10:29-30). You have given me permission to test You and prove You to see if what You promise is true.

I have tested You many times, Lord, and You have consistently proven that You do what You say You will do. The thousands of miles that I have traveled on the highways over the years and never once had a car break down or be stranded is proof. You said train up a child in the way he should go, then You made it possible for all of my five children to go to church school. When I said, "Lord, my nephew needs a house," You told me to turn around, and there was a sign pointing to a house for sale. You enabled me to purchase it for a good price, and two years later, the house appraised at almost three times what I paid for it. You said if I eat right and take care of my body, You would help keep me healthy. I became a vegetarian at age ten. I have no medical diseases, and I am not on any medications. You told me that You would contend with those that contend with me and You will save my children. Isaiah 49:25, You have never lied to me. You have consistently demonstrated that You do exactly as You say. I humbly ask, knowing that You keep Your promise, that You save my children, just like You said You would do.

Love looks like _____

My strength in this area _____

My weakness in this area _____

Dear God, You have promised _____

You have told me that it is in my best interest to _____

I praise Your name for helping me to _____

YT "Through it all" Andre Crouch
YT "Try me" James Brown

I know my value

1 Samuel 16:7, "But the LORD said unto Samuel, Look not on his countenance, or on the height of his stature; because I have refused him: for the LORD seeth not as man seeth; for man looketh on the outward appearance, but the LORD looketh on the heart."

Matthew 10:29-31, "Are not two sparrows sold for a farthing? and one of them shall not fall on the ground without your Father. But the very hairs of your head are all numbered. Fear ye not therefore, ye are of more value than many sparrows."

Isaiah 43:4, "Since thou wast precious in my sight, thou hast been honourable, and I have loved thee…"

Christ valued me enough to die for me while I was still a sinner. He chose me before He created the world. He made me in His image. I am adopted as His son because Jesus paid a high price for me when He died on the cross, His life. He was resurrected. He lives. Because He lives, I am free to live as His valued child. He gives me an inheritance. "In Him also we have obtained an inheritance, being predestined according to the purpose of Him who works all things according to the counsel of His will, that we who first trusted in Christ should be to the praise of His glory" (Ephesians 1:11, 12). He gives me the desires of my heart. I have permission to ask Him for anything I need and He will give it to me. He is able to do exceedingly more than I can ask or think, consequently I live my life in abundance.

I walk worthy of what He has called me to be. I know I am of infinite worth, and I am humbled by it, so that I walk humbly in faith with Him. I am intentional about recognizing who I am in Christ Jesus. I allow the value He has placed on me to influence others and help them to know their value. Because of my value and worth, by faith, I continue to grow in grace and in the knowledge of my Lord and Saviour moving towards my high calling in Christ Jesus. Through His Spirit, I am filled with all the fullness of God. I experience the width and depth and the length of His love. By His power, I live my life to the praise of His glory. I remember that He makes me more precious than gold. "I will make a man more precious than fine gold; even a man than the golden wedge of Ophir" (Isaiah 13:12). I have confidence in the abilities He has given me. I recognize the difference that He helps me make in the world. The same God that made me made you, and we are equal in His sight. I have courage to speak up when it is necessary. External validation is good, but because I know my value, I know that I can survive without it. I am God's child, heir to His throne. "I will praise thee; for I am fearfully and wonderfully made: marvellous are thy works; and that my soul knoweth right well" (Psalm 139:14).

Love looks like _____

My strength in this area _____

My weakness in this area _____

Dear God, You have promised _____

You have told me that it is in my best interest to _____

I praise Your name for helping me to _____

YT "More precious than silver" Lynn Deshazo
YT "You give good love" Whitney Houston

I HAVE NO FEAR OR SHAME.

Isaiah 41:10, "Fear thou not; for I am with thee: be not dismayed; for I am thy God: I will strengthen thee; yea, I will help thee; yea, I will uphold thee with the right hand of my righteousness."

Psalm 34:4, "I sought the LORD, and he heard me, and delivered me from all my fears."

Fear – I give respect to something that I believe has control over me usually manifested as an emotional response to a perceived threat.

God came down into the Garden of Adam and called Adam by name. "Adam, where are you?" The first response of Adam to God after he disobeyed God and ate the fruit was "I hid myself because I was afraid" (Genesis 3:10). The purpose of fear physiologically is to protect me from danger, real or perceived. Fear warns me to pay attention to what is going on around me and assumes that I have power to check whatever is threatening me. But God has commanded me not to fear. "But now thus saith the LORD that created thee, O Jacob, and he that formed thee, O Israel, Fear not: for I have redeemed thee, I have called thee by thy name; thou art mine" (Isaiah 43:1). Isn't it remarkable that God does the same for me as He did for Adam in the Garden of Eden – calls me by my name. I hear Him saying to me You are My child and no child of Mine has a need to fear anything. I formed you I redeemed you. I called You by name. You are Mine. Inherent in every command that He gives is the promise of the power and whatever is needed to carry it out.

Stress is fear-based. I worry about things that I have no control over. I worry whether you are going to approve of what I do. I do things because I fear you do not like me. I fear that things are not going to turn out the way I want them to. My fear leads me to act. The fear that God commands me not to have leads me to "freeze, fight, flight, fright." I stop what I am doing to try to figure out what's going on. I then decide to fight or fun to attempt to protect myself. My last action is that I am frightened by what is going on, but I do nothing but think about it, I take no definitive action. God knows that there are times when I am going to be afraid and gives me an alternative to all of these. "What time I am afraid, I will trust in thee" (Psalm 56:3). He tells me "…Fear God, and keep his commandments…" (Ecclesiastes 12:13). I fear God, I give respect to Him because I believe Him and have submitted my will to His.

I feel shame and guilt because I know that I have done wrong or behaved foolishly. God tells me, "If we confess our sins, he is faithful and just to forgive us our sins, and to cleanse us from all unrighteousness" (1 John 1:9). There is no reason for me to feel guilty. I confess my wrong doing. God forgives me. He does not want me to go around with my head hung down feeling like He does not want to have anything to do with me. He loves me. He forgives me and still wants to talk to me and for me to talk to Him. I have no fear or shame. "… Be strong and of a good courage; be not afraid…" (Joshua 1:9).

Love looks like _____

My strength in this area _____

My weakness in this area _____

Dear God, You have promised_____

You have told me that it is in my best interest to_____

I praise Your name for helping me to_____

YT "My life is in Your hands" Kurt Franklin"
YT "I surrender" Brooklyn Tabernacle Choir

Chapter 6
I love you as I love myself

I LOVE YOU LIKE I LOVE MYSELF

1 Samuel 18:1, "And it came to pass, when he had made an end of speaking unto Saul, that the soul of Jonathan was knit with the soul of David, and Jonathan loved him as his own soul."

"To be loved as an equal, to be the embodiment of everything one holds dear in this world, the physical manifestation of one's highest values, most treasured virtues, and deepest desires, to be appreciated for your greatness and not your faults by someone who mirrors the greatness that they see in you, and to be loved for who you are rather than what you sacrifice is the purest, most honest, and most powerful form of love that can ever be offered from one human being to another" (Brian Underwood, The Mendenhall, Feb. 14 2011).

I love you like I love myself. We are equals, both children of God, created in His image. I love you because I love myself. The same Holy Spirit that dwells within me dwells within you.

Am I being honest with myself and with you when I say to you that I love you like I love myself? What does it really mean that you are my equal? We are both children of God, created in His image. How do I know that the Holy Spirit is in you when you just lied on me? How do I know that you are my equal? I mean, after all, I have this fantastic college degree, and you didn't even graduate from high school. You are known to be a liar. You have that six-figure job while I only make a small salary. You are known to be a wife-abuser. How can I possibly love you like I love myself? Jesus said, "Greater love hath no man than this, that a man lay down his life for his friends." John 15:13. Ah! That's the standard. I want life for you like I want life for myself. The same things that

I want for myself, I want for you. I want respect. I want you to have respect. I want love. I want you to have love. I want to be treated kindly. I want you to be treated kindly. But even though I want those things for you, Paul tells me in Romans 7: 23-25, "But I see another law in my members, warring against the law of my mind, and bringing me into captivity to the law of sin which is in my members. O wretched man that I am! Who shall deliver me from the body of this death? I thank God through Jesus Christ our Lord. So then with the mind I myself serve the law of God; but with the flesh the law of sin." The truthfulness of it is, I can't love you like I love myself. I don't know how. It is God in me that loves you and works with me to show me how to show His love to you. "The Jesus in me loves the Jesus in you, so easy, easy to love."

Love looks like _____

My strength in this area _____

My weakness in this area _____

Dear God, You have promised _____

You have told me that it is in my best interest to _____

I praise Your name for helping me to _____

YT 'THE JESUS IN ME LOVES THE JESUS IN YOU"
YT "THIS OLD HEART OF MINE" ISLEY BROTHERS

I WANT TO KNOW YOU.

Proverbs 2, "My son, if thou wilt receive my words, and hide my commandments with thee; So that thou incline thine ear unto wisdom, and apply thine heart to understanding; Yea, if thou criest after knowledge, and liftest up thy voice for understanding; If thou seekest her as silver, and searchest for her as for hid treasures; Then shalt thou understand the fear of the LORD, and find the knowledge of God. For the LORD giveth wisdom: out of his mouth cometh knowledge and understanding. He layeth up sound wisdom for the righteous: he is a buckler to them that walk uprightly. He keepeth the paths of judgment, and preserveth the way of his saints. Then shalt thou understand righteousness, and judgment, and equity; yea, every good path. When wisdom entereth into thine heart, and knowledge is pleasant unto thy soul; Discretion shall preserve thee, understanding shall keep thee: To deliver thee from the way of the evil man, from the man that speaketh froward things; Who leave the paths of uprightness, to walk in the ways of darkness; Who rejoice to do evil, and delight in the frowardness of the wicked; Whose ways are crooked, and they froward in their paths: To deliver thee from the strange woman, even from the stranger which flattereth with her words; Which forsaketh the guide of her youth, and forgetteth the covenant of her God. For her house inclineth unto death, and her paths unto the dead. None that go unto her return again, neither take they hold of the paths of life. That thou mayest walk in the way of good men, and keep the paths of the righteous. For the upright shall dwell in the land, and the perfect shall remain in it."

In this chapter in Proverbs, God helps me to understand why it is so important that I get to know you. I must incline my ear unto wisdom. I have to hear what you have to say. I must apply my heart to understanding. I must invest my feelings into knowing you. If I "cry" after knowledge and ask questions to help me know you, God says I will understand and find knowledge for He will give me the wisdom to know you. He provides sound judgment in my interactions with you. He will help me to understand righteousness, judgment, and how to treat you fairly. He promises me that when I have wisdom and knowledge about you, then I will know how to be discrete and preserve our relationship. He further tells me that that knowledge will deliver you and me from the way of the evil man. I will be able to discern and be delivered from those that speak unhealthy and unholy things, who walk in paths that will lead me in the wrong way. I will be able to discern crooks and avoid strangers who flatter me for no good end.

Just as God came down every evening to talk to Adam and Eve, so that they could know Him, I must spend time talking to you. Listening to you. Seeing you. I must be present in your physical, mental, emotional space, and spiritual space, so that I can know you. You must be willing to allow me that privilege. And indeed it is a privilege that God has given to love you and to know you. He promises to help me. Will you allow me the privilege and honor of knowing you, so that I can love you like I love myself?

Love looks like _____

My strength in this area _____

My weakness in this area _____

Dear God, You have promised_____

You have told me that it is in my best interest to_____

I praise Your name for helping me to_____

YT "You know my name" Brooklyn Tabernacle Choir

Can you tell me what you want out of our relationship?
Colossians 3:12, "Put on therefore, as the elect of God, holy and beloved, bowels of mercies, kindness, humbleness of mind, meekness, longsuffering."

Peter asked Jesus after giving up everything to follow Him, "What's in this for me?" It's a legitimate question of you to ask me. Jesus promised Peter a hundred-fold return on his investment and eternal life. I can't promise you either of those, but if you are willing to share with me what you want out of the relationship and what that looks like for you, I am sure that we can come to agreement on what's in this for both of us.

As an elect of God, He has told me that I am holy and beloved. Consequently He has told me to be merciful, kind, humble, meek, and longsuffering. I offer those to you. What I need for you to do is tell me what those things look like to you.

Many perceptions of what mercy is exist among people. God's mercy is displayed by not giving me the punishment I deserve when I disobey His law of love. What does mercy look like to you? Is it giving you my seat when there are no others available? Is it staying quiet when you are having a meltdown? Share with me, so that I know how to be merciful to you.

Kindness is another area where there are many different concepts of what it looks like. In biblical days, it often referred to providing help to someone needing help or resources. In today's environment, you often hear it associated with the words and temperament in which we interact with others along with the deeds of help. How will you help me to know when I am being kind or unkind to you?

Humility is recognizing that God is in charge. Meekness is the position and behaviors that result from that recognition. Longsuffering results from having those characteristics. He is King of kings and Lord of lords, and I am created a little lower than the angels, a servant in His great kingdom. I am a servant in my love relationship with you. Tell me what I can do with and for you. Share with me how you want me to do it.

What else do you want in this relationship? Would you like to experience joy, peace, gentleness, honesty, tenderness? How do you want to grow in this relationship? Tell me what you want this relationship to look like.

Love looks like _____

My strength in this area _____

My weakness in this area _____

Dear God, You have promised _____

You have told me that it is in my best interest to _____

I praise Your name for helping me to _____

YT "I WANNA BE" MANHATTANS

How can I best show you that I love you?
Colossians 2:2, "That their hearts might be comforted, being knit together in love, and unto all riches of the full assurance of understanding, to the acknowledgement of the mystery of God, and of the Father, and of Christ."

I want you to feel comforted in my presence. I want us to be united. I want to feel as we are one. I want our hearts to be knit together in love. I need to know what that looks and feels like to you.

Smiling, dilated pupils, and a happy countenance suggests feeling of comfort. Sitting at the same level and looking in my face helps provide me with comfort. What do I need to do to make you feel comfortable? Is it the music? Is it the light in the room? Is it the tone of my voice? Tell me, what do I need to do to make you feel comfortable.

God and His Son are one. They want us to have the same oneness in our relationship. I need to be on the same page with you. What are our goals and plans? How shall we evaluate where we are? What do we do with the information we get from evaluating where we are? Ultimately I want to spend eternity with you. That starts here. The unity and oneness that we develop here, we will carry onto the streets of gold. The communication that we develop here, we will use in heaven.

God tells me that if I love Him, I will keep His words in my heart. I need you to speak words to me that I can keep in my heart. Will you share your deep thoughts with me? When I repeat them back to you months, years later, you will know indeed that I have kept them in my heart and I do love you.

God tells me that if I love Him, I will keep His commandments of love. He tests me to see if indeed I keep those love laws. He will finally decide if the relationship I have with Him will endure throughout eternity based on how I respond to those love laws. Will you tell me what your "love laws" are so that I can be sure to keep them? What boundaries do you want me to maintain? What can I ask you about? What "test" are you willing to give me to evaluate our relationship? Will you let me know when I am violating your "love laws?" Can I have a second chance if I accidentally mess up? Tell me what I need to do to show you that I love you.

Love looks like _____

My strength in this area _____

My weakness in this area _____

Dear God, You have promised _____

You have told me that it is in my best interest to _____

I praise Your name for helping me to _____

YT "The Love of God " Wintley Phipps
YT "I want to know what love is" Foreigner

I want to have an environment with you where the angels join us in singing.

Job 38:7, "When the morning stars sang together, and all the sons of God shouted for joy?"

Angels praise God and rejoice in singing. I want an environment with you where the angels join us in singing. Can you imagine what kind of environment that will be? We are so united and joyful that the angels sing with us when we raise our voices in praising God!

We start here on earth and we continue that tradition in heaven with the twenty-four elders and the heavenly host. "When He had taken the book, the four living creatures and the twenty-four elders fell down before the Lamb, each one holding a harp and golden bowls full of incense, which are the prayers of the saints. And they sang a new song…" (Revelation 5:8-11). Do you know how to play a harp yet? The twenty-four elders have bowls of incense, which are our prayers, yours and mine. That means when you receive me into your house and we pray, our prayers go the Father as sweet smelling incense! He wants us to pray to Him, to talk to Him, together.

"…I will come again and receive you unto myself that where I am, there ye may be also…" (John 14:3) If you will receive me into your life, I will be humble with you. I will not judge you. I embrace you as you are. I want your face to shine when I am in your presence. I will be honest with you. I will forgive you if you hurt me. I will be patient with you. I will delight in your success. I promise to build you up by talking about your strengths and successes. I will be honest with you about what I perceive as your weaknesses in such a way as to build you up, not cut you down. I will be empathetic and comfort you.

Is it okay if I touch you? I need your permission, but I long to touch you. To hold you. To kiss you. To reassure you that I am yours and you are mine.

I will be there for you when you need me. I will stand by your side when you need me to. I will sacrifice for you. I am your servant. I will be patient and not rush you. I will love you unconditionally. I will not wrong you. I will not give up on you.

I will treat you like I want to be treated. I will not demand to have my way with you. If you give me permission, I will tell others about you.

I will be your friend forever. Forever. We will start here and continue as friends in eternity. Together, we can create an environment where the angels will sing with us – now and forever.

Love looks like _____

My strength in this area _____

My weakness in this area _____

Dear God, You have promised _____

You have told me that it is in my best interest to _____

I praise Your name for helping me to _____

YT "Angels we have heard on high"

Chapter 7
Sex and Love

GOD DOES NOT WANT ME TO BE ALONE.
Genesis 2: 18, "And the LORD God said, It is not good that the man should be alone; I will make him an help meet for him."

When God made the world during creation week, at the end of each day, He looked at everything that He had done and said, "It is good." He made male man first, Adam. He gave Adam a chance to look at the pairs of other animals and notice that he didn't have a mate. I wonder what his thoughts were as he named the animals and saw that each one had a partner and he didn't have one. Why did God choose to do it this way? Was it possibly to give Adam time to reflect on his own needs? Good question to ask Jesus when I have an opportunity to sit down and talk with Him in eternity.

The fascinating part of this is right from the sixth day of creation, before sin, the God who made me knew that it was not in my best interest to be alone! He knew my physical needs and how He had made me. He knew my emotional needs and what would be needed to support them. He knew my social needs and how best to meet those. He knew my spiritual needs and the best way to make sure those were met. He said that it was not good that the man should be alone, even in the perfect state with the indwelling Spirit in him that He had created. So what did He do? He put Adam to sleep, took a rib, crucial part of Adam, and made Eve, female man. In His own image, created He them. Man, male man, female man. "…Let us make man in our image, in our likeness… God created man in His own image, in the image of God He created him; male and female He created them" (Genesis 1:26-27). Then "God saw all that He had made, and it was very good…" (Genesis 1:31).

He made us in His image, physical, spiritual, emotional, social, all interacting in such a way as to be in unity with Him and each other. This need did not change after sin but became distorted in the interaction of the components needed to maintain unity.

Love looks like _____

My strength in this area _____

My weakness in this area _____

Dear God, You have promised _____

You have told me that it is in my best interest to _____

I praise Your name for helping me to _____

YT "I'M SO TIRED OF BEING ALONE" AL GREEN
YT "I JUST DON'T WANNA BE LONELY" MAIN INGREDIENT

THE 1ST STEM CELL TRANSPLANT - GOD GAVE EVE ADAM'S DNA. Genesis 2: 20-23, "And Adam gave names to all cattle, and to the fowl of the air, and to every beast of the field; but for Adam there was not found an help meet for him. And the LORD God caused a deep sleep to fall upon Adam, and he slept: and he took one of his ribs, and closed up the flesh instead thereof; And the rib, which the LORD God had taken from man, made he a woman, and brought her unto the man. And Adam said, This is now bone of my bones, and flesh of my flesh: she shall be called Woman, because she was taken out of Man."

Stem cells are cells that can differentiate themselves into different types of cells in the body to support areas of growth and replacement of cells. Around 2006, stem cells started to be transfused into humans to treat disease. Stem cells are made and have their start in bone marrow. This exchange is first seen biblically when God took one of Adam's ribs and made Eve. Science bears out that stem cells are made in the bone marrow and then are transported in the blood, bearing witness to the testimony of the bible, life is in the blood. Stem cells grow up and differentiate into the type of cell needed to support the body's various functions. They may mature into muscle cells, nerve cells, liver cells, whatever the body needs to maintain its homeostatic functions. Stem cells contain DNA (deoxyribonucleic acid), the genetic component that makes individuals unique and is passed on to future generations. God's marvelous work of creation recognized by David. "I will praise thee; for I am fearfully and wonderfully made: marvellous are thy works; and that my soul knoweth right well" (Psalm 139:14).

When God took one of Adam's ribs to make Eve, He essentially gave Eve Adam's DNA. Truly we all come from one man, male man, Adam, and female-man, Eve just as the bible says. Adam recognized that when he saw her and understood the process by which God had created her. Bone of my bones and flesh of my flesh, "she" is "me." I wonder what Adam's thoughts were when he looked at that beautiful woman. I wonder if his heart beat increased when he looked in her eyes and saw himself looking back at him. I wonder what he felt like when he held her in his arms for the first time. Kissed her. Ran his fingers through her hair. I wonder if they sang songs together. I wonder what Eve thought about when she found out how she had been created from Adam. I wonder if she rubbed the muscles in his arms. Interesting conversations for future engagement with Adam and Eve walking down the streets of gold or sitting under the Tree of Life.

Love looks like _____

My strength in this area _____

My weakness in this area _____

Dear God, You have promised _____

You have told me that it is in my best interest to _____

I praise Your name for helping me to _____

YT "Make us one" Philip Bailey
YT "Stone in love with you" Stylistics

When he finds a wife, he finds a good thing.

Proverbs 18:22, "Whoso findeth a wife findeth a good thing, and obtaineth favour of the LORD."

After God made Adam and Eve "God saw all that he had made, and it was very good..." (Genesis 1:31). Good, perfect, excellent, efficient, useful, healthy, morally upright. Created in the image of God. He knew that it was not good for man to be alone. He made him a companion and said it was very good. After sin His intentions remain and His love commands tell us that whoso findeth a wife, finds a good thing. The same applies to the woman that finds a husband. She finds a good thing. God's intentionality in not being alone resulted from knowing what He had created when He made us in His image. A man needs a wife and a woman needs a husband. When he finds one, he finds a good thing AND he obtains the favor of the Lord. Although sin has impaired what God originally intended to accomplish by this, marriage has not fallen out of favor with God. He made us. He knew what we needed, even before sin and those needs have not changed but only increased after sin.

Finding a spouse. Great implications in those words. This means some searching is done as part of the process. It is true in science that opposites attract, but in marriage, those attractions often turn into heated debates. Social research suggests that it is wiser to find someone as much like you as possible. One must also ask him/herself what am I bringing to the table. What kind of person am I? I need to be the kind of partner that I want my spouse to be. I need to be emotionally healthy. Have a good understanding of who I am and what I value. What I want. Knowing who I am, then empowers that search to be focused and intentional, then I can "find that good thing" and I will have God's favor, tangible evidence that I have His approval, His demonstrable delight.

It was after Adam sinned that fear entered the human experience. A fear primarily associated with being alone, being abandoned, being separated from love. It was that fear that Jesus experienced in the Garden of Gethsemane the night before the crucifixion and that same deep emotional separation that forced the words "My God, My God! Why has thou forsaken Me?" from His lips on the cross. God does not want me to be alone. He came down into the Garden and talked to Adam and Eve every evening. He created us in His image. He knows and does not want me to be alone.

Love looks like _____

My strength in this area _____

My weakness in this area _____

Dear God, You have promised _____

You have told me that it is in my best interest to _____

I praise Your name for helping me to _____

YT "United" Peaches and Herb
YT "Endless love" Lionel Ritchie/Diana Ross
YT "I'm looking for a love" Bobby Womack
YT "Searchin' for my baby" Manhattans

THE TWO SHALL BECOME ONE FLESH.

Ephesians 5:31, "For this cause shall a man leave his father and mother, and shall be joined unto his wife, and they two shall be one flesh."

He shall be joined unto his wife. The "S" word that our society struggles to have a good conversation about. SEX. God gave it to us. He told us the conditions under which we should engage in it. He told us what happens as a consequence. The two shall be one flesh.

Physiologically when a man joins with his wife sexually and ejaculates, he deposits some forty million to 200 million of his sperm cells inside her vaginal tract each time he ejaculates. When these cells die, the debris from those cells are used by the woman's cells and become part of her makeup. This includes the DNA in his sperm cells. She literally becomes him. Remember the rib taken from Adam to make Eve? The rib contained bone marrow where cells are made. Sexual intercourse exchanges DNA. When he ejaculates, his penis acts like a vacuum that sucks up what is in her vaginal canal, including any of her cells that may have sloughed off during the friction of intercourse. He gets far fewer of hers than she gets of his, but nonetheless he gets her cells and DNA and whatever else may be in her vaginal tract. The two become one.

Look at what God tells me. "So ought men to love their wives as their own bodies. He that loveth his wife loveth himself" (Ephesians 5:28). No different than when Adam looked into Eve's eyes and she looked back at him, seeing him through his own eyes. "If you say my eyes are beautiful, it's because I'm looking at you. My eyes are just a window for my feelings to shine through" (Jermaine Jackson and Whitney Houston).

Sexual intercourse brings two together as one flesh. So loving his wife is the same as loving himself. When he mistreats his wife, he is mistreating himself. When he is unfaithful to his wife, he is being unfaithful to himself. Look at how this fits into the command to love thy neighbor as thyself.

God's intended purpose from the very beginning was that the two become one flesh. He gave us sexual intercourse to bring together those parts of our being to unite us to become one in the marriage. He made it enjoyable and made sure that the experience would be one in which we would want to engage.

Love looks like _____

My strength in this area _____

My weakness in this area _____

Dear God, You have promised _____

You have told me that it is in my best interest to _____

I praise Your name for helping me to

YT "IF YOU SAY MY EYES ARE BEAUTIFUL" JERMAINE JACKSON/WHITNEY HOUSTON
YT "MAKE US ONE" PHILIP BAILEY

Sex before and after sin.
Genesis 2:25, "And they were both naked, the man and his wife, and were not ashamed."

Imagine that first encounter between Adam and Eve. They were both naked and were not ashamed.

Look at the change after sin. "…I heard thy voice in the garden, and I was afraid because I was naked; and I hid myself." Fear and hiding. Because I was naked. And the pattern after sin continues. Fear, hiding, shame. I hide myself from you, emotionally, physically, mentally, spiritually, because of fear of being rejected. Fear of not being loved. Fear of being abandoned. The same fear that Adam had after sin, I feel. The fear from separation from God that Adam felt activated Jesus' sympathetic nervous system in the Garden of Gethsemane the night that He sweat great drops of blood before the crucifixion. The same fear that Adam felt, Jesus experienced when He was on the cross and said just before dying, "My God! My God! Why hast Thou forsaken me?"

The tremendous amount of difficulty in attaining the unified relationship that God clearly intended to establish when He made a helpmate for Adam demonstrates itself in a greater than fifty percent divorce rate in first time marriages in our society. The role that women are forced to play, not as helpmates at the side of the husband but often times crushed underneath his feet, is only a small part of the fear, hiding, and shame that resulted after Adam sinned. I have heard many times the statement "behind every good man, there is a good woman." God never placed her behind man, He placed her at his side. He gave us the delightful joy of sexual intercourse intended to help mediate the physiological, emotional, mental, and spiritual aspects of our nature to bring about the unity He knew that we needed because of the way in which He made us.

God's intentionality in accomplishing unity between man and woman united in becoming one flesh has been tarnished by the ubiquitous role that multiple partners play in sexual relationships that exist in our society. Yet God has not abandoned His desire for the two becoming one flesh and the unity that He intended to accomplish. He has told me that even while I live in a sinful world, how to best accomplish that unity. He completely authorizes the two becoming one flesh, knowing that it is in my best interest. He has told me not to commit adultery. He has told husbands to love their wives, even as Christ loved the church AND GAVE HIMSELF FOR IT (that part is often missed and omitted), when we quote the last part, woman, submit yourself unto your husband as unto the Lord. He has told me not to be unequally yoked because He who made me understands the exchange of DNA that occurs during sexual intercourse and what happens in that process long-term. The God who made me, loves me, and knows how best to keep me in this sinful world. What He asks me to do is trust His love enough to do what He commands, even if I don't understand it. Even when I don't feel like it.

YT "You're my first, last, everything" Barry White
YT "Reunited" Peaches and Herb

I AM FEARFULLY AND WONDERFULLY MADE TO ENJOY SEX AND ITS BENEFITS. (1)
Psalms 139:14, "I will praise thee; for I am fearfully and wonderfully made: marvelous are thy works..."

When I understand many of the physiological processes that happen during the act of sexual intercourse, I better understand why God says to me what He does about relationships in His word.

God has made me so that chemicals released in my body impact cells and organs by binding to sites on the cell to tell the cell and organ what to do and what not to do. During the act of sexual intercourse, endorphins, oxytocin, prolactin, epinephrine, dopamine, serotonin, and testostrone are released. Endorphins are the body's "feel good" hormones that also increase the immune response. They are the body's natural opioids. Oxytocin increases the bonding and trust that occurs between humans. It is also released in the new mother to stimulate the release of breast milk, as well as bond the mother to the new born baby emotionally. Prolactin induces sleep. Epinephrine raises the heart rate and blood pressure. Dopamine is part of the "reward system" that elevates your mood. The integration of these hormones helps make sex not only an enjoyable experience but works to protect the body, produce positive health outcomes, and mediate the unity God intended between husband and wife.

It turns out that Marvin Gaye and Aretha Franklin were right. "Sexual healing" is good for me. "Doctor Feelgood" in the morning works in my behalf. I can't use "headache" as an excuse. The endorphins released take care of pain. Ejaculation decreases the risk factor for my husband getting prostate cancer. The heart benefits of sex are well documented. When he turns over and goes to sleep afterwards, I have done a good job in releasing prolactin. When I get up in the morning singing in the shower, I know he has released those endorphins and activated the dopamine! Thirty minutes of sex or walk two miles, same exercise benefit for the cardiovascular system. Fewer colds and infections occur because sex also protects and enhances my immune system. Even in old age, Sarah and Abraham!

Solomon said he would rather be on the rooftop than in the room with an angry woman. Although he was the best looking black man ever, he really couldn't take care of the needs of 700 wives and 300 concubines. That means even if he was capable of performing every day, each woman's needs were met once in two years. Not enough by any stretch of the imagination! Sex elevates mood and decreases depression. I will ask Jesus to help Solomon understand in heaven why those women were so irritable.

It is well to note that the best health outcome results are found in married couples in a one-partner, stable relationship. Research bears out the predictability, reliability, and validity of what God told me from the very beginning: my best mental, physical, spiritual, and emotional outcomes result from one husband, one wife.

Love looks like _____

My strength in this area _____

My weakness in this area _____

Dear God, You have promised _____

You have told me that it is in my best interest to _____

I praise Your name for helping me to _____

YT "Sexual healing" Marvin Gaye
YT "Dr. Feelgood" Aretha Franklin

I AM FEARFULLY AND WONDERFULLY MADE TO ENJOY SEX AND ITS BENEFITS. (2)

Psalms 139:14, "I will praise thee; for I am fearfully and wonderfully made: marvellous are thy works…"

In the physiological exchange of body cells during sex, God's marvelous work of creation can be readily seen. In the normal exchange of cells in humans, God has placed within us the immune system complex, so that cells that enter my body from another source are recognized, rejected, and attacked via the inflammatory process. That is how an immunization works. Cells with the DNA of the virus or bacteria is injected into my body. My immune system takes "fingerprints" of the foreign object and builds antibodies and a system, so that if the microorganism comes back again, my body will recognize the organism, and I will resist the disease taking place in my body. That is also the reason that a person that gets a transplanted kidney from another person has to take anti-rejection drugs for life, so as not to attack and reject the transplanted kidney.

But look at how God has so structured me to enable me to have sex! He has so made me that when the sex cells of my husband enters my body, my body begins to recognize his cells as my cells. Through what is called the MHC (major histocompatibility complex), my body begins to recognize his cells as my cells and I accept them into my body. When the immune function fails to work, my body can start to attack its own organs in what we call autoimmune diseases. Lupus and rheumatoid arthritis are two of those diseases. When his cells die within my body, God has made me such an efficient organism that the material from those dead cells, including his DNA, through a process called apoptosis is recycled to continue the cycle of life by being used by my cells as nutrients to continue to grow and function in my body.

Have you ever wondered why people that have been married start to look alike? Research has recently found male DNA (genes) in the brains of women. Although more research needs to be done to confirm this transfer, this fits very much with what the Bible says about the two becoming one flesh. Remember she gets more of his DNA (40-200 million of his sperm cells with each ejaculation) than he gets of hers. Do you begin to understand the implications that this has for, "thou shalt not commit adultery?" The implications for "can two walk together unless they be agreed?" The implications for "not being unequally yoked?" The implications for "submission?" When God said the two shall become one flesh, He knew indeed what He had put together and how it worked. Research findings in science are shedding light on the validity of what God has said to us in His word. When the integration of those chemicals and hormones has enhanced my femininity and moved me towards God's intended unity, my response is, "Thank You, Jesus!"

Love looks like _____

My strength in this area _____

My weakness in this area _____

Dear God, You have promised_____

You have told me that it is in my best interest to_____

I praise Your name for helping me to_____

YT "I believe" Wintley Phipps
YT "Love won't let me wait" Luther Vandross

Husband, love me like Jesus loved the church and I will submit to you like Sarah did to Abraham. I will wash your feet with my tears and dry them with my hair like Mary did Jesus.

Ephesians 5: 21-26, "…Wives, submit yourselves unto your own husbands, as unto the Lord. For the husband is the head of the wife, even as Christ is the head of the church: and he is the saviour of the body. Therefore as the church is subject unto Christ, so let the wives be to their own husbands in everything. Husbands, love your wives, even as Christ also loved the church, and gave himself for it…"

God has placed mechanisms within me and my husband to mediate physiologically much of what is said in these verses during the act of sexual intercourse. I don't have to be ashamed to be "naked" anymore. " I will greatly rejoice in the Lord, my soul shall be joyful in my God; for he hath clothed me with the garments of salvation, he hath covered me with the robe of righteousness, as a bridegroom decketh himself with ornaments, and as a bride adorneth herself with her jewels" (Isaiah 61:10).

In the physiology of submission, at ejaculation, 40 to 200 million of his sperm cells with his DNA (genetic blueprint that determines who he is) is placed in my body. When those cells die within me, those cells, including the DNA, are recycled as nutrients by my cells. I become one with him. Because I get far more of his DNA than he gets of mine, he has the control. In his DNA are his thoughts, his memories, his personality, who he is. When I incorporate his DNA into my cellular structure, I have the same response that Eve had when Adam's rib with his DNA was used in making her. So as time passes, we look alike. We begin to think alike. He can start to speak and I can finish the sentence. This submission is to my OWN husband, not men in general as so many males interpret it.

"Unto the woman he said…**thy desire shall be to thy husband, and he shall rule over thee**" (Genesis 3:16). God knew what He was talking about because He made us. 40-200 million of his cells, two to three times a week gives him quite a bit of control when his DNA is incorporated into my cellular structure. My submission is supported physiologically through the act of sexual intercourse.

The condition for my submission is very clear. Husband, love me as Christ loved the church, and gave Himself for it. What are you willing to give up to be with me? Christ gave His life. Are you prepared to give up everything to be with me, including your life? That is the condition that God has placed on you when He gave me instructions to submit. He has placed sex in our lives to help mediate that process.

Love looks like _____

My strength in this area _____

My weakness in this area _____

Dear God, You have promised _____

You have told me that it is in my best interest to _____

I praise Your name for helping me to _____

YT "I surrender" Brooklyn Tabernacle Choir
YT "Make me yours" Betty Swann
YT "Can't get enough of your love, baby" Barry White

WHEN YOU ARE UNFAITHFUL TO ME, YOU ARE UNFAITHFUL TO YOURSELF. Exodus 20:14, "Thou shalt not commit adultery." **I Corinthians 6: 16-18,** "What? know ye not that he which is joined to an harlot is one body? for two, saith he, shall be one flesh… Flee fornication. Every sin that a man doeth is without the body; but he that committeth fornication sinneth against his own body.

Whoever I choose to have sexual intercourse with, I am choosing to become one flesh with them. The implications of that have so many outcomes that God has warned me about in His words of love to me. I take on their DNA, so the potential for influencing my thoughts and feelings is there. That's why He tells me to "Be ye not unequally yoked" (2 Corinthians 6:14). Every woman that he has slept with and she slept with, I now have not only whatever microorganisms that inhabited her vaginal tract to produce sexually transmitted diseases, I have their DNA, which I pass on to my children when I give birth. And we wonder why our kids act the way they do! Amazing!

Not only is he sinning (violating the laws of love) against God and me, he is sinning against his own body. So ought men to love their wives as their own bodies. He that loveth his wife loveth himself" (Ephesians 5:28) for when I have sex with him, I become one with him as well.

When a person has multiple sex partners, the body's immune system gets confused. The MHC (major histocompatibility complex) that helps the body recognize his sex cells as her cells is overwhelmed and the immune system begins to malfunction. Prostitutes are well known to get diseases a lot easier than those in the general population as are men who frequent them. A compromised immune system is one of the reasons that this occurs. Not only is a person that is unfaithful to their mate compromising him/herself, that person is also compromising the immune response of the spouse. God, who made me, knew all this when He gave me instructions on how to handle my relationships. I show my love for Him, for myself, and for others when I follow the instructions He has given me.

Love looks like _____

My strength in this area _____

My weakness in this area _____

Dear God, You have promised _____

You have told me that it is in my best interest to_____

I praise Your name for helping me to_____

YT "He's been faithful to me" Brooklyn Tabernacle Choir
YT "Just be true" Betty Everett/Jerry Butler

Thank You, Jesus, for sex! Your mercy endureth forever!
Genesis 1:28-29, "And God blessed them, and God said unto them, Be fruitful, and multiply, and replenish the earth, and subdue it… And God said, Behold, I have given you every herb bearing seed, which is upon the face of all the earth, and every tree, in the which is the fruit of a tree yielding seed; to you it shall be for meat."

God gave sex to accomplish His purpose of multiplying and replenishing the earth. He made it enjoyable, so that I would be willing to participate. Note how the efficiency of God's creative power persists even in a sinful world. There is one day out of the month (add two days if you want to include the days that a sperm can live inside her body) when a woman can become pregnant. It takes only one sperm to fertilize an egg. Yet, there are over seven billion people living on the planet at this time. What a God I serve! Note also the intentionality of God to perpetuate and sustain life. In all forms of life that He created, plants, animals, fish, He put in place the mechanisms to both perpetuate life and support life. He even called fruit and herb bearing seed "meat" and gave us the diet that would best support His goals of sustaining and perpetuating life!

Look at how David praises Him for what He put in place that sustains and supports life in Psalms 136. 3 O give thanks to the Lord of lords: for his mercy endureth forever. Mercy enables eternal life. 5 To him that by wisdom made the heavens: for his mercy endureth forever. The air we breathe sustains life. Without it we live for about six minutes. 6 To him that stretched out the earth above the waters: for his mercy endureth forever. My body is sixty to seventy percent water. Without water, I will die. 8 The sun to rule by day: for his mercy endureth forever. The trees grow ever upward toward the light of the sun. Light is needed for life. Fruit from the trees is needed to sustain life. 9 The moon and stars to rule by night: for his mercy endureth forever. Sleep and rest is needed to sustain life. Growth hormone and other hormones are secreted at night during sleep. One thing that David left off this list is sex, so I will ask God's permission when I see Him in heaven to add this as verse 10: O give thanks to the Lord of lords to Him that gave sex, and made it enjoyable, to reproduce and replenish the earth and protect my health: for His mercy endureth forever.

Love looks like _____

My strength in this area _____

My weakness in this area _____

Dear God, You have promised _____

You have told me that it is in my best interest to _____

I praise Your name for helping me to _____

YT "I believe" Wintley Phipps
YT "Let it be me" Betty Everett/Jerry Butler

Chapter 8
Music and the Expression of love

MUSIC AND THE EXPRESSION OF LOVE
Psalm 95:1, "O come, let us sing unto the LORD: let us make a joyful noise to the rock of our salvation." **Ephesians 5:19,** "Speaking to yourselves in psalms and hymns and spiritual songs, singing and making melody in your heart to the Lord." **Psalm 150:4,** "Praise him with the timbrel and dance: praise him with stringed instruments and organs."

"Music is one of the fairest and most glorious gifts of God, to which Satan is a bitter enemy, for it removes from the heart the weight of sorrow, and the fascination of evil thoughts," **Martin Luther**

The same God that knew that sexual intercourse was in my best interest also gave me music to support accomplishing unity and oneness in my loving you as I love myself. Remember He made me to feel good. Research documents that appropriate music accomplishes just that.

Music can impact the heart rate, blood pressure, and other body functions. It can elevate mood and relieve depression. Music improves memory and recall, especially when associated with emotional events, such as weddings and graduations. Classical music is known to increase the number of brain waves associated with increased learning and intelligence.

I feel like floating and moving with music. I love dancing, moving in coordination with music. David must have liked it as well as he was overcome with joy and danced in the streets when the ark was finally returned to its rightful place. When his wife told him how disgusted she was with what he had done, he rebuked her and told her it was before the Lord and that he was willing to get even more base and vile before the Lord if necessary. "And David said unto Michal, It was before the LORD, which chose me before thy father, and before all his house, to appoint me ruler over the people of the LORD, over Israel: therefore will I play before the LORD. And I will yet be more vile than thus, and will be base in mine own sight" (1 Samuel 14:22-23).

I catch the emotions of others when perceiving their emotional expressions when listening to music. This assists in understanding the feelings of others. Think of what happens when I am sitting in the room with someone that I care deeply about and we are listening to music together. Think of what happens when I sit in church and the congregation is brought together in unity and harmony when we sing songs of praise together. My emotions are influenced by the emotions of others. I don't live in a vacuum in isolation. I breathe in the air that you breathe out. Mirror neurons in my brain connect me to you through a brain mechanism designed to facilitate imitating and mimicking. If I sit across from you long enough and I am engaged in our conversation, if you cross your legs, my automatic response is to cross my legs. The same process happens when I am in an encounter with you and we are listening to music.

Love looks like _____

My strength in this area _____

My weakness in this area _____

Dear God, You have promised _____

You have told me that it is in my best interest to _____

I praise Your name for helping me to _____

YT "DANCE TO THE MUSIC" SLY/FAMILY STONE

Psalm 71:23, "My lips shall greatly rejoice when I sing unto thee; and my soul, which thou hast redeemed."

During my growing up years, rock and roll music came heavily onto the scene. Christians were discouraged from listening to this kind of music, and I was often told as a young adult that this was the devil's music. When I listen to some of those songs now, I hear a deep spiritual message often of people searching or experiencing the benefits associated with love or the collateral torments associated with fear. I hear words of love that help me to understand the kind of relationship that Jesus wants me to have with Him and with those that He loves and died for. I hear the torments associated with the fear that resulted when Adam sinned. I hear man trying to get from other humans what he can only get from God. Love and its attributes are expressed in the words of many "secular" songs, songs written by men and women who often in their present or past history have had a deep relationship with God or have been in a love relationship with someone else. These are songs with words and music often gifted by God to help us understand and obey His command to love Him supremely and our neighbor as ourselves. The Holy Spirit guides me to discern which are words of love by opening up my eyes to the word of God, the Bible. He empowers me to understand that if what I am hearing is not what God has told me in His word, I need to avoid it. Please read the following verses then listen to the YouTube song associated to hear the message of love.

"There is no fear in love; but perfect love casteth out fear: because fear hath torment. He that feareth is not made perfect in love" (1John 4:18). **YT "Stoned Love" Supremes**

"By this shall all men know that ye are my disciples, if ye have love one to another" (John 13:35). **YT "I want a love I can see" Temptations**

"Behold, I stand at the door, and knock: if any man hear my voice, and open the door, I will come in to him, and will sup with him, and he with me" (Revelation 3:20). **YT "Open the door to your heart" Darrell Banks**

"Every good gift and every perfect gift is from above, and cometh down from the Father of lights…" (James 1:17) "Be strong and of a good courage, fear not, nor be afraid of them: for the LORD thy God, he it is that doth go with thee; he will not fail thee, nor forsake thee" (Deuteronomy 31:6) **YT "I wanna be your everything" Manhattans "Let it be me" Betty Everett/Jerry Butler**

"And all mine are thine, and thine are mine; and I am glorified in them" (John 17:10) **YT "Make me yours" Betty Swann**

"And the Lord God said, It is not good that the man should be alone; I will make him an help meet for him" (Genesis 2:18). **YT "I just don't want to be lonely anymore" Main Ingredient "If I were your woman" Gladys Knight/Pips**

"The Lord hath appeared of old unto me, saying, Yea, I have loved thee with an everlasting love…" (Jeremiah 31:3). **YT "I've been loving you to long" Otis Redding**

God who loves me, has given me music to help me know how to love Him, and others as I love myself.

Chapter 9
Where do I go from here?

CHOOSE.
Joshua 24:15 "… choose you this day whom ye will serve (love)…but as for me and my house, we will serve (love) the LORD."

God loves me. God offers me the choice to love Him back. A choice that I make and renew every day that I live. Choose love and live or choose its opposite, hate, and die. Choose eternal life or choose eternal death, separation from Him who loves me forever. He leaves that choice in my hands. He has told me throughout His written word what love is, what it looks like, and how to execute that choice. He shares His love with me in nature; when I look at how He cares for the trees and animals, I see how He cares for me even more. When I look at the stars, it is a revelation of His love for me. When I look at His Son, sent to be bone of our bones and flesh of our flesh, on that cross crying out, "My God, My God Why hast Thou forsaken me. I gasp at the depth of His love for me. He makes Himself available to me every second of the day. He has set aside time just to be with me, to reveal Himself to me, so that I may know Him that I may have eternal life. He wraps His warm and loving arms around me. He comes to sup and abide with me. He lays down with me at night to bring joy, peace, comfort, and safety. He is coming back to get me, so that I can be forever in His space. Choose Him, choose life. He articulates very clearly the outcomes of my choices, intermittent, short-term, and long-term outcomes. He tells me how to love Him, myself, and others throughout His word. Inherit in every love promise and command, is His power, through His indwelling Spirit, to carry out the command. He uses those same love commands to evaluate whether I have lived by the choice I made. He is doing that evaluation now and when He comes He will bring my reward with Him because through His power alone, I shall have demonstrated to Him that I love as He loves. I will be like Him when He comes.

"Thou shalt love the Lord thy God with all thine heart…and thy neighbor as thyself." Love God. Love others as I love myself.

Solomon summarizes it for us in Ecclesiastes 12:13, "Let us hear the conclusion of the whole matter: Fear (love) God, and keep his commandments: for this *is* the whole *duty* of man."

YT "How Great thou Art" Whintley Phipps
YT "I hope you dance" Gladys Knight